PREDESTINATION

Books by the Author Translated into English

God, His Existence and His Nature: A Thomistic Solution of Certain
Agnostic Antinomies (1914)

Christian Perfection and Contemplation, according to St. Thomas
Aquinas and St. John of the Cross (1923)

The Love of God and the Cross of Jesus (1929)

Providence (1932)

Our Savior and His Love for Us (1933)

Predestination (1936)

★The One God (1938)

The Three Ages of the Interior Life: Prelude of Eternal Life (1938)

The Three Ways of the Spiritual Life (1938)

★The Trinity and God the Creator (1943)

★Christ the Savior (1945)

The Priesthood and Perfection (1946)

Reality: A Synthesis of Thomistic Thought (1946)

Life Everlasting (1947)

★Grace (1947)

The Priest in Union with Christ (1948)

The Mother of the Saviour and Our Interior Life (1948)

★The Theological Virtues—Vol. 1: Faith (1948)

★Beatitude (moral theology, 1951)

Last Writings (spiritual retreats, 1969)

Books by the Author Not Translated into English

Le sens commun: la philosophie de l'être et les formules dogmatiques (1909)

Saint Thomas et le neomolinisme (booklet, 1917)

De Revelatione per ecclesiam catholicam proposita (1918)

De methodo sancti Thomae speciatim de structura articulorum summae
theologicae (booklet, 1928)

Le réalisme du principe de finalité (1932)

Le sens du mystère et le clair-obscur intellectuel: nature et
surnaturel (1934)

Essenza e attualità del Tomismo

Dieu accessible à tous (booklet, 1941)

★De Eucharistia: Accedunt de Paenitentia quaestiones dogmaticae (1942)

Les XXIV Theses Thomistes pour le 30e Anniversaire de leur
Approbation (booklet, 1944)

Verite et immutabilite du dogme (booklet, 1947)

★De virtutibus theologicis (1948)

★*Commentaries on St. Thomas Aquinas'* Summa Theologica.

PREDESTINATION

By
Fr. Reginald Garrigou-Lagrange, O.P.

Translated by
Dom Bede Rose, O.S.B., D.D.

TAN Books
Charlotte, North Carolina

Nihil Obstat: P. Jerome Wespe, O.S.B.
                       Censor Deputatus

Imprimi Potest: ✠ Thomas Meier, O.S.B.
                       Abbot

Nihil Obstat: F. J. Holweck
                       Censor Librorum
                       St. Louis, Missouri
                       September 1, 1939

Imprimatur: ✠ C. H. Winkelmann
                       Vicar General
                       St. Louis, Missouri
                       September 2, 1939

Library of Congress Catalog Card No.: 98-61398

ISBN: 978-0-89555-634-9

Cover illustration by Janssens.

Printed and bound in the United States of America.

TAN Books
Charlotte, North Carolina
www.TANBooks.com
2013

To
The Holy Mother of God
Mother of Divine Grace
as a
Token of Gratitude and
Filial Obedience

PREFACE

In two works [1] published some years ago, we discussed the fundamentals of the teaching on predestination, but we did not come directly to grips with this famous question, and a separate study of it was felt necessary. The opportunity presented itself when we had to write on Predestination, Providence, and Premotion for the *Dictionnaire de théologie,* several articles that had previously been published on these problems in different reviews.[2] The purpose of the present work is to give substantially and in compact form the result of those labors. St. Augustine's phrase, "The predestination of the saints," reminds us that predestination to grace alone, which does not in fact bring us to eternal life, is not in the true sense predestination, since this latter includes the gift of final perseverance.

In the first part of this book our studies will be concerned with the meaning of predestination according to Scripture and the teaching of the Church. Then we shall consider the principal difficulties of the problem, the method to be followed, the classification of the theological systems, and the stand taken by St. Augustine.

In the second part we shall give the history of the various solutions of the great problem, insisting upon the teaching of St. Thomas, which we shall compare with the tentative solutions proposed by theologians of later date, and especially with the solutions proposed by the post-Tridentine theologians.

In the third part we shall treat of grace, especially of effica-

[1] *Dieu* and *Providence.* Both have been published in English translation.
[2] Cf. *infra.* p. 292, note 29.

cious grace, by which the effects of predestination are realized in this life. These are vocation, justification, and merit. We shall make a special study of efficacious grace in its relation to sufficient grace that is offered and even given to all.

The scope of this book from beginning to end is the reconciliation of the two principles of divine predilection and possible salvation for all. On the one hand, "no one thing would be better than another, if God did not will greater good for one than for another." [3] On the other hand, God never commands what is impossible, but makes it possible for all who have come to the use of reason to fulfil the precepts that are of obligation, at the time they are of obligation, when and as these are known by them.

The intimate reconciliation of these two principles is beyond our power of perception. Before our admission to the beatific vision, this would be impossible for any created intellect, either angelic or human. But we must attach equal importance to both principles. They counteract each other, and the history of theology as well as a thorough knowledge of the teaching of St. Thomas, enables us to estimate each principle at its true value, so that we vaguely foresee how infinite mercy, justice, and sovereign liberty are intimately reconciled in the eminence of the Deity, or of the intimate life of God.

It will serve a useful purpose to study these great questions again at the present time, all the more so as people today very often are not aware of the reality and value of divine grace; for without it we can do nothing in the way of saving our souls. The eternal reality of the problem studied in these pages becomes more strikingly evident from the light thrown on it by the following reflections taken from the fine book recently published by a friend of ours. [4] "The mystery of the incarnation," says St. Thomas, "is considered as a condescen-

[3] Cf. St. Thomas, Ia, q.20, a.3.
[4] J. Maritain, *Science et Sagesse,* pp. 43–47.

sion of the fulness of the Godhead into human nature rather than as the promotion of human nature already existing, as it were, to the Godhead." [5]

"There are thus two movements in the Christian world. The movement by which it ascends to God is but the result of the movement by which God descends into it, and this is the first movement. And the more it yields to this movement by which God gives Himself to it, the more the movement is awakened in it by which it gives itself to God. For grace has a vivifying effect, and is not, as Luther thought, a mantle cast over a dead person. The creature, profoundly stirred to act, arises from sleep and becomes all vigilance and activity. In its final stage this activity is one of pre-eminence, of loving contemplation, and of superabundance. But at the same time it is also a moral, ascetic, practical, and militant activity. . . .

"A time came when man took this second movement for the first. In the age of anthropocentric humanism, which is Pelagianism in action, man forgot that God is the first Mover in the act of love, as He is the first Cause of being. Man acted as if the creature owed its advancement to itself and not to the operation of the divine plenitude in it. When these conditions prevailed, the Christian world,[6] laboring under the triple ferment of the Renaissance, of rationalism, and of its contrary Jansenist or Protestant tendency (which, as it seeks to nullify man's efforts as regards the supernatural, in the same degree seeks to exalt them in the natural order), was inevitably doomed to disintegration.

"Even though as Christians we remain truly loyal and obedient to all that has been revealed, since grace is something hidden, the movement by which we ascend to God, that is,

[5] St. Thomas, IIIa, q.34, a.1 ad 1um.

[6] By this expression the author does not mean the Church, but Christendom; that is to say, the assembly of nations united officially even by their legislation to the Church, and it refers especially to the condition that prevailed in Europe before the coming of Protestantism.

our indispensable effort to attain spiritual perfection, may veil from our eyes the descending movement and the gift of uncreated love in us. Then is struck a discordant note, increasing in volume, between life as we Christians should live it and our consciousness and interpretation of it. Religion tends to become less and less existential; it is swept away by appearances, and we live but a superficial life. We shall always believe in grace, but we shall act as if it were but the pediment of an edifice, and as if, even without it, on the chance supposition that it did not operate, things would still be the same, because of precautions taken by human aids and conditions deemed to be sufficient. When such periods occur, which act as counter currents to grace, should we be astonished at their anemia?

"To be sure, the Middle Ages were not such a period. The enormous activity manifested during that period, though it may deceive the historian, did not deceive the period itself. The Middle Ages knew that this great and constructive work was but the mask cloaking an invisible mystery of love and humility. Those ages obeyed the law of the incarnation, which continued to accomplish its effects in them. . . . Medieval Christianity knew in a practical way that the Word came down and was made flesh, that the Holy Spirit, following this movement, also comes down. Medieval Christianity opened the world of knowledge to the stream which coursed through it gradually. Thus the world was enabled to know the order of wisdom, and for a time it experienced in itself the realization of the peaceful encounter and harmony of the three wisdoms: the infused, the theological, and the metaphysical."

We should like to set forth here the nature of the union of these three wisdoms, as described by St. Thomas apropos of one of the greatest problems, of this most exalted part of divine providence—predestination.

When we consider the disorder in Europe at the present time, and when we think of what has been happening in

Russia and in Mexico for the past several years and of what has happened in Spain, it is good to recall our Lord's words about predestination, words that will infallibly be fulfilled in spite of all difficulties: "My sheep hear My voice. . . . I give them life everlasting, and they shall not perish for ever. . . . No one can snatch them out of the hand of My Father." [7] It occurs also at an appropriate time for us to remember that St. Paul sees in predestination a great motive for hope, when he writes: "We know that to them that love God all things work together unto good, to such as according to His purpose are called to be saints. For whom He foreknew He also predestinated to be made conformable to the image of His Son. . . . And whom He predestinated, them He also called . . . justified . . . and glorified." [8] St. Paul also says: "Blessed be God . . . who hath blessed us in heavenly places. As He chose us in Him before the foundation of the world, that we should be holy and unspotted in His sight . . . unto the praise of the glory of His grace, in which He hath graced us in His beloved Son." [9]

[7] John 10: 27–29.
[8] Rom. 8: 28–30.
[9] Eph. 1: 3–6.

TRANSLATOR'S PREFACE

WITH his accustomed keenness of penetration and precision of thought, Father Garrigou-Lagrange has discussed this engrossing problem of predestination. It is more, of course, than a problem; it is one of the mysteries of revelation. For this reason there must ever remain points about it that are obscure.

It would be absurd for anyone to expect that in this work all difficulties are removed, and that everything is explained or proved by reason. As Father Garrigou-Lagrange so wisely points out, it is only when, by God's grace, we shall be admitted to the beatific vision, that we shall see how infinite justice, mercy, and goodness are intimately reconciled in the eminence of the Deity. Predestination is a subject that closely concerns these divine attributes.

The author wrote this work primarily for students of theology. Gradually and carefully he has traced for us the development of thought on this subject. Beginning with the decisions of the Church in the earliest councils, continuing with the statements of the Church Fathers, and ending with the views of the leading theologians, especially of St. Thomas Aquinas, we have presented to us in this work a body of doctrine that is a guide for every student and diligent inquirer in the search for truth. In this book a sincere and, I believe, successful effort has been made to give the true and unadulterated doctrine of St. Thomas. To interpret aright the mind of the Angelic Doctor is not always an easy matter, as is evident from the history of the conflicting opinions even among the Thomists. The various errors and heresies on this subject of predestination have been clearly set forth and condemned on the authority of the Church without the slightest hesitation.

In conclusion I wish to express my thanks and deep appreciation to the Reverend Newton Thompson, S.T.D., for his careful revision of the manuscript and his valuable suggestions.

Predestination is a translation of *La prédestination des saints et la grace,* by Rev. Reginald Garrigou-Lagrange, published by Desclee, De Brouwer & Cie, Bruges, Belgium.

CONTENTS

PART I

THE TEACHING OF THE CHURCH AND THE THEOLOGICAL SYSTEMS

PART II

THE PRINCIPAL SOLUTIONS OF THE PROBLEM

CONTENTS

PART III

GRACE AND ITS EFFICACY

PREDESTINATION

PART I

THE TEACHING OF THE CHURCH AND THE THEOLOGICAL SYSTEMS

In the first part we shall direct attention first to the idea of predestination as presented to us in the Scripture. Then we shall inspect the declarations of the Church formulated on the occasion of conflicting heresies. Thus we shall perceive more clearly the point at issue and what precisely constitutes the chief difficulty of the problem. Then there will be a classification of the various theological opinions to be explained in the course of this work. At the end of this first part we shall remind our readers of the stand taken by St. Augustine and his first disciples, since this exerted a very profound influence on the whole of medieval theology.

CHAPTER I

The Significance and Reality of Predestination According to Scripture

The Gospel is the good tidings of the redemption of the human race which must be preached to all, for our Savior said: "Going therefore, teach ye all nations: baptizing them in the name of the Father and of the Son and of the Holy Ghost. Teaching them to observe all things whatsoever I have commanded you. And behold I am with you all days even to the consummation of the world." [1] St. Paul says in like manner: "God will have all men to be saved and to come to the knowledge of the truth. For there is one God, and one mediator of God and men, the man Christ Jesus, who gave Himself a redemption for all." [2]

God never commands what is impossible and He makes the fulfilment of His precepts really possible for all, both when they are of obligation and according as they are known. However, there are souls that through their own fault are lost; and souls, at times, that have enjoyed a close intimacy with the Savior, as was the case with the "son of perdition." There are others, the elect, who will infallibly be saved. Among these are children who die shortly after being baptized, and adults who, by divine grace, not only can observe the commandments, but actually do so and obtain the gift of final perseverance. Jesus in His sacerdotal prayer said to His Father: "Those whom Thou gavest Me have I kept, and none of them is lost, but the son of perdition, that the Scripture may be

---

[1] Matt. 28: 19–20.
[2] I Tim. 2: 3–5.

3

fulfilled." [3] Speaking in more general terms, Jesus says again: "My sheep hear My voice. And I know them, and they follow Me. And I give them life everlasting: and they shall not perish for ever. And no man shall pluck them out of My hand. That which My Father hath given Me is greater than all, and no one can snatch them out of the hand of My Father. I and the Father are one." [4] There are elect chosen by God from all eternity. Jesus spoke of them on several occasions. Once He said: "Many are called, but few are chosen." [5] He announced the destruction of Jerusalem, the distress of those times of trial, and He added: "Unless those days had been shortened, no flesh should be saved; but for the sake of the elect those days shall be shortened." [6]

The precise meaning of these utterances of our Savior are made known to us by what St. Paul tells us about predestination, by which God directs and brings the elect infallibly to eternal life. In one of his epistles we read: "What hast thou that thou hast not received? And if thou hast received, why dost thou glory as if thou hadst not received it?" [7] It is but the comment on the words of the Master, who said: "Without Me you can do nothing." [8] St. Paul also says: "For it is God who worketh in you, both to will and to accomplish, according to His good will." [9] When writing to the Ephesians, he speaks explicitly about predestination. "Blessed be the God and Father of our Lord Jesus Christ," he says, "who hath blessed us with spiritual blessings in heavenly places in Christ. As He chose us in Him before the foundation of the world, that we should be holy and unspotted in His sight in charity. Who hath predestinated us unto the adoption of children

[3] John 17: 12.
[4] *Ibid.*, 10: 27–30.
[5] Matt. 22: 14.
[6] *Ibid.*, 24: 22.
[7] I Cor. 4: 7.
[8] John 15: 5.
[9] Phil. 2: 13.

through Jesus Christ unto Himself, according to the purpose of His will. Unto the praise and glory of His grace, in which He hath graced us in His beloved Son." [10] Again, with more clarity of precision, he writes: "We know that to them that love God all things work together unto good: to such as according to His purpose are called to be saints. For whom He foreknew, He also predestinated to be made conformable to the image of His Son, that He might be the firstborn amongst many brethren. And whom He predestinated, them He also called. And whom He called, them He also justified. And whom He justified, them He also glorified." [11]

With St. Augustine, St. Thomas, and St. Bellarmine, we must remark that in this last text the words, "whom He foreknew, He also predestinated," do not refer to the divine foreknowledge of meritorious acts. Nowhere in St. Paul do we find any foundation for this interpretation, and it would contradict several of his texts, especially this one and the ones we are about to cite. The meaning is: "those whom God foreknew, looking favorably upon them," which is a frequent acceptation of the verb "to know" in the Bible, as in the text: "God has not cast away His people which He foreknew." [12] This exegesis of St. Augustine, St. Thomas, and St. Robert Bellarmine is upheld at the present day by Lagrange, Allo, Zahn, Julicher, and others. [13]

[10] Eph. 1: 3-7.

[11] Rom. 8: 28-30.

[12] Rom. 11: 2; cf. Matt. 7: 23; Gal. 4: 9; I Cor. 8: 3; 13: 12; II Tim. 2: 19; Ps. 1: 6.

[13] Father Lemonnyer, O.P., has explained the deep significance of this standard text of Rom. 8: 28-30, in his article entitled: "Prédestination," which was written for the Dict. de théol. cath. He remarks that God's intention is manifested in this text by two acts: first, there is the act of foreknowing: "those whom He foreknew" (29); then the act of predestinating: "whom He predestinated" (30). But the act of first intention seems to be passed over in silence. As a matter of fact, remarks Father Lemonnyer, it is indicated in the final clause of v. 29: "that He might be the firstborn amongst many brethren." Here we have this divine intention. . . . This presupposed intention suffices to provide the means for its realization, that is, the discerning and decreeing of the putting of it into effect. This discernment is the foreknowledge, and

In the Epistle to the Romans (chaps. 9–12), St. Paul in plain terms also sets forth God's sovereign independence in the dispensation of His graces. The Jews, who were the chosen people, are rejected because of their unbelief, and salvation is announced to the Gentiles as a result of Israel's obduracy. The Apostle prophesies, however, the final conversion and salvation of the Jews, and he formulates the principle of predilection, which is applied to nations and individuals: "What shall we say then? Is there injustice with God? God forbid! For He saith to Moses: I will have mercy on whom I will have mercy. And I will show mercy to whom I will show mercy. So then it is not of him that willeth nor of him that runneth, but of God that showeth mercy." [14]

Hence the Apostle's conclusion: "O the depth of the riches of the wisdom and of the knowledge of God! How incomprehensible are His judgments, and how unsearchable His ways! For who hath known the mind of the Lord? Or who hath been His counsellor? Or who hath first given to Him, and recompense shall be made him? For of Him and by Him and in Him are all things. To Him be glory for ever. Amen." [15]

We shall return later on to a discussion of the literal meaning and scope of these texts, when we present the scriptural background for the teaching of St. Thomas. It suffices for the present to point out with the Thomists and St. Robert Bellarmine,[16] what Scripture has to say about the gratuitousness of predestination to eternal life. Such is the teaching of Scripture, which declares three indisputable things on this point, namely: (1) God has chosen certain persons to constitute the

---

this decree is the predestination. Both are evidently acts of the practical reason moved by a preconceived intention."

Father Lemonnyer insists upon the gratuitous character of the divine purpose, which is the reason of our salvation and our call. It seems that this gratuitousness must be extended to predestination. Cf. II Tim. 1: 9; Eph. 1: 11; Tit. 3: 5.

[14] Rom. 9: 14–17; cf. Lagrange, *Epitre aux Romains*, 1916, chap. 9, p. 244.
[15] *Ibid.*, 11: 33–36.
[16] *De gratia et lib. arb.*, Bk. II, chaps. 9–15.

elect.[17] (2) He has caused this election to be efficacious so that they will infallibly get to heaven: "My sheep shall not perish for ever. And no man shall pluck them out of My hand." [18] "Whom He predestinated, them He also called. And whom He called, them He also justified. And whom He justified, them He also glorified." [19] (3) God's choice of the elect was entirely gratuitous and previous to any consideration of foreseen merits: "Fear not little flock, for it hath pleased your Father to give you a kingdom." [20] "You have not chosen Me, but I have chosen you; and have appointed you, that you should go and should bring forth fruit and your fruit should remain." [21] "Even so then, at this present time also, there is a remnant saved according to the election of grace. And if by grace, it is not now by works, otherwise grace is no more grace." [22] "As He chose us in Him before the foundation of the world, that we should be holy," [23] and not because we were so, or because He foresaw that we would be so by our own efforts. "For whom He foreknew (in His benevolence), He also predestinated to be made conformable to the image of His Son." [24]

From all these passages of Scripture, St. Augustine formulated this classical definition: "Predestination is the foreknowledge and preparedness on God's part to bestow the favors by which all those are saved who are to be saved." [25] St. Augustine is still more explicit on this point when he writes: "God already knew, when He predestined, what He must do to bring His elect infallibly to eternal life." [26]

[17] Matt. 20: 16; 24: 31; Luke 12: 32; Rom. 8: 33; Eph. 1: 4.
[18] John 10: 27 f.; cf. Matt. 24: 24; John 6: 39.
[19] Rom. 8: 30.
[20] Luke 12: 32.
[21] John 15: 16.
[22] Rom. 11: 5.
[23] Eph. 1: 4.
[24] Rom. 8: 29.
[25] De dono perseverantiae, chap. 14.
[26] De praedestinatione sanctorum, chap. 10.

CHAPTER II

THE TEACHING OF THE CHURCH

THE teaching of the Church on this subject was formulated on the one hand against Pelagianism, and on the other against predestinarianism, Protestantism, and Jansenism.

DECLARATIONS OF THE CHURCH AGAINST
PELAGIANISM AND SEMIPELAGIANISM

The meaning and scope of the declarations of the Church against Pelagianism and Semipelagianism are evident, if we bear in mind the principles of these condemned doctrines and the bearing they have on predestination.

1) The Pelagians held that grace is not necessary for the observance of the precepts of the Christian law, but merely for greater facility in their observance, and that by our naturally good works we may merit the first grace. Hence they said the foreknowledge of good works, whether natural or supernatural, is the cause of predestination. Pelagianism was first condemned in the two councils of Carthage and Milevi (416). It was afterward condemned in the Council of Carthage held in 418, but the canons of this council have been assigned by mistake to the Second Council of Milevi. Canon 6 especially has in mind this false teaching, that "without grace we can keep the commandments . . . and that grace is not necessary except for making it easier to keep them."

2) The Semipelagians, as we see from the letters of SS. Prosper and Hilary to St. Augustine, admitted: (1) that man does not need grace for that beginning of faith and good will

spoken of as the "beginning of salvation," and that he can persevere until death without any special help; (2) that God wills equally the salvation of all, although special graces are granted to some privileged souls; (3) consequently predestination is identical with the foreknowledge of the beginning of salvation and of merits by which man perseveres in doing good without any special help; negative reprobation is identical with the foreknowledge of demerits. Thus predestination and negative reprobation follow human election, whether this be good or bad.

Such an interpretation eliminates the element of mystery in predestination spoken of by St. Paul. God is not the author but merely the spectator of that which distinguishes the elect from the rest of mankind. The elect are not loved and helped more by God.

Concerning children who die before the age of reason, the Semipelagians said that God predestines or reprobates them, foreseeing the good or bad acts they would have performed if they had lived longer. That means a foreknowledge of the conditionally free acts of the future or of the *futuribilia,* previous to any divine decree. This reminds us of the theory of the *scientia media,* which was proposed later by Molina. The opponents of this doctrine reply that such an interpretation would mean that children are marked for reprobation on account of sins they did not commit.

Against these principles, St. Augustine, especially in his writings toward the end of his life,[1] shows from the testimony of Holy Scripture that: (1) man cannot, without a special and gratuitous grace, have the "beginning of salvation," and that he cannot persevere until the end without a special and gratuitous grace; (2) that the elect, as their name indicates, are loved more and helped more, and that the divine election is therefore previous to foreseen merits, which are the result of grace; (3) that God does not will equally the salvation of all.

[1] *PL,* XLIV, 959; XLV, 993.

The Council of Orange (529), in condemning Semipelagianism, took many of its formulas from the writings of St.
Augustine and St. Prosper. All historians agree that it disap-
proved of the Semipelagian denials of the gratuitousness of
grace and of its necessity for the beginning of salvation and
for final perseverance.[2]

That is the minimum and it is admitted by all. But many
historians and theologians, among whom are the Thomists
and Augustinians, considering the obvious sense of the terms
employed by the Second Council of Orange and of the various statements of St. Paul, see therein an additional affirmation of the intrinsic efficacy of grace, presupposed by the
principle of predilection.

We shall return to this point. But in any case, from this
minimum admitted by all we get three propositions to which
all Catholic theologians subscribe. They are: (1) Predestination to the first grace is not because God foresaw our naturally
good works, nor is the beginning of salutary acts due to
natural causes; (2) predestination to glory is not because God
foresaw we would continue in the performance of supernaturally meritorious acts apart from the special gift of final
perseverance; (3) complete predestination, in so far as it comprises the whole series of graces from the first up to glorification, is gratuitous or previous to foreseen merits. These three
propositions are admitted by all Catholic theologians. But
Thomists and Augustinians on the one hand, and Molinists
and congruists on the other, differ in their interpretation of
them.

a) The first proposition which concerns the beginning of
salvation is understood by Molina, in accordance with his
principle, as meaning that "whenever the free will by its own
natural powers attempts to do what it can, God bestows the
prevenient grace, on account of Christ's merits." [3] The Thom-

---

[2] Denz., nos. 176, 177, 179, 183, 806.
[3] *Concordia*, disp. 10, q.14, a.13 (1876 ed., p. 564).

ists and Augustinians understand this proposition in a different sense, so that it reads: To the man who does what he can with the help of actual grace, God does not refuse habitual grace. This safeguards much better the gratuity of both actual and habitual graces, as defined by the Council of Orange.[4]

b) The second proposition, which concerns final perseverance, is understood by Molinists and congruists as meaning that the actual grace of final perseverance is extrinsically efficacious inasmuch as our consent is foreseen by means of the *scientia media*. On the contrary, Thomists and Augustinians understand this grace to be intrinsically efficacious; and this seems to be far more in agreement with the tenor of canon ten of the Council of Orange which reads: "God's help is always to be sought even for the regenerated and holy, that they may come to a happy end, or that they may continue in the performance of good works."[5] This canon summarizes the teaching of St. Prosper.[6] Now St. Prosper follows St. Augustine, who considers the great grace of final perseverance as belonging properly to the elect, and as efficacious of itself. "It is a grace," he says, "that is spurned by no one whose heart is hardened, and it is therefore given that the hardness of heart may first be eliminated."[7] Molina, admitting his departure from the teaching of St. Augustine, in opposition to him says: "It may happen that two persons receive in an equal degree the interior grace of vocation; one of them of his own free will is converted, and the other remains an infidel. It may even happen that one who receives a far greater prevenient grace when called, of his own free will is not converted, and another, who receives a far less grace, is converted."[8] It seems difficult to reconcile this with what the Council of Trent affirms of the great gift of final persever-

4 Denz., nos. 176–78, 199, 200.
5 *Ibid.*, no. 183.
6 *PL*, XLV, 1815.
7 *De praed. sanct.*, chap. 8.
8 *Loc. cit.*, disp. 12, p. 51.

ance, stating that it is a "gift which cannot be obtained from any other than from Him who is able to establish him who standeth [9] that he stand perseveringly, and to restore him who falleth." [10] All these expressions seem to denote a grace that is efficacious of itself and not because of our foreseen consent. The Council of Trent, too, calls this grace "that great and special gift of final perseverance." [11] It is hard to see how this can finally be construed as a case of being placed in favorable circumstances in which God foresaw that of two persons who receive equal help from Him, one would persevere, and the other would not. Is not any devaluation of God's gift a corresponding devaluation of the mystery?

The Council of Trent also says: "No one, moreover, so long as he is in this mortal life, ought so far to presume as regards the secret mystery of divine predestination as to determine for certain that he is assuredly among the number of the predestined; as if it were true that he who is justified either cannot sin any more, or, if he do sin, that he ought to promise himself an assured repentance. For except by special revelation it cannot be known whom God hath chosen unto Himself." [12]

In favor of the Augustinian and Thomist doctrine, the following argument has also in all fairness been brought forward that, according to the Council of Trent, the grace of final perseverance cannot be merited, at least *de condigno;* for the council states that the just man can merit eternal life, "provided he die in the state of grace." [13] Now this latter cannot be merited, for the state of grace and continuation in the same, since these are the principle of merit, cannot be merited. From this it follows that predestination to the grace of final perseverance, by which one is ultimately disposed for heav-

[9] Rom. 14: 4.
[10] Denz., no. 806.
[11] *Ibid.,* no. 826.
[12] *Ibid.,* no. 805.
[13] *Ibid.,* no. 842.

enly glory, is not because of foreseen merits. Therefore predestination to heavenly glory, which is included in the former, is also gratuitous.

If then we wish to affirm that predestination to heavenly glory is the result of foreseen merits, we must add what would seem to nullify this affirmation and say: provided that God gratuitously maintains us in the possession of these merits until death. As a matter of fact, Molina says, true to his principle —and it is the indispensable minimum—provided that God, according to His entirely gratuitous good pleasure, wills to place man in those circumstances in which He foresees by His *scientia media* that this man will persevere. From this and from his pact theory concerning the beginning of salvation,[14] Molinism avoids Semipelagianism; the Thomists, however, think it seems to depreciate the first grace and that great and special gift of final perseverance.

c) The third proposition. In this last case we are concerned with complete predestination, which includes the whole series of graces. All theologians are unanimous in saying against the Semipelagians, that this is gratuitous or previous to foreseen merits. Molina admits it, but he adds: "To the foreknowledge which is included in predestination on the part of the intellect, there is attached the condition of the use of free will without which there would have been no preordaining by God." [15] Contrary to this, Augustinians and Thomists understand complete predestination as it is explained by St. Thomas: "It is impossible that the whole of the effect of predestination in general should have any cause as coming from us; because whatsoever is in man disposing him toward salvation, is all

---

[14] This pact theory between God and Christ the Redeemer is thus expressed in Molina's *Concordia*, disp., 10, p. 43: "Among the laws which Christ and the eternal Father decreed concerning the aids and gifts which Christ merited for us simply and freely to be bestowed upon us, there is one which was most in conformity with reason, and it is this, that as often as we attempt to do what we can by our own natural powers, the assistance of grace is at our disposal for us to succeed in doing those things we ought for our salvation.

[15] *Concordia*, q. 23, sept. concl., p. 516.

included under the effect of predestination; even the preparation for grace." [16] Thus even the free determination disposing
one toward salvation is entirely included in the effect of
predestination. "There is no distinction," says St. Thomas,
"between what flows from free will, and what is of predestination; as there is no distinction between what flows from a
secondary cause and from a first cause." [17]

It is clear that this way of interpreting complete predestination presupposes the intrinsic efficacy of the divine decrees
and of grace. It also includes, as a natural consequence, the
absolute validity of the principle of predilection; whereas
these are not presupposed in the interpretation given by
Molinists and congruists. Now St. Thomas is apparently per-
suaded that the proposition "whatsoever is in man disposing
him toward salvation, is all included under the effect of predestination," as well as the intrinsic efficacy of grace and the
principle of predilection express the teaching of St. Augustine and of the Second Council of Orange. We shall leave this
for the reader to judge, and all that we shall do is to quote
the principal canons of this council.

The whole process of salvation and each of its salutary acts,
with all the goodness in them, is attributed to God by the
council. Canon 9 reads: "It is God's gift when we think aright
and restrain ourselves from walking in the path of error and
corruption. As often as we do good, it is God who works in
us and with us enabling us to act." [18] This canon is a recapitu-
lation of Prosper's twenty-second sentence, which repeats the
teaching of St. Augustine.

It concerns efficacious grace by which we not only can but
actually do what is right. The fact that God operates in us,
enabling us to act, is verified in every free act disposing us
to salvation. We cannot at all see how this free determination
disposing us to salvation, as a free determination, should es-

[16] *Summa theol.*, Ia, q.23, a.5.
[17] *Ibid.*
[18] Denz., no. 182.

cape the divine causality. The obvious sense of the text is, that God works in us and with us, as St. Paul says: "It is God who worketh in you, both to will and to accomplish." [19] There is a grace that is efficacious in this sense that it is effective of the act, although it does not exclude our co-operation, but in a mysterious way starts it. Canon twelve formulates the principle of predilection: "God so loves us, as we shall be by the gift of His grace, not as we are by our own merit." Taken from Prosper's fifty-sixth sentence, it follows immediately from this that God so much the more loves us, as we shall be better by the gift of His grace. In other words, no one would be better than another, if he were not loved more by God. In the quotation of this canon,[20] there is reference in the margin to the "Indiculus," on the Grace of God,[21] where it is said: "There is no other way by which anyone is pleasing to God except by what He Himself has bestowed." Therefore, one is not more pleasing to God than another, without having received more from Him. If, on the contrary, grace became efficacious *in actu secundo* by our consent, then it would follow that of two men who received equal help, one would become better, and this without having been loved more, helped more, or having received more from God. This is not what the Council of Orange declares, or the "Indiculus" on grace, which latter is a collection of the declarations of the Roman Church, compiled in all probability by the future pope St. Leo I. This collection of declarations by the Church met with universal reception about the year 500.[22] If it be so, how is it

[19] Phil. 2: 13.
[20] Denz., no. 185.
[21] *Ibid.*, no. 134.
[22] As a proof of this, consult the *Indiculus*, Denz., nos. 131, 133. The opening words of this latter canon are: "It is only by Christ's help that anyone makes good use of free will." Cf. also nos. 134, 135, 137, 141. In this last reference we read: "By God's help free will is not taken away but made free. . . . He acts, to be sure, in us so that what He wills, we both will and do." In no. 142 we read: "There must not be the least disparagement of the effect and esteem of God's grace."

possible for the salutary act, in so far as it is a free determination, not to depend upon the efficacy of grace, but to be the cause of this efficacy?

There are still other ways in which the Council of Orange has expressed the principle of predilection. Canon sixteen reads: "Let no one glory in what he may seem to have, as if he had not received it." And canon twenty states: "God does many good things in man, which man does not accomplish; but there is no good work done by man which God has not assisted him to do." [23]

Taken from St. Augustine and the three hundred and twelfth of Prosper's sentences, these canons point out that all good comes from God either as the author of nature or of grace; hence it is only through having received more from God that one is better than another. This is also the meaning of canon twenty-two, which reads: "No man can claim as his own anything except lying and sin. If a man hath anything of truth and righteousness it is from that fountain which it behoves us to thirst after in this desert that being, so to speak, refreshed with some of its drops we may not faint by the way." [24] This canon which is taken from the writings of St. Augustine,[25] speaks of God as the author of good things both in the order of nature and of grace; and this is more clearly expressed in canon nineteen.[26] Hence it does not follow that all the works of infidels are sins. Some of them are morally good in the natural order, such as paying one's debts and providing for the support of one's children. But even this natural goodness comes from God, who is the author of all good; and it is not independently of Him that such a naturally good act is performed by this particular man and not by that other, who is permitted to act contrariwise and sin.

All these canons of the Council of Orange, which are taken

[23] Denz., nos. 189, 193.
[24] *Ibid.*, no. 195.
[25] Hom. on John 5: 1.
[26] Denz., no. 192.

from the writings of St. Augustine or of St. Prosper show that the least we may say is what H. Leclercq affirms in his French translation of Hefele's work. He writes: "What seems to be an undeniable fact is, that the Church adopted (in the Second Council of Orange) the Augustinian theory in its defense of the fundamental principles against the Pelagians and Semipelagians, of original sin, of the necessity and gratuitousness of grace, and of our absolute dependence upon God for every salutary act." [27] There is no reason therefore to be astonished that Augustinians and Thomists detected from the obvious sense of the terms of this council the principle of predilection, this principle which presupposes the intrinsic efficacy of grace. They also detect this principle in the epistles of St. Paul, for he says: "It is God who worketh in you, according to His good will. For who distinguisheth thee? Or what hast thou that thou hast not received? [28]

Is it not this that the Semipelagians denied in saying that God wills to save equally all men and that He is not the author but the onlooker of what distinguishes the just from the impious, and the elect from the rest of mankind?

DECLARATIONS OF THE CHURCH AGAINST PREDESTINARIANISM

The declarations of the Church in the Council of Orange express one aspect of the great mystery with which we are concerned; the other is presented to us by what the Church taught first of all against predestinarianism, and then against Calvinism, Bajanism, and Jansenism.

1) In the fifth century. Lucidus, a priest of the Catholic Church who was accused of having taught predestinarianism or predestination to evil, made a retractation of his teaching in the Council of Arles, which was held in the year 473. His

---

27 Cf. *Histoire des conciles*, II, 1102 note.
28 Phil. 2: 13; I Cor. 4: 7.

opinion, as formulated by the council, reads as follows: "That Christ the Lord, our Savior, did not die for the salvation of all mankind; . . . that God's foreknowledge forcibly impels man to everlasting death, or that those who are lost, are lost by God's will. . . . Likewise I reject the opinion of one who says that some are destined to everlasting death and others are predestined to everlasting life." [29] In his retraction, Lucidus affirmed that he who is lost could have been saved.[30] We must beware of attaching too much importance to the decisions made against Lucidus. They are the result, it has been said, of an anti-Augustinian environment.

2) In the ninth century. As for the controversies of the ninth century in connection with predestination, we must by all means quote the decisions of the councils of Quierzy (853),[31] Valence (855),[32] Langres, Toul, and finally Thuzey.[33] From these divers texts it follows: (1) that God wills in a certain way to save all men; (2) that there is no such thing as predestination to evil, but that God decreed from all eternity to inflict the penalty of damnation for the sin of final impenitence, a sin which He foresaw and in no way caused but merely permitted.

From the canons of the above-mentioned councils we see the meaning and scope of these two propositions. Predestination to evil is clearly excluded in the first canon of Quierzy. As for predestination to eternal life, it is viewed as a grace, a special mercy as regards the elect whom God by His grace has predestined to life, and to eternal life. The second canon reads: "Our will, aided by prevenient grace and concomitant is free to do what is good; and our will, forsaken by grace, is free to do what is evil." These latter words indicate that sin does not happen without God's permission, who justly al-

---

29 Denz., no. 3026.

30 For an explanation of this episode, consult the *Dict. de théol. cath.*

31 Denz., no. 316.

32 *Ibid.*, no. 320.

33 *PL,* CXXVI, 123. Cf. *Dict. de théol. cath.,* art. "Prédestination."

lows it to happen in one, while mercifully preserving another from it. This truth is brought out more clearly in the following canon, and what is of essential significance is that portion of it which states: "Almighty God wills without exception, all men to be saved, though not all are saved. That some are saved, however, is the gift of Him who saves; if some perish, it is the fault of them that perish." This canon is taken from the writings of St. Prosper. From this third canon of Quierzy we see that, if the will to save is universal, it is not equally so for all, as the Pelagians wanted it to be. It is efficacious only as regards the elect, and that in virtue of a special gift; but there is no predestination to evil. The two aspects of the mystery are affirmed in plain language, but we fail to perceive the mode of their intimate reconciliation. The fourth canon of Quierzy affirms that Christ died for all men.

The third Council of Valence (855) insisted more strongly on the gratuity of predestination to eternal life in so far as it is distinct from simple foreknowledge, for this latter also extends to evil. According to the declarations of this council, the least good and the least punishment that is justly inflicted, never occur without a positive and infallible decree from God, and no sin is committed, and nowhere by preference, without His foreknowledge and permission.[34]

We know that after the Council of Langres (859), the discussions concerning predestination between Hincmar, the great opponent of Gottschalk, and the Church of Lyons, were terminated at Thuzey in the year 860. The synodal letter, approved in this council, contains the following affirmations.[35] (1) Whatsoever the Lord pleased He hath done in heaven and on earth. For nothing is done in heaven or on earth, except what He Himself is pleased to do, or justly permits to be done. This means that all good things, whether easy or difficult to accomplish, whether natural or supernatural, come

[34] Denz., nos. 321–22.
[35] *PL*, CXXVI, 123.

from God, and that sin does not occur, nor in this one rather than in the other, without His divine permission. Countless consequences evidently are included in this absolutely general principle. The Thomists see in it the equivalent of the principle of predilection. The other assertions of this synodal letter are derived from this general principle. They are as follows: (2) God wills all men to be saved and no one to perish . . . nor after the fall of the first man is it His will forcibly to deprive man of free will. (3) That those, however, who are walking in the path of righteousness, may continue to do so and persevere in their innocence, He heals and aids their free will by grace. (4) They who go far from God, who is desirous of gathering the children of Jerusalem that wills it not, will perish. (5) Hence it is because of God's grace that the world is saved; and it is because man has free will that the world be judged. (6) Adam, through willing what is evil, lost the power to do what is good. . . . Wherefore the whole human race became a mass of perdition. If no one had been rescued from it, God's justice would not have been to blame. That many are saved, however, is due to God's ineffable grace. This last statement repeats what SS. Augustine and Prosper said. Thus at the end of these conferences of the ninth century, the bishops, assembled in council at Thuzey, rejected absolutely the theory of predestination to evil and affirmed God's universal will to save, as Prosper had done. God never commands the impossible, but He wills to make it possible for all to fulfil His precepts and obtain salvation. That is what all the bishops assembled in this last mentioned council affirmed with SS. Augustine and Prosper. But they do not deny, on that account, the other aspect of the mystery, to wit: the absolute gratuity of predestination, of true predestination as opposed to reprobation.

3) In the sixteenth and seventeenth centuries. This teaching of the Church was confirmed both by the decisions of the Council of Trent against the errors of Protestantism and by

the condemnation of Jansenism. The Church again declares that man, though having contracted the stain of original sin, is free to do good by the aid of grace, consenting to co-operate with it, though at the same time he can resist it.[36] From this it follows that God predestines no one to evil; [37] but He wills, on the contrary, the salvation of all men; and Christ dies for all, although all do not receive the benefit that is the fruit of His death, "but only those to whom the merit of His passion is communicated." [38] In the case of adults good works are necessary for salvation, and, in the order of execution, heavenly glory is the reward granted at the end of their probation for meritorious acts.

It is likewise declared against Jansenism that Christ did not die only for the predestined, or only for the faithful; [39] that there is a grace which is truly sufficient, and which makes the fulfilment of God's precepts possible for all those on whom these precepts are imposed. The Church, quoting the words of St. Augustine, says again in refuting the Protestants and Jansenists: "God commands not impossibilities, but, by commanding, both admonishes thee to do what thou art able, and to pray for what thou art not able to do." [40] She also says that "God does not abandon the just without previously having been abandoned by them." [41] It is only mortal sin that deprives them of sanctifying grace, and they are deprived of certain actual graces necessary for salvation only because they resisted sufficient graces. God does not permit us to be tempted beyond our powers of resistance; [42] the grace of conversion is offered to sinners,[43] and only those are deprived of it who, failing in their duty, refuse it, this being

---

36 Denz., no. 797; cf. no. 816.
37 *Ibid.*, no. 827.
38 *Ibid.*, no. 795.
39 *Ibid.*, nos. 1096, 1294, 1380 ff.
40 *Ibid.*, no. 804.
41 *Ibid.*, nos. 804, 806, 1794.
42 *Ibid.*, no. 979.
43 *Ibid.*, no. 807.

something which God permits, but of which He is by no means the cause.[44] The Church, however, though affirming that God by a sufficient grace makes the fulfilment of His precepts possible for all, none the less affirms the efficacy of grace that actually is productive of good works. The Council of Trent declares that "God, unless men be themselves wanting to His grace, as He has begun the good work, so will He perfect it, working in them to will and to accomplish." [45]

What are we to conclude then from the teaching of the Church against the conflicting heresies of Semipelagianism and predestinarianism, heresies that were renewed by Calvinism and Jansenism?

To sum up: Against Semipelagianism, we must say that the Church affirms particularly three things: (a) The cause of predestination to grace is not the foreknowledge of naturally good works performed, nor is it due to any preliminary acts of the natural order that are supposed to prepare for salvation. (b) Predestination to glory is not due to foreseen supernatural merits that would continue to be effective apart from the special gift of final perseverance. (c) Complete predestination, which comprises the whole series of graces, is gratuitous or previous to foreseen merits. And St. Thomas understands this to mean that "whatsoever is in man disposing him towards salvation, is all included under the effect of predestination." [46] In a word: "that some are saved is the gift of Him who saves." [47]

4) Against predestinarianism and the doctrines of Protestantism and Jansenism that revive it, the Church teaches: (a) God wills in a certain way to save all men and He makes the fulfilment of His precepts possible for all; (b) There is no predestination to evil, but God has decreed from all eternity to inflict eternal punishment for the sin of final impenitence

[44] *Ibid.*, nos. 816, 827, 1677.
[45] *Ibid.*, no. 806; Phil. 2: 13.
[46] *Summa theol.*, Ia, q.23, a.5.
[47] Denz., no. 318.

which He foresaw, He being by no means the cause of it but merely permitting it.

We see that the teaching of the Church against these conflicting heresies may be summed up in these profound words of St. Prosper, which the Council of Quierzy makes its own. Against Pelagianism and Semipelagianism the council says: "That some are saved, is the gift of Him who saves." Against predestinarianism it says: "That some perish, is the fault of those who perish." Holy Scripture expressed the same thought in these words: "Destruction is thy own, O Israel; thy help is only in Me." [48]

There is no difference of degree between the assent of the Christian mind unhesitatingly given to these two great and indisputable truths, and the mysterious mode of the intimate reconciliation.

[48] Osee 13: 9.

CHAPTER III

The Principal Difficulties of the Problem and the Method of Procedure

THE DIFFICULTIES

FROM what has just been said we see that the first difficulty was always how to reconcile predestination with God's will to save all mankind. On the one hand Scripture declares that God wills all men to be saved; [1] on the other hand, it says that all are not predestined, but that "whom He predestined, them He also called . . . and also justified . . . and glorified." [2] It even says that "He hath mercy on whom He will. And whom He will, He hardeneth." [3] Therefore the predestined will infallibly be saved, and the others not. Hence arises the difficulty. How can predestination, which is infallible in its effect, be reconciled with the will to save all mankind, since the salvation of many will not be realized?

Is it human effort that makes God's help efficacious, or is it the intrinsic efficacy of God's help that prompts human effort? And if grace is of itself efficacious, how is it that God mercifully grants it to the elect and justly refuses it to the rest? We see that this mystery concerns the intimate reconciliation of God's infinite mercy and justice, and the free manifestation of these divine perfections. Philosophy, confronted with a difficulty of the same kind, has to explain how the presence of evil, especially moral evil, can be reconciled with God's infinite goodness and omnipotence.

[1] I Tim. 2: 4.
[2] Rom. 8: 29 ff.
[3] *Ibid.* 9: 18.

A second difficulty of this problem is that it is no longer a question of the two groups of human beings, the elect and those not among the elect, but of individuals. The question is this. Why has God placed in the number of the elect this person and not that other? Why has He chosen Peter rather than Judas, and not vice versa? Seemingly unjust is this unequal distribution of such gifts to human beings who are equal both by nature and by reason of original sin.

This is the difficulty that St. Paul expresses when he writes: "What shall we say then? Is there injustice with God? God forbid. For He saith to Moses: I will have mercy on whom I will have mercy. And I will shew mercy to whom I will shew mercy." [4] St. Paul thus answers the difficulty by affirming the principle of predilection, or of the gratuity of grace to which we can have no claim. Further on he states: "O the depth of the riches of the wisdom and of the knowledge of God! How incomprehensible are His judgments, and how unsearchable His ways!" [5] St. Augustine expresses the mystery in these words: "Why He draweth one and not another, seek not to judge if thou dost not wish to err." [6]

St. Thomas called special attention to these two great difficulties in the mystery of predestination; one difficulty is general in scope, the other of particular interest. He says: "The reason for the predestination of some, and the reprobation of others, must be sought for in the goodness of God. . . . God wills to manifest His goodness in men; in respect to those whom He predestines, by means of His mercy, in sparing them; and in respect of others, whom He reprobates, by means of His justice in punishing them. . . . Yet why He chooses some for glory and reprobates others, has no reason except the divine will. . . . Neither on this account can there be said to be injustice in God, if He prepares unequal lots for

4 *Ibid.* 9: 14.
5 *Ibid.* 11: 33.
6 *On St. John,* hom. 26, the beginning.

not unequal things. . . . In things which are given gratuitously a person can give more or less, just as he pleases (provided he deprives nobody of his due), without any infringement of justice." [7]

The answers given by St. Paul, St. Augustine and St.
Thomas show there is no contradiction. But underlying these
two aspects there is an inscrutable mystery because it is essentially supernatural and also because the divine intervention is supremely free. This mystery is supernatural not only
modally like a miracle that can be known by natural means,
but it is supernatural because by its very nature it belongs
to that class of mysteries which concerns the intimate life
of God, such as the Trinity, and it thus transcends the natural powers of every intellect whether human or angelic, of
every created and creatable intellect. Moreover, in this mystery there is the intervention of God's supremely free good
pleasure, the *divinum beneplacitum* which St. Paul speaks
of. This good pleasure, which is not at all a caprice—for it
is the very essence of wisdom and holiness—is for us, as everything is which concerns God's sovereign liberty, a profound
mystery. By this good pleasure God mercifully grants His
grace to one of the two thieves crucified with the Savior,
whereas in justice He permits the other to resist to the very
end, and so lets him remain in sin.

Hence we see in this mystery an intervention of infinite
mercy and justice and of sovereign liberty, all of which absolutely transcend the powers of every created and creatable intellect. St. Thomas calls attention to this obscurity, which
comes either from the essentially supernatural nature of the
object, or from the fact that the truth pertains to the contingent order and as yet is undetermined. He says that there
are things far removed from our knowledge, either spatially
or because of their supernatural transcendence, such as the
mystery of the Trinity, which is absolutely determined and

[7] *Summa theol.,* Ia, q.23, a.5 ad 3um.

knowable in itself, but not to us. Then there are things which, since they are not of themselves determined, are not knowable in themselves, such as future contingent things, the truth of which can be determined and known by God in His supremely free decree.[8]

Such is the difficulty of the problem, or rather the great obscurity of the mystery and dogma which claims our attention. The theologian, seeking the method to be followed, must bear in mind what St. Thomas said: "In questions of sacred doctrine we may have recourse to philosophy in order to refute what is said against the faith, either by showing it to be false, or of no consequence."[9] Theology thus averts the evident contradiction; but it is not its province to prove philosophically the intrinsic possibility of mysteries. Just as the reality of the mysteries of the Trinity, incarnation, and predestination remains obscure to us in this life, so does their intrinsic possibility. (Cf. Vatican Council; Denz., no. 1795 f.)

Thus we see the whole difficulty of the problem, and consequently how easily we may be deceived unless we follow faithfully the teaching of Holy Scripture, the councils, and the great doctors of the Church. It is easy to favor one or other of the contrary heresies, for instance, by speaking of the will to save mankind in a manner that savors of Semipelagianism, which denies the dogma of predestination; or, on the other hand, we may speak of predestination in a manner and tone that savors of predestinarianism, which denies the will to save mankind. A slight exaggeration, by the addition of some adverb, suffices to incline one toward either of the opposing heresies, just as the introduction of a single note suffices to modify one of Beethoven's symphonies, so as to destroy its harmony. How is the theologian to proceed in the midst of these difficulties?

[8] *Loc. cit.*, IIa IIae, q. 171, a. 3.
[9] *In Boetium de Trinitate*, q. 11, a. 3.

THE METHOD TO BE FOLLOWED

On this point the theologian must bear in mind what the Vatican Council says: "Reason, indeed, enlightened by faith, when it seeks earnestly, piously, and calmly, attains by a gift from God some, and that a very fruitful, understanding of mysteries; partly from the analogy of those things which it naturally knows, partly from the relations which the mysteries bear to one another and to the last end of man. But reason never becomes capable of apprehending mysteries as it does those truths which constitute its proper object." [10]

The theologian must also bear in mind that just as God permits evil only for the sake of a greater good, so He permits conflicting heresies for the sole reason that thus the sublimity and value of truth may, by way of contrast, stand out more prominently. We must then profit by these opposing heresies, but never at the expense of detracting from the sublimity of the mystery about which we are seeking to acquire some understanding.

A watchful theologian will observe that in this difficult question, as in all the great problems of philosophy and theology, the human mind, inclined to systematize and forgetting that the tendency to synthesize is superior to the tendency to systematize, is at first inclined to posit an extreme thesis, which at times seems to express a profundity of thought, but which in reality is superficial, as in the cases of Pelagianism and Semipelagianism. Then, by way of reaction, the mind inclines to an antithesis just as extreme and superficial, as in the case of predestinarianism and the errors revived by it.

Furthermore, the theologian must take note of the attempts at reconciliation proposed by eclecticism, which, without any guiding principle, selects what appears to it to be the truth from the two opposing camps. By this means it gets the impression that the solution is to be found not only mid-

[10] Cf. *Ibid.*, no. 1796.

way between the extreme errors, but that it is far above them, and also above all eclectic reconciliations, and in this respect it is like the culminating point reached by the great doctors of the Church, who derived their spiritual sustenance from the substantial nourishment of Scripture and tradition.

Whereas eclecticism does not go more than halfway, these great doctors reached that higher synthesis in which the various aspects of the real are reconciled by the light of the sublimest and most universal of principles. Was this not what St. Augustine did? St. Thomas did so, too, though with greater precision, when he brought out the full sublimity and universality contained in the principle that *the love of God is the cause of all good.* Hence it follows that God wills to save all men, by making it really possible for all to keep His commandments, and hence it follows that one would not be better than another, unless he were loved more by God.[11]

We shall insist on these principles when we come to classify the various theological systems, and from this classification the culminating point of the mystery will be more clearly seen. Here we merely say that often, after we have discovered a synthesis of a truly higher order that safeguards in its entirety God's revealed word, the human mind, like one tired out, descends from its halfway post to consider the more or less arbitrary combinations and fluctuations of eclecticism, which substitutes for the divine obscurity of the mystery an apparent clarity that is without any real foundation. Hence the necessity of returning to the teaching of the great doctors of the Church, who were not merely learned historians and capable reasoners, but by the gifts of the Holy Ghost were great contemplatives, with a profound knowledge of God's revelation.

Certainly we would not form a true idea of the mystery of predestination by depreciating God's infinite mercy, either as regards all human beings (the will to save mankind) or as re-

11 *Loc. cit.,* Ia, q.20, a.3, 4.

gards the elect (gratuity of election). Nor would we do so by depreciating His justice which gives to all what they absolutely need and which cannot punish anyone for doing what could not be helped, since such acts would not be sins.

In the course of his investigation the theologian must not forget that several great contemplatives, such as St. Theresa, have declared that the greater the obscurity in the mysteries, the greater was their attachment to them, because faith is of things unseen and because this obscurity results not from the absurdity or incoherence of the mysteries, but from the presence of a light too great for our feeble vision. Lastly, the theologian must bear in mind what the great masters of the spiritual life, such as St. John of the Cross, have said about the passive purifications of the soul in which, as a rule, the mystery of predestination appears in all its transcendent obscurity, so that the soul which has gone through this ordeal may feel the necessity of rising above all human conceptions with their apparent clarity, and thus abandon itself completely to God in sentiments of pure faith, filial confidence, and love.

St. Thomas, too,[12] says that the gift of understanding purifies the mind of the believer—and therefore of the theologian —of that too great attachment to sensible images and to those things that tend to lead them into error, thus enabling them to penetrate beyond the meaning of Holy Scripture and enter into the spirit of the mysteries, perceiving them in their supernatural sublimity. Such is the method of procedure not only in speculative theology, but also in contemplation, in which no aspect of the mystery is unduly limited by the restrictions of reasoning. This goes to show, especially in the case of these sublime and difficult questions, the necessity of reading first of all the works of the great theologians who were also great contemplatives. These excelled in both kinds of wisdom spoken of by St. Thomas: [13] acquired wisdom, which is

12 *Ibid.*, IIa IIae, q.8, a.7.
13 *Ibid.*, q.45, a.2.

according to the perfect use of reason, and the gift of wisdom, which is the principle of a quasi-experimental knowledge that has its foundation in the special inspiration of the Holy Ghost and in the connatural disposition of charity for the things that pertain to God. Is not this what the Vatican Council alludes to in the words already quoted, when it says: "Reason, indeed, enlightened by faith, when it seeks earnestly, piously, and calmly, attains by a gift from God some, and that a very fruitful, understanding of mysteries"?

In such an atmosphere we no longer feel inclined to say that thinking about these inscrutable mysteries is useless. On the contrary, we see that they constitute the final goal of all things spiritual and that they are increasingly the object of contemplation in proportion as the Lord purifies the soul.

CHAPTER IV

The Classification of the Theological Systems

THE revealed doctrine of predestination and of the will to save mankind is like a mountain peak towering above the two precipices of Pelagianism and Semipelagianism on the one hand, and predestinarianism on the other.

This representation makes it easier to see how the different theological systems are at variance with one another. There seems to be nothing wrong in saying that on one side of this mountain, halfway up, we find Molinism, and a little farther up the congruism of Suarez. On the other side we have the rigid systems of Augustinianism and Thomism, which modify, so it seems, God's universal will to save by making negative reprobation consist in the positive exclusion from heavenly glory as from a favor to which one is not entitled. Still midway between the two sides we find the eclecticism of the congruists of the Sorbonne, who admitted the efficacy of grace for difficult salutary acts and not for those easy of accomplishment.

The mountain peak, which is above the various systems, seems inaccessible to the pilgrim here on earth, to any created intellect, even enlightened by supernatural faith and the gifts of the Holy Ghost. To see this culminating point, the light of glory would be indispensable, that light by which the blessed in heaven see directly the divine essence, the Deity, which contains eminently and formally the attributes of infinite mercy, justice, and sovereign liberty, without any real distinction between them.

This peak is inaccessible to earthly pilgrims. Before it is

reached, there is a doctrine which directs us unfailingly to it, and which, though we do not see the peak, enables us to determine its exact location. It is the doctrine that rests upon the most sublime and universal of principles which mutually adjust one another. It is a doctrine that deducts nothing from these principles and that by means of them surmises where the culminating point is to be found from which these principles are derived and toward which all things converge.

Is not this the doctrine whose major principle is that "the love of God is the source of all good"? Subordinate to it and offsetting each other are two other principles: God by His love makes it possible for all to obey His precepts and attain salvation; one person would not be better than another, unless he were loved more by God.

We are thus led to a methodical classification of the systems. It is not from the defense of any Scholastic doctrine that this classification must receive its inspiration, but this must come from the two great principles of our faith. The first is the omnipotence of God, who in His sovereign goodness predestines and who is the author of all salvation. The second principle is His will to save all men.

The theological systems relative to predestination have been classified in three ways. The first classification, which is the one more commonly proposed, considers not so much the principles as the conclusions of the theologians. The second, proposed by Father Billot, S.J., is from the Molinist point of view and considers rather the principles adopted by the theologians. The third, proposed by Father del Prado, O.P., is from the Thomist point of view and likewise considers not so much the conclusions as the principles of the theologians.

1) According to the commonly proposed classification, there are two tendencies. Some say the predestination of adults to glory is the result of foreseen merits; these are sponsors of the purely Molinist view, such as Vasquez, Lessius. Others say that the predestination of adults to glory is previ-

ous to foreseen merits, and that negative reprobation or non-election is previous to foreseen demerits. This view is upheld by the Thomists, the Augustinians, the Scotists, and even those congruists who are of the Bellarminian and Suarezian type.

But of these theologians who admit the absolute gratuity of the predestination of adults to glory, almost all of the old school, i. e., the Thomists, the Augustinians, and the Scotists, hold that this predestination has its foundation in the divine predetermining decrees, whereas the congruism of Bellarmine and Suarez rejects these decrees and retains the theory of the *scientia media* to explain the distribution of the grace that is called "congruent," and God's certain knowledge of the consent given by the elect.

2) A second mode of classification was proposed by Father Billot.[1] Whereas for some, he says, the foundation of foreknowledge, which implies predestination, is in the divine predetermining decrees, for others it is in the *scientia media*. Among these latter Father Billot distinguishes between those who, like Vasquez and Lessius, admit the predestination of adults after foreseen future merits, and the non-election of certain ones after foreseen future demerits. He also distinguishes between those who, like Suarez, say that the predestination of adults to glory is even before conditionally future foreseen merits, and that negative reprobation or non-election is even before conditionally future foreseen demerits. Lastly, he distinguishes between those who hold that the predestination of adults to glory is after foreseen merits as conditionally future, but not as simply future. Father Billot admits the last opinion, maintaining that it is the one Molina taught. In other words, for Father Billot, what is absolutely gratuitous is the divine choice of circumstances in which God places a certain person, after having foreseen by the *scientia media* that in these circumstances the consent would be freely given.

[1] *De Deo Uno,* p. 290 (last ed.).

As for individual cases of negative reprobation or non-election, Father Billot's view does not differ much from that of Vasquez, which latter is very difficult to establish.

3) A third classification has been proposed by Father del Prado, O.P.[2] He also takes especially into consideration the principles of the two leading schools, according as they admit either the divine predetermining decrees or the *scientia media*. But he insists that only the theologians admitting the divine predetermining decrees are faithful followers of St. Thomas, who wrote: "Whatsoever is in man disposing him toward salvation, is all included under the effect of predestination, even the preparation for grace."[3] This includes, therefore, even the free determination of the salutary act in so far as it is in this one rather than the other, and not vice versa. This is truly what St. Thomas meant, who previously in the article just quoted had written: "Now there is no distinction between what flows from free will, and what is of predestination; as there is no distinction between what flows from a secondary cause and from a first cause."

Let us add to this what Father del Prado elsewhere points out, that only the theologians who admit the intrinsic efficacy of the divine decrees and of grace recognize the absolute and universal validity of the principle of predilection formulated by St. Thomas in these words: "Since God's love is the cause of goodness in things, no one thing would be better than another, if God did not will greater good for one than for another."[4] Further on in the same work St. Thomas likewise wrote: "He who is better prepared for grace, receives more grace. Yet it is not man who prepares himself for grace, except inasmuch as his free will is prepared by God. Hence the first cause of this diversity is to be sought on the part of God, who dispenses His gifts of grace variously."[5] Similarly St.

[2] *De gratia et libero arbitrio,* III, 188.
[3] *Summa theol.,* Ia, q.23, a.5.
[4] *Ibid.,* q.20, a.3.
[5] *Ibid.,* Ia IIae, q.112, a.4.

Thomas says: "He who make a greater effort does so because of a greater grace; but to do so, he needs to be moved by a higher cause." [6] This principle of predilection, as we shall see, presupposes that the divine decrees concerning our future salutary acts are intrinsically and infallibly efficacious. Otherwise the case might arise in which of two persons who are loved and helped to the same extent by God and who are placed in the same circumstances, one would correspond with the grace received and the other would not. Thus without having been loved and helped more by God, one would prove to be better than the other by doing something either easy or difficult to perform, whether this be the first or final act. This is what, in opposition to St. Thomas, Molina maintained. He thus reduced the principle of predilection to the choice of favorable circumstances in which God places those whom He foresaw by His *scientia media* will of necessity make good use of the grace in these circumstances.

THE SYSTEMS COMPARED

This comparison, after what has just been said, brings us back to the question of the value of the principle of predilection, namely, "that one thing would not be better than another, if God did not will greater good for one than for the other." [7] Is this principle of absolute and universal validity, as the early theologians maintained, or has it merely a relative and restricted value, as the Molinists and the congruists think?

As we shall see when we come to explain the doctrine of St. Thomas, in the philosophical order this principle seems to be a corollary from the principle of causality applied to God's love which is the cause of all good: "Since God's love is the cause of goodness in things," [8] says St. Thomas. In the super-

[6] *Com. in Matt.* 25: 15.
[7] *Loc. cit.,* Ia, q.20, a.3.
[8] *Ibid.,* Ia, q.20, a.3.

natural order this principle of predilection has been revealed. St. Paul expresses it in these terms: "For who distinguisheth thee? Or what has thou that thou hast not received?" [9] He finds the answer in the Old Testament, saying: "For He saith to Moses: I will have mercy on whom I will have mercy. And I will show mercy to whom I will show mercy." [10] It is to this principle of predilection that St. Augustine appeals in support of all his opinions. When the occasion arises he applies the principle even to the angels, remarking that, if the good and bad angels were created equally good, the former were more abundantly assisted and attained eternal happiness, whereas the latter, through their own defectibility, fell from grace.[11] Hence St. Augustine's famous saying: "Why He draweth one and not another, seek not to judge, if thou dost not wish to err." [12]

Moreover, this principle of predilection is absolutely universal. That is why St. Thomas formulates it in the neuter: "One thing would not be better than another, if God did not will greater good for one than for another." [13] This principle is true in every order. It is true of plants with reference to minerals, of animals, of human beings, of angels and their acts, of things in which there is less of perfection or of goodness. It is also true of every man who, from whatever point of view, is better than another, whether this is because of a naturally or supernaturally good act performed, of an act easy or difficult to perform, of an act begun or sustained, of a first or final act.

We shall see that the attempts at synthesis proposed by the Molinists and the congruists after the time of St. Thomas, far from rising to the loftiness of these higher principles formulated by him, failed to realize the sublimity and univer-

9 I Cor. 4: 7.
10 Rom. 9: 15.
11 *De Civ. Dei,* XII, 9.
12 *On St. John,* hom. 26, the beginning.
13 *Loc. cit.,* Ia, q.20, a.3.

sality of these principles as well as their philosophical and theological validity. The principle dominating the whole question is this: "God's love is the cause of all goodness." [14] It follows first of all from this that God, by reason of His love, wills to make it possible for all to obey His commandments and be saved. This real possibility is a good that is the result of God's love or of His universal will to save mankind. It is not effective, however, in all cases, and sometimes God permits the presence of evil in view of a greater good, which often eludes us, and the reason for which we shall see clearly only in heaven. There is in this a very great mystery.

Since God's love is the cause of all goodness, it follows that one thing would not be better than another if God did not will greater good for one than for another. From this principle of predilection St. Thomas deduces all his conclusions about predestination. For them it is like the keystone of an arch, the principle upon which they depend for their preservation and unity.

[14] *Ibid.,* a.2.

CHAPTER V

THE STANDPOINT OF ST. AUGUSTINE AND HIS FIRST DISCIPLES

ST. AUGUSTINE pointed out repeatedly that the fathers who wrote before the rise of the Pelagian heresy touched only incidentally upon the problem of predestination. This circumstance was noted also by St. Robert Bellarmine,[1] who quotes, however, St. John Chrysostom. The latter, commenting on St. Paul's words, "For who distinguisheth thee?" says: "Therefore thou hast what thou hast received, and not only this or that, but whatever thou hast. These are not thy merits, but God's gifts." [2]

We must also observe that the fathers previous to the time of St. Augustine, especially the Greek fathers, often interpreted predestination as meaning the will to give glory after this life. They scarcely spoke of it except by way of exhortation, and then they had in mind the preconceived order of execution in which merits precede glory, whereas as intended by God it happens in the inverse order.[3] In the order of intention God wills the end before the means; that is why He wills

---

[1] *De gratia et libero arbitrio*, II, 14.

[2] *In I Cor.*, 4: 7, hom. 12.

[3] Cf. *Dict. de Théol. Cath.*, art. "Prédestination," by Father Simonin, O.P.
We are aware of the two different interpretations of the teaching of the Greek fathers on this point. Petavius is of the opinion that they side with those who believe in predestination *after foreseen merits.* Thomassin maintains they taught predestination *before foreseen merits.*

In the above-mentioned article Father Simonin concludes that the Greek fathers "neither stated nor solved the problem of predestination, as to whether this is *before or after foreseen merits;* for this often presupposes a conjecture that directly concerns the divine intention." They considered rather in a concrete and practical manner the execution of the divine plan.

to save the good thief to whom He grants the grace of final perseverance. But in the order of execution He gives eternal life as the reward of meritorious acts.

This distinction between the two orders of intention and execution, is a distinction which, taken in general or as regards human affairs, appeals to common sense. What the mason has in mind is the end of his labor, which is the house to be built, although this end is attained after the completion of the work. We cannot conceive of this plan of divine providence apart from this elementary condition. God from all eternity wills first the final end of the universe, which is the manifestation of His goodness, and He ordains the means which concur in this end. This will be fully realized at the end of time, when the elect, who were chosen from all eternity, have reached the end of their course.

As it always happens in such a case, this distinction between intention and execution was only gradually applied to the problem of predestination. At first it was applied obscurely by St. Augustine, and then more and more explicitly by the Scholastic theologians. Only with the rise of the Pelagian heresy did an understanding gradually develop of the necessity of considering predestination, not only in the order of execution, by way of exhortation, but also in the order of intention, so that everything pertaining to our salvation should be attributed to God. This explanatory formula we find in the writings of the earlier fathers, especially in St. John Chrysostom's commentary on the words of St. Paul: "For who is it that distinguisheth thee? Or what hast thou that thou hast not received?" [4] The principle of predilection was already obscurely expressed in these words. It thus became increasingly certain that our Lord's granting of the grace of final perseverance to the good thief in preference to the other was because He willed efficaciously to save him, and this efficacious will was from all eternity.

[4] I Cor. 4: 7.

THE GRATUITY OF PREDESTINATION ACCORDING TO
ST. AUGUSTINE

Among the theologians who in recent times have made a study of St. Augustine's teaching about predestination, Father Cayre [5] and Father J. St. Martin,[6] both of them Augustinian Assumptionists, confirmed the traditional interpretation of St. Augustine's writings. We endorse their conclusions.[7]

This doctrine was more fully discussed in the treatises that St. Augustine wrote toward the end of his life.[8] It was implicitly contained in the following formula: "Lord, give what Thou commandest, and command what Thou wilt." [9]

We remarked above, at the close of the first chapter, that St. Augustine deduced from the New Testament texts referring to this problem, the following definition: "Predestination is the foreknowledge and the preparation of those gifts of God whereby they who are delivered are most certainly delivered." [10] In this definition the word "foreknowledge" is not taken as meaning that God foresees the merits of the elect, but that He foreknows and prepares the gifts by which

---

[5] *Précis de patrologie,* I, 664–77.

[6] *Dict. de théol. cath.,* art. "Prédestination."

[7] Father J. St. Martin *(loc. cit.,* col. 2853) insists, and rightly so, upon the importance of knowing whether the predestined are predestined for grace only or also to glory. This knowledge is necessary even for a delineation of St. Augustine's teaching. Let us recall here the question that gave rise to so much dispute. The Semipelagians did and could admit only predestination to grace. It was a grace, too, which, according to their interpretation, depended for its efficacy on free will alone. St. Augustine was particularly vehement in refuting this theory, for he knew quite well that this was the summing up and pivotal point of the error. According to the teaching of St. Augustine, the reality of predestination consists in the gift of final perseverance, and without this latter there is no predestination, notwithstanding all the other graces received. The holy doctor is not in the least doubt about this.

[8] Cf. *De correptione et gratia; De dono persever., De praed. sanct.*

[9] *Ad Simplicianum,* Bk. I; *De dono persever.,* no. 53; *Confessions,* X, 37, no. 60.

[10] *De dono persever.,* chap. 14.

the elect will actually be saved in the order of execution. St. Augustine clearly says the same: "By His predestination God foreknew what He had to do," [11] so as to direct His elect infallibly to eternal life. Our Lord's words are equivalent to this, for He said: "My sheep . . . shall not perish for ever. And no man shall pluck them out of My hand." [12]

For St. Augustine, predestination presupposes a decisive and definite will on God's part to sanctify and save freely all the elect.[13] God knows them individually and He wills to have them perform meritoriously acts that are required for entering heaven. He wills to give them the grace to persevere until the end, this being what St. Paul means when he says: "For it is God who worketh in you, both to will and to accomplish according to His good will." [14] The fact that God foresees our salutary and meritorious acts presupposes, according to the teaching of St. Augustine, the decree of the divine will as regards these acts.[15] Father Portalié considers that St. Augustine favors the theory of the *scientia media* because of the following sentence: "Far be it that man should have the power to frustrate the intention of the omnipotent Being who has foreknowledge of all things." [16] We know, on the contrary, that for St. Augustine the foreknowledge of our salutary acts refers to what God has decreed that created wills should do. The words that immediately follow the text quoted by Father Portalié prove this to be so, for we read: "These have but a faint conception of so great a question, or what they have does not suffice, who think that the omnipotent God wills something and is powerless to effect it because of weak man preventing Him." Father Portalié should have remarked that

11 *De praed. sanct.*, chap. 10.
12 John 10: 27–28.
13 Cf. *Enchiridion*, chap. 100, no. 26.
14 Phil. 2: 13; cf. *De praed. sanct.*, XVIII, 41; *De dono persever.*, XXIII, 63.
15 *De dono persever.*, XVII, 41, 47; XIX, 48; XX, 50; *De praed. sanct.*, XVII, 34; XVIII, 37.
16 *Dict. de théol. cath.*, art. "Augustin." This sentence is taken from St. Augustine's *Opus imperfectum contra Julianum*, I, 93.

Molina, on the other hand, reproved St. Augustine for not having known of the *scientia media.*[17]

To what cause must we assign, according to the great doctor's opinion, the efficacy of grace that is granted to the elect? The principles laid down by him reveal his mind on this point. God's will, he says, is omnipotent and efficacious (most efficacious).[18] We read in one of his treatises as follows: "There is no doubt that human wills cannot resist (*in sensu composito*) the will of God, who hath done whatsoever He willed in heaven and on earth, in that He does what He wills and when He wills. Undoubtedly He has the power to move the human heart to submit, as it pleases Him, to His omnipotent will." [19] From this we see that, in St. Augustine's view, the decrees of the divine will are infallible not because God foreknows that we will give our consent, but because He is omnipotent. He also says: "The wills of men are more in God's power than in their own." [20] In another of his works he says: "There is no doubt that we will whenever we will, but He is the cause of our willing what is good; . . . there is no doubt that we act whenever we act, but He is the cause of our acting, by most efficaciously strengthening our will." [21] Still more clearly when speaking professedly on this subject of predestination, he says that "no one who is hardened in heart rejects grace, because it is primarily given to remove this hardness of heart." [22]

---

17 Cf. *Concordia,* ed. 1876, p. 546.

18 Cf. *Enchiridion,* chaps. 95 ff.

19 *De correptione et gratia,* chap. 14.

20 *Ibid.,* cf. *De civitate Dei,* V, 9.

21 *De gratia et libero arbitrio,* chap. 16.

22 *De praed. sanct.,* chap. 8. In his tractate *ad Simplicianum,* Bk. I, q.2, no. 13, St. Augustine speaks of a congruent grace that is adapted to the dispositions of the individual, these being known by God. Some have sought to interpret this as meaning a congruent grace that is not intrinsically efficacious, such as we shall see later on Suarez conceives it to be. Father Guillermin pointed out (*Revue Thomiste,* 1902, p. 658) that St. Augustine has in mind "an active and victorious congruency." In a word, the grace is intrinsically efficacious.

Lastly, St. Augustine repeatedly teaches that predestination is gratuitous. And he means predestination as he defined it, which is not only to grace but also to glory; for predestination to grace alone does not lead one effectively to eternal life. It has but the name of predestination, since it belongs equally to those who, after being justified, do not persevere.

This gratuity of predestination is peculiarly stressed by him. In discussing the gift of perseverance, he says: "Of two children equally held captive by original sin, why is one taken and the other left? And of two wicked persons already advanced in years, why is one called and the other not? All this pertains to the inscrutable judgments of God." [23] He also says: "Why God draws this one and not that other, seek not to judge, if thou wilt not err." [24]

What precisely constitutes the crux of the mystery, according to St. Augustine's opinion, is man's inability to find out the reasons for the divine choice. He is continually harking back to this impossibility, and his opponents find no avenue of escape from it. This impossibility is a pledge of his fidelity to the teaching of St. Paul. It is, so to speak, the theme of his teaching. [25]

Tixeront wrote: "St. Augustine's views, considered as a whole, direct us toward the doctrine of predestination to glory *before foreseen merits.* . . . Were it a question of the full predestination to efficacious grace, final perseverance, and glory, and not of predestination to glory alone, there would be no room for doubt: the Bishop of Hippo insists again and again upon its absolute gratuitousness." [26]

---

[23] *De dono persever.,* chap. 9.

[24] *In Joan.,* tr. 26.

[25] *De dono persever.,* VIII, 17; IX, 12, 21; XI, 25; XII, 30. *De praed. sanct.,* VIII, 16; XIV, 26. *De correptione et gratia,* VIII, 17, 19 (in the order of execution).

[26] *History of dogmas,* Bk. II, p. 503; cf. *Enchiridion,* chaps. 98, 99; *Ep.,* 186, no. 15; *De dono persever.,* chaps. 17, 25.

ST. AUGUSTINE'S FIRST DISCIPLES

1) St. Prosper of Aquitaine. After St. Augustine's death an anonymous pamphlet appeared that distorted his doctrine of predestination. St. Prosper thereupon defended the teaching of his master.[27] St. Prosper went to Rome and obtained from Pope St. Celestine in 431 a letter in which the Pontiff boldly affirmed the orthodoxy of the Bishop of Hippo, at the same time requesting the French bishops to put an end to this calumniation of St. Augustine. But St. Prosper, upon returning to France, had to refute another pamphlet that seems to have been written by St. Vincent of Lerins. This saint thought the Augustinian doctrine denied God's will to save all men and that it implied that God is the author of sin. St. Prosper refuted these conclusions; [28] about 433 he wrote a book against Cassian, in which he discusses anew the problem of grace and free will.[29]

Some Pelagians put a wrong construction upon St. Paul's text that "God will have all men to be saved," [30] and claimed that God wills equally the salvation of all. In reply to these heretics St. Augustine, arguing from the fact that all men are not saved and from the principle of the infallible efficacy of the divine will, had repeatedly spoken of a restricted will to save. By this he meant the infallibly efficacious will that leads the elect to eternal life. St. Prosper, replying to the objections made against the teaching of his master, insists upon another aspect of this doctrine. St. Augustine had clearly affirmed that "God does not command what is impossible, but in commanding admonishes thee to do what thou canst and to ask for

---

27 *PL*, LI, 155–75. Pro Augustino responsiones ad capitula objectionum Gallorum calumniantium.

28 Cf. *ibid.*, 177–86; Pro Augustino responsiones ad capitula objectionum vincentianarum.

29 Cf. *Liber ad collatorem, ibid.*, 213–76.

30 I Tim. 2: 4.

what thou canst not do." [31] God never commands what is impossible, otherwise no one could avoid committing actual sin, which in this case would no longer be a sin, and the divine chastisements inflicted for such would be a manifest injustice. To say that God never commands the impossible means that He wills to make it really possible for all to comply with the precepts imposed upon them and to do so when they are imposed. Thus He wills to make their salvation really possible, though He does not lead them all efficaciously to eternal life. Moreover, St. Augustine again and again, without adding any restrictions, explained St. Paul's text that "Christ dies for all." [32]

True to the teaching of his master, St. Prosper wrote as follows: "We must most sincerely believe and profess that God wills all men to be saved. For this, indeed, is the mind of the Apostle, who most urgently commands, what is a most devout custom in all the churches, that suppliant prayers be offered to God for all men. That many of these perish is the fault of those who perish: that many are saved is the gift of Him who saves." [33]

In these words of St. Prosper we have formulated the two extreme aspects of the mystery. On the one hand we have God's will to save all men, and on the other hand we have the mystery of predestination, namely, that many are saved is the gift of Him who saves.[34] Concerning predestination in the strict sense of the term, St. Prosper is equally firm in his defense of St. Augustine's opinion, and he refuses to identify predestination with foreknowledge, because God foresees the bad no less than the good acts, but He positively wills and is

[31] De natura et gratia, PL, XLIII, 50; XLIV, 271.

[32] II Cor. 5: 15; cf. PL, XLIV, 825; XLV, 1217.

[33] PL, LI, 179; cf. Resp. ad 8 obj. Gallorum vincent., ibid., 162.

[34] Concerning St. Prosper's point of view on this question, consult P. M. Jacquin's article entitled "La question de la prédestination aux Ve et VIe siècles, "in the Revue d'hist. eccles., VII, 269–300; J. Tixeront, History of dogmas, III, pp. 283–93; Cayré, Précis de patrologie, II, 180–85.

the cause of only the latter.[35] He is the author of all good, and it cannot be said that, irrespective of His divine will, one particular person is better than another. Predestination implies, therefore, along with foreknowledge a love of predilection or the will to effect in a particular person and by means of him in preference to a certain other, this salutary good by which such a person will actually merit and attain eternal life.[36] Therefore predestination of the elect is gratuitous, as St. Augustine had said.

If St. Prosper mitigated his master's teaching on any point, it was on the question of reprobation. He is not satisfied with merely speaking of souls left by God in the *mass of perdition,* for he considers that reprobation is the result of personal sins foreseen by God.[37] This way of viewing it cannot be maintained as the reason for the non-election of children who die without being baptized. As for the reprobate adults, it leaves the question still shrouded in obscurity: their personal sins, which are foreseen by God, could not happen without His divine permission. Again, why has God permitted certain individuals to commit sins without efficaciously intending that their sins should be actually forgiven, whereas He permits sins in the case of the elect only to bring them to a truer humility, by which their love becomes purer?

We shall see farther on that many of St. Augustine's disciples who, considering themselves to be interpreting the mind of their master more faithfully, distinguish between negative reprobation (non-election and the will to permit sins that will not be forgiven), and positive reprobation (eternal decree to inflict the punishment of damnation for sins foreseen). Negative reprobation, so they say, cannot be the result of personal sins foreseen by God as not calling for His

[35] *PL,* LI, 170.
[36] *Ibid.,* 174. Resp. ad cap. Gall.
[37] *Ibid.,* 161.

forgiveness; for it means nothing else but God's permission of these sins which, unless He permitted them, could not be foreseen by Him. This proved, later on, to be the teaching of St. Thomas,[38] and it seems to be fully in agreement with what St. Augustine taught.[39]

2) The author of a certain treatise [40] written between 430 and 460—which was about the period in which St. Prosper lived—like a true disciple of St. Augustine, admits God's will to save all men, at the same time maintaining the gratuity of predestination. To explain this will to save all men, he insists upon a general grace for salvation that is offered to all, and he distinguishes between this and a special and entirely gratuitous grace that is given to those who are actually saved. In addition to these general gifts . . . there is the liberal bestowal of a special grace.[41] This special grace is the effect of a divine predilection.

3) St. Fulgentius. At the end of the sixth century the controversies on grace and predestination were resumed after the death of the Semipelagian bishop Faustus of Riez. St. Fulgentius of Ruspe then wrote a little treatise on this subject.[42] He followed this up with an important letter on the question of grace [43] and wrote a work comprising seven books in direct refutation of the teachings of Faustus. Of this work only one treatise remains.[44] Last of all he wrote a work in vindication of the truth of predestination and grace.[45] St. Fulgentius, who is called "Augustine in miniature," adopts as his own the whole of St. Augustine's teaching on grace and its gratuity.[46]

---

[38] Summa theol., Ia, q.23, a.5 ad 3um.

[39] PL, XLIV, 580, 965.

[40] Ibid., LI, 647–72. De vocatione omnium gentium.

[41] Ibid., 711.

[42] PL, LXV, 451–93. Liber de incarnatione et gratia Domini nostri Jesu Christi.

[43] Ibid., 435–42.

[44] Ibid., 151–206, Ad Monimum. Columns 153–78 are concerned with predestination.

[45] Ibid., 603–72.

[46] Ibid., Ad Monimum, 157–60, 162–63.

He accepts, too, everything his master teaches about predestination. Complete predestination, which means to glory and to grace, is considered by him to be absolutely free, certain, and restricted. It is absolutely free because grace, without which man is incapable of performing any salutary good work, is purely a gift of God's mercy.[47] Predestination is a certainty in virtue of God's omnipotent and unchangeable will.[48] Finally, it is restricted to the elect, who are called in manifestation of God's merciful goodness in their behalf.[49]

Concerning God's will to save, in those texts in which St. Fulgentius speaks of the divine and infallibly efficacious will to save, he limits it, as St. Augustine did.[50] He does not deny, however, this other point of Augustinian teaching, that "God does not command what is impossible." He really wills to make it possible for all to fulfil His precepts, for this is the way by which one attains eternal life. St. Fulgentius positively rejects predestination to sin,[51] and he explains that those whom God has not elected are justly abandoned by Him either because of original sin, or because of pride which is the result of this sin.[52]

4) St. Caesarius of Arles (470–543). His sermons are also a faithful reflection of St. Augustine's teaching on predestination. Father Lejay says: "The problem of both salvation and damnation is solved in the same way as St. Augustine solved it. If the wickedness of sinners induces to hardness of heart, it is God who removes this by His grace. If we ask why God gives grace to some and refuses it to others, Caesarius answers by saying with St. Augustine: As a rule God's judgments are hidden from the knowledge of men, but they are not unjust. Like St. Augustine, he counterattacks by quoting the well-

47 *Ibid.,* 603–27, *De veritate praed.*
48 *Ibid., Ad Monimum,* 161.
49 *Ibid., Ad Monimum,* 172–74; *De verit. praed.,* 644–45.
50 *Ibid.,* 658 ff. Ep. 441.
51 *Ibid., Ad Monimum,* 155–57, 166–78.
52 *Ibid.,* 166.

known Pauline texts: O the depths of the riches of the wisdom and of the knowledge of God! O man who art thou that repliest against God?" [53]

From this we see, however, that St. Caesarius, like his master, distinguishes between God's permission of sin, without which this would not happen, and the withdrawal of His grace which, as a just punishment, presupposes on the contrary that God foresees the sin. With this in mind he writes: "Pharao is hardened in heart by the withdrawal of grace, but also because of his wickedness." [54] In this there is a mystery, that God permits sins that will not be forgiven. God often remits sins which He has permitted, often enough, but not always. This, too, is a mystery.

5) The Second Council of Orange (529), in which the influence of St. Caesarius of Arles preponderated, put an end to the heated discussions between the Augustinians and the anti-Augustinians in France, by approving the fundamental points maintained by St. Augustine. The first eight canons of the council were taken by St. Caesarius from St. Augustine's works. Another proposition was added by the Bishop of Arles (c. 10), and then there are sixteen propositions (c. 9 and 11–25) compiled by St. Prosper from St. Augustine's works and sent by Pope Felix IV. Pope Boniface II, his successor, confirmed (January 25, 531) these decisions in which Rome had already played an important part, and he declared the profession of faith formulated by the synod to be in agreement with the Catholic principles of the fathers.

These canons of the Council of Orange clearly affirm not only the necessity of grace for every supernaturally good work, but also its gratuity. By this ruling the council definitely steered clear of Semipelagianism. On the question whether the efficacy of grace, of which the council speaks, is intrinsic

[53] Cf. *Dict. de théol.*, II, 2178; Caesarius of Arles, *Sermons*, XXII, 4; CCLXXV, 1; Rom. 11: 33; 9: 20.
[54] *Sermon* XXII.

or extrinsic, in other words, whether or not it depends upon the fact that God foresees our consent, modern theologians are not in agreement. Those who, like the Augustinians and the Thomists, admit the intrinsic efficacy of grace, quote especially the following canons: (3) "If anyone says that God's grace can be conferred by the invocation of man, and that this, however, is not caused by grace itself, such a person contradicts the prophet Isaias or the Apostle who says: I was found by them that did not seek Me: I appeared openly to them that asked not after Me." [55] (4) "If anyone says that God waits for us to will that we may be cleansed from sin, and who does not confess that even our wish to be cleansed from sin is the effect of the infusion and operation of the Holy Spirit who by the mouth of Solomon says: The will is prepared by the Lord, and also the Apostle proclaiming for our benefit that: it is God who worketh in you, both to will and to accomplish according to His good will." [56] (6) "If anyone . . . does not consent to believe it to be the gift of grace itself, that we be obedient and humble, resists the Apostle who says: What hast thou that thou hast not received? and By the grace of God I am what I am." [57] (9) "For as often as we do what is good, God works in and with us that we may do it." [58] (10) "We must always implore God's help even for those who have been baptized and cured of their spiritual infirmities, whether this be that they may persevere in the performance of good works or that they may die a happy death." [59] (12) "God loves us because of what we will be by the gift of His grace, not because of what we are by our own merit." [60] (20) "There is no good act done by man which God does not help man to do." [61] (22) "No one has for one's own anything but lying and

[55] Denz., no. 176; cf. Rom. 10: 20; Is. 65: 1.
[56] *Ibid.*, no. 172; Prov. 8: 25; Phil. 2: 13.
[57] *Ibid.*, no. 179; I Cor. 4: 7; 15: 10.
[58] *Ibid.*, no. 182.
[59] *Ibid.*, no. 183.
[60] *Ibid.*, no. 185.
[61] *Ibid.*, no. 193.

sin." [62] Later on theology stated more precisely that man can perform no supernaturally good act except by God's supernatural help, and no morally good deed without a help in the natural order.

The Council of Orange makes no positive affirmation about predestination to glory and grace; but we see that this is the logical result of the canons just quoted, especially of canons twelve and twenty. The latter canon reads: "There is no good act done by man which God does not help man to do." Canon twelve declares that "God loves us because of what we will be by the gift of His grace, not because of what we are by our own merit." These two statements along with the Pauline text: "What has thou that thou hast not received?" [63] are tantamount to saying that one would not be better than another if one were not loved more and helped more by God, and that in the work of salvation everything comes from God, in this sense that we cannot detect therein the least good which could be said to be exclusively from ourselves and not from Him.

The *Indiculus de Gratia Dei,* appended to Pope Celestine's twenty-first letter, said the same: "For the acknowledgment of God's grace, the operative power and dignity of which must not in the least be undervalued, we believe that whatever the canons have taught us in accordance with the aforesaid rules laid down by the Holy See is amply sufficient: so that we absolutely do not think is Catholic what has clearly been seen to be contrary to the foregoing decisions." [64]

Finally, the Council of Orange distinctly disapproves of predestination to evil. On this point it says: "That some are predestined by divine power to evil, not only we do not believe this, but also, if there are any willing to believe so great an evil, in all detestation we anathematize them." [65] In the

[62] *Ibid.,* no. 195.
[63] I Cor. 4: 7.
[64] Denz., nos. 134, 135, 139, 142.
[65] *Ibid.,* no. 200.

same paragraph the council affirms that all the baptized can be saved if they will keep the commandments, for we read: "This also we believe according to Catholic faith, that all those who have received grace by being baptized, Christ helping and co-operating with them, if they have willed to labor faithfully, can and ought to put into effect those things that pertain to the salvation of their souls." [66] This is what St. Augustine said, whom the Council of Trent quoted against the Protestants as follows: "God does not command what is impossible, but in commanding advises you to do what you can and to ask for what you cannot do," [67] and again when he said: "God does not abandon those whom He has once justified by His grace, unless He is first abandoned by them." [68]

Thus the two extreme aspects of the mystery were affirmed: on the one hand, the gratuity and necessity of grace; and on the other, the real possibility of salvation, at least for all the baptized.

6) After the Council of Orange. St. Gregory the Great is also distinctly of the Augustinian school. He teaches the necessity of a prevenient grace for the beginning of good works and faith,[69] and that predestination to grace and eternal life is absolutely gratuitous, as in the case of the good thief.[70] In the seventh century, St. Isidore of Seville also taught that the elect are gratuitously predestined to heaven,[71] and that God has prepared for the reprobates the punishments they have deserved for their sins which have been permitted by Him. To the question why God has freely chosen some and not others, St. Isidore answers by saying: "In an obscurity so great as this it is of no avail for man to investigate the divine dis-

66 Ibid.
67 Ibid., no. 804; cf. PL, XLIII, 50.
68 PL, XXVI, 29.
69 Ibid., LXXV, 1135.
70 Ibid., LXXVI, 436–37.
71 Ibid., LXXXIII, 606.

pensation and examine the secret arrangements of predestination." [72]

Such is the teaching of St. Augustine's disciples. They affirm the two extreme aspects of the mystery: the gratuity of predestination and the real possibility of salvation for at least all baptized adults. Moreover all agree in saying that no one in this life can see how these two truths are intimately reconciled, for that would be to see how God's infinite justice, infinite mercy, and sovereign independence or liberty are intimately reconciled. The just mean was found in the affirmation of these two extreme aspects of the mystery and in the higher contemplation of God's infinite goodness, which is equally the principle of His mercy and that of His justice. On the one hand, God's sovereign goodness is diffusive of itself, it being the principle of His mercy; on the other hand, it has the right to be loved above all things, it being the principle of His justice.

St. Augustine's disciples steered a middle course by a loving contemplation of these truths in the obscurity of faith. This middle course was compromised in the ninth century by the assertions of Gottschalk, which necessitated many a struggle for its restoration. [73]

[72] *Ibid.*, 606, no. 6.
[73] *Ibid.*, CXXI, 347–66.

PART II

THE PRINCIPAL SOLUTIONS OF THE PROBLEM OF PREDESTINATION

SECTION I

The Views of Predestination Held by the Scholars of the Middle Ages

The question of predestination was studied by the scholars of the Middle Ages. They were guided by the principles which St. Augustine formulated in defense of the teachings of the Gospel and of St. Paul against the Pelagians and Semipelagians. After the time of St. Anselm several theologians, like Peter Lombard, were satisfied with a compilation of the principal teachings of St. Augustine, explaining some of them by others and reviving the memory of predestinarianism, a heresy in direct opposition to that of Pelagianism. Not a few theologians sought also to reconcile St. Augustine's doctrine with what St. John Damascene wrote concerning God's will to save all men, which he calls His antecedent will.

To see more clearly the meaning and scope of these works of the Middle Ages, we should recall that St. John Damascene and St. Augustine held different views on this subject of predestination. The former [1] almost always considered the question from the moral point of view, in its relation to God's goodness and men's sins. If God is supremely good, he asks, how does it happen that not all are saved? He answers this question by saying that some sin and remain in sin. Consequently God punishes them; but previous to the sin, God wills the salvation of all, because He is supremely good. If He punishes after the sin, it is because He is also supremely just.

This answer given by St. John Damascene, which is accord-

[1] *De fide orth.*, II, 29.

ing to common sense and is Christian in sentiment such as
to be naturally understood by the faithful, somehow did not
take into consideration God's omnipotence and the efficacy of
grace. It also failed to solve from the speculative point of view
many difficulties, even those to which St. Augustine replied
in his contest against the Pelagians. These heretics, denying
the mystery of predestination, claimed that God wills equally
the salvation of all, and thus they misconstrued St. Paul's text
on this point.[2]

Certainly St. John Damascene had clearly affirmed in the
same passage that "every good comes from God" and that no
evil can happen unless it is permitted by Him. But many persons, after they read his distinction between the *antecedent*
and *consequent* wills in God, asked this question: If God is
omnipotent, how are we to explain that His antecedent will
for the salvation for all is only partly realized? Does the divine
will meet with an insurmountable obstacle in the malice of
some? Looking at it in this way, what becomes of the revealed
mystery of predestination, which does not allow of our affirming with the Pelagians that God wills equally or in the same
way the salvation of all?

Whereas St. John Damascene insisted on God's will to save
all mankind, St. Augustine, to correct the Pelagian and Semipelagian interpretations of St. Paul's text, which states that
"God will have all men to be saved," [3] stressed the mystery
of predestination. At the same time he maintained that God
never commands what is impossible, and thus He wills and
actually makes it really possible for all who are bound to observe the precepts to be saved.

Thus the two extreme aspects of the mystery were affirmed.
It was for the theologians to endeavor to formulate them so
well that one should not exclude the other. They all agreed
that the mode of their intimate reconciliation is just as much

2 I Tim. 2: 4.
3 *Ibid.*, 2: 4.

beyond our powers of perception as is that of God's infinite mercy and justice.

CHAPTER I

THE THEOLOGIANS PRIOR TO ST. THOMAS

ST. ANSELM

IN his treatise *De concordia praescientiae et praedestinationis nec non gratiae Dei cum libero arbitrio*.[1] St. Anselm examines the question of predestination. We know from Eadmer [2] that St. Anselm wrote this work toward the end of his life. The title indicates that the treatise is divided into three questions. We shall give a summary of the tenor and contents of the second question, *De concordia praedestinationis cum libero arbitrio*,[3] which unfortunately is the shortest question in the treatise.

Chapter I. It is concerned with the problem arising from the agreement between predestination and human liberty. After giving the commonly accepted definition of predestination, the author stresses the difficulty of perceiving how this latter does not conflict with our free will. If God predestines both the good and the bad, then nothing is left to free will, and everything happens from necessity. If He predestines only the good, then free will would have for its scope everything that is bad. The two alternatives seem to exclude each other.

Chapter II. St. Anselm then investigates in what sense we may speak of the predestination not only of the good, but also of the bad. "God predestines the bad and their bad deeds," he says, "when He does not correct them and their bad deeds. But more especially He predestines in the case of

[1] *PL*, CLVIII, 507–42.
[2] *Ibid.*, 114; *Vita S. Anselmi.*
[3] *Ibid.*, 519–21.

those who perform good deeds . . . because in these He is the cause not only of their entity but also of their goodness; but in the case of bad deeds He is the cause of their entity, not of their badness."

Chapter III. The author finally comes to the crucial point: in the accomplishment or in the effects of predestination, how is it that the divine action does not intervene alone, but is accompanied by man's co-operation, without one of the factors eliminating the other? In replying to this, St. Anselm has recourse especially to affirmative statements. He says: "There is no justice in one who does not adhere to it freely." Then he adds that "certain things . . . which are predestined, do not happen by reason of that necessity which precedes and is the cause of the occurrence, but by reason of that which follows it." After this comes the distinguishing feature of the author's doctrine. He remarks that God, when He predestines, does not do so by forcing the human will or resisting it, but He *leaves it master of itself.* And although our will makes use of its power, in the case of the good, however, nothing is done by it except as the result of God's grace; so that in the case of the bad, sin must be imputed solely to their will.

We understand the method of procedure adopted by St. Anselm. It is a very just but perhaps too restricted application of his previous exposition of the divine foreknowledge. God foresees infallibly the free acts of the future, at the same time leaving their contingency intact. Therefore He can predestine a person to perform these acts. It is possible that the effects of this predestination will or will not be realized in time, if we consider their cause, which is our free will. They are foreseen and ordained by God from all eternity, being irrevocable and necessary in virtue of a necessity of consequence. In this third and most important chapter of his treatise, the author shows clearly the necessity of our free co-operation with grace.

So we see that St. Anselm seeks the solution of the problem from the teaching of St. Augustine. Previous to this, however,

Scotus Eriugena and Gottschalk had interpreted the mind of the Bishop of Hippo. Something more definite might have been expected concerning the difficulties raised by them. But the texts already quoted show how tenaciously and unequivocally St. Anselm adheres to certain great principles. These principles he maintains along with almost all his predecessors and contemporaries. He holds that every good comes from God, that the free determination of a salutary act in all that constitutes it as such, is a good that comes entirely from God, just as it comes entirely from us as a secondary cause.[4] Another principle enunciated in the same passage is, that it does not happen independently of God's action that this free determination of a salutary act comes or will come from this man rather than from a certain other, whom God will permit to fall into sin, the cause of which, however, will be solely because this other willed it.

PETER LOMBARD

The Master of the Sentences has the same view as St. Augustine about predestination and reprobation, for he says: "By predestination God foreknew those things which He Himself would do; but He foreknew also those things which He will not do, that is all evil things. He predestined those whom He chose, but the rest He rejected as reprobates, that is He foreknew they would sin and be condemned to eternal death." [5] God predestined those whom He chose, and this suggests no passivity or dependence upon foreknowledge on the part of any determination of the created order. He did not choose the others, but foresaw and permitted their obduracy in sin, and for this they are deservedly condemned to eternal punishment. In like manner, he says: "Since predestination is preparation by God's grace, or divine election, by

---

4 Cf. chap. 3: *De concordia praedestinationis cum libero arbitrio.*
5 Cf. I *Sent.,* d. XL, 1.

which He chose those whom he willed before the foundation of the world, as the Apostle says (Eph. 1: 4): on the other hand, by reprobation is to be understood the foreknowledge of the wickedness of certain persons and eternal punishment prepared for them . . . and the former, that is their wickedness, He knows and does not prepare; the latter, that is, eternal punishment, He foreknows and prepares." [6]

Predestination does not presuppose, therefore, the foreseeing of the merits. On this point Peter Lombard writes: "But if we ask why some deserve to be left in their obduracy and others to obtain mercy (or to be predestined), we find the reason for the former, but not for the latter; for there is no question of mercy being merited, for grace would cease to be grace if it were not freely given, but were bestowed on account of merits." [7] Peter Lombard then puts an objection which has its foundation in an opinion St. Augustine held shortly after his conversion. According to this opinion the reason for the election of some and the non-election of others would be because of certain merits very difficult to detect. But he replies that St. Augustine later on gave up this opinion.[8] Peter Lombard insists especially on this: That reprobation is not likewise the cause of evil, as predestination is the cause of good.

As for God's will to save all mankind, he considered it [9] not only as St. John Damascene does, in its relation to God's sovereign goodness, but also, with St. Augustine, in its relation to the divine omnipotence and the efficacy of prayer. On this point Peter Lombard writes as follows: "For who is so irreverent and foolish as to say that God cannot turn men away from willing what is evil to will what is good, if, when, and where He has so willed it." [10] And therefore, he adds,

6 *Ibid.*, d. XL, 4.
7 *Ibid.*, d. XLI.
8 *Retract.*, I, 23.
9 *Loc. cit.*, d. XLVI, XLVII.
10 *Ibid.*, d. XLVI, 3.

when we read that "God wills to save all men," [11] we must not take this to mean that His omnipotence meets with an insurmountable obstacle in the malice of some persons; but with St. Augustine we must interpret this as meaning that no one is saved unless God willed it.

In addition to this, Peter Lombard firmly maintains that God never commands what is impossible, but makes it possible for all to observe His commandments; hence this includes the possibility for them to save their souls. In this sense he recognizes with St. Augustine that God wills the salvation of all those who are bound to observe the precepts, although there may be some difficulty in the case of children who die without being baptized.[12] Thus we see that the two aspects of the mysteries are clearly affirmed by Peter Lombard.

ALEXANDER OF HALES

This theologian quotes the current definition of predestination among the Augustinians, and these presuppose no passivity or dependence on God's part.[13] A little farther on,[14] asking whether merits are the cause of predestination, he replies: "By the term predestination is meant the preparation of the divine helps, united to foreknowledge and its effects, namely, grace and glory, which latter will be given to the elect. Now merits are only the cause of the conferring of glory, and not of God's eternal choice, or of the conferring of grace."

If Alexander says that "foreknowledge of the merits may be the reason for the conferring of grace and glory,"[15] he certainly does not mean this in the Pelagian sense, in that the sinner can merit justification, but he merely means that he can dispose himself for it under the influence of actual grace. This was the comment of the editors of St. Bonaventure's

[11] I Tim. 2: 4.
[12] Loc. cit., XLVI, 11.
[13] Summa theol., Ia, q.28, memb. 1, a.1–3.
[14] Ibid., memb. 3, a.1.
[15] Ibid., ad 2um.

works,[16] and they point out that Alexander of Hales, St. Bonaventure, and St. Albert the Great are in agreement on this point. The difficulties presented by this doctrine are cleared up by what Alexander says farther on in his theological treatise.[17]

ST. BONAVENTURE

He retains the Augustinian definition of predestination. In that it is the preordainment of the elect to glory, together with those helps that most certainly will enable them to attain it, preordainment presupposes election.[18] This very election presupposes a gratuitous and special dilection, and this applies not only to God's antecedent will but also to His consequent will to save.[19] Concerning election, St. Bonaventure writes: "There are two kinds of election. One is caused by the diversity and pre-eminence of the eligibles, and this is a consequence of the eligibles, as in the case of human election; the other accounts for the diversity in choosing, and this is divine election, which is concerned with different natures, not as they are but as they will be. Such election precedes and is eternal.[20] Very numerous texts in St. Bonaventure's works

[16] I *Sent.*, d. XLI, a.1, q.2, scholion no. 2 (Quaracchi).

[17] *Loc cit.*, q.30, a.1; q.31, membr. 3: Whether God loves equally every creature? Q.32, membr. 1: Whether among human beings God's love is greater for the one whom He foreknew to be at the present moment in a state of grace, than for the one who is predestined, though he is at the present moment in a state of sin? He replies in accordance with the principle: God's love is greater for those to whom He wills a greater good; and one would not be better than another unless He had been loved more by God.

[18] I. *Sent.*, d. XL.

[19] *Ibid.*, a.3, q.1. In this article St. Bonaventure teaches clearly the principle of predilection. Like St. Albert the Great and St. Thomas, he holds that divine predilection, contrary to ours, is the cause of the greater or less goodness found in creatures and in the elect. Here we have the great and traditional principle, namely, that one would not be better than another, unless one were loved more by God.

[20] *Ibid.*, a.3, q.1, no. 4. The editors of the Quaracchi edition of St. Bonaventure's works, in commenting on this passage (*ibid.*) state that "it is confirmed by the Council of Orange, canon twelve, which reads: God loves us such as we will be by the gift of His grace, not as we are by our own merit."

refer to the principle of predestination.[21] There is therefore no passivity or dependence in God's foreknowledge concerning a free and salutary determination of the created order.

Guided by the light of this principle, what answer does he give to the question whether foreseen merits are the cause of predestination? He answers [22] that predestination implies three things: an eternal design, and then its effects: justification and glorification. Now the merits of the elect are the cause of the subsequent glorification, but not of the eternal design which precedes them. As for justification this cannot be merited *ex condigno,* but only *ex congruo,* that is, by a merit improperly so called, in so far as God does not refuse sanctifying grace to the sinner who does what he can to obtain it. But in virtue of the principle of predilection previously enunciated by him, St. Bonaventure holds that of two sinners, one does not become better than another by disposing himself for conversion, unless he has been loved more by God and helped more by actual grace. This is the constant teaching of St. Augustine and, as we shall see, St. Thomas adopted it,[23] so St. Bonaventure writes concerning salutary acts that the total effect is from the created cause and likewise from the uncreated will.[24]

However, St. Bonaventure seeks to discover some motive for this choice on God's part. If this particular man has been chosen in preference to a certain other, Peter in preference to Judas, is not this because of some suitable quality in him unknown to us, and not because of any merit on his part? He replies in the affirmative: "If coming to particular cases, we ask why He wills more to justify one than another, when evidently the two are equally eligible, we must say that there can be many reasons of congruence for this, so that there is no objective certainty. Therefore, since our knowledge is de-

---

[21] Consult index of Quaracchi edition under the heading "Dilectio."
[22] *Loc. cit.,* d. XLI, a.1, q.1.
[23] *Summa theol.,* Ia, q.23, a.5.
[24] *Loc. cit.,* d. XLV, a.2, q.2 ad 1um.

pendent upon objective certainty, we can discover no certain reason for this, unless it be revealed by Him in whom there are no doubts but only certainties.[25] St. Albert the Great says practically the same.[26]

Contrary to this, in virtue of the principle of predilection, St. Thomas said: "Why He chooses some for glory, and reprobates others, has no reason except the divine will . . . as from the simple will of the artificer it depends that this stone is in this part of the wall, and that in another." [27] Scotus held the same view as St. Thomas on this point, and affirmed God's sovereign liberty in the choice of the elect.[28]

Is the reason given by St. Bonaventure to be taken as applying to the future merits of the elect, when he says that the choice is one of fittingness and not of merit? He says it would be rash to affirm this.[29] In any case, he maintains the principle of predilection, which we have seen so emphatically affirmed by him. It is that one would not be better than another unless one were loved more by God (for divine love is not caused by the diversity of eligibles, but is the cause of them).

All these theologians, moreover, agree on this, that just as God would have suffered no inconvenience if He had not created, so there would have been no inconvenience to Him if He had placed Judas in preference to Peter among the elect, and granted him the graces that would have infallibly led him to merit freely eternal life and persevere unto the end. As St. Bonaventure says: "Although there can be others and more than are predestined, yet there never will be; and if there were, then they were from all eternity predestined. And therefore in this there can be no change." [30] His conclusion is that

25 *Ibid.*, d. XLI, a.1, q.2.
26 *Summa theol.*, Ia, tr. 16, q.65.
27 *Summa theol.*, Ia, q.23, a.5, ad 3um.
28 I *Sent.*, d. XLI, q.1.
29 *Loc. cit.*, d. XLI, dub. 1, ed. Quaracchi, I, 742.
30 *Ibid.*, d. XL, a.2, q.2, no. 5. When St. Bonaventure says that there can be others and more, he is speaking of the certainty of salvation. He points out that since salvation, objectively considered, depends upon the use of free

God wills to save all men in so far as He has given all the human nature, and offers to all by Christ the grace necessary for salvation.[31]

ST. ALBERT THE GREAT

This doctor has discussed predestination and God's will to save all mankind in two of his works,[32] and his teaching on this subject is substantially the same as St. Bonaventure's.

He states positively that divine knowledge is the cause of things, and is not measured by them.[33] It does not, however, prescribe the characteristic trait of necessity for all things; for there may be, as Aristotle says, a *necessity of consequence* without a *necessity of consequent,* according to the following example given by Boethius: What I see must be; now I see Peter walking; therefore he must be walking, although he is doing this freely. Thus God has infallibly foreseen contingent events.[34] In like manner, God willed efficaciously from all eternity the conversion of the good thief, and he was infallibly converted without being in the least way compelled.[35]

He says, too, with St. Bonaventure, that predestination to glory presupposes election, and this latter presupposes divine predilection: "Love tends to show a preference between persons, and to love the one preferred in view of eternal life. Therefore love precedes election, and election precedes predestination on the part of Him who loves, elects, and predes-

---

will, then it is to be classed among other uncertain and contingent events of life. But on God's part the number does not admit of either increase or decrease, since the certainty in question here depends upon His foreknowledge, which is not subject to error. (Tr.)

[31] *Ibid.,* d. XLVI, a.1, q.1.

[32] Cf. *Com. on Sentences,* I, d. XLVI, XLVII; *Summa theol.,* Ia, q.62, 64. This latter work was written in 1270 after the first part of St. Thomas' theological summa had appeared.

[33] I *Sent.,* d. XXXVIII, A, a.1; D, a.3.

[34] *Ibid.,* d. XXXVIII, E, a.4.

[35] *Ibid.,* d. XLVI, C, a.1; d. XLVII, A, a.1 ad 1um. Also *Summa theol.,* Ia, tr. 15, q.61, m. 2, 5, 8.

tines.[36] This doctrine affirms the principle of predilection, that no created being would be better than another unless it were loved more by God.

What conclusion do we come to when we ask whether anything we do contributes as a meritorious cause of predestination? St. Albert answers this question.[37] Subsequently he gives a clearer solution to this problem in his theological treatise. In this latter work he says: "It is of Catholic faith that the only cause of or good reason for predestination is the will and love of Him who predestines. . . . Furthermore, it is of Catholic faith that merit does not come before grace. . . ."[38] However, St. Albert affirms that "What is added to grace, is an act that takes place in time and is measured by time, and cannot be caused; there can, however, be a reason that may make it appear reasonable: and this reason is not antecedent but concomitant. Hence the reason for this may be the knowledge of merits, because, to be sure, He gives grace to the one whom He well knows will make good use of it." [39]

These concluding words remind us of one of Henry of Ghent's opinions quoted and discussed by Cajetan.[40] But St. Albert attaches much less importance to them, saying: "Sometimes God gave grace to one whom He knew would make a bad use of it, as in the case of Judas." [41] Similarly he says: "Sometimes God gives grace to one whom He knows will make a bad use of it, on account of some useful purpose it will serve; thus He made use of the betrayal by Judas so as to accomplish the redemption of the human race. But He would not be a good dispenser if, without any thought of the advantage to be gained therefrom, He gave grace to one who will make a bad use of it." [42]

[36] *Ibid.,* d. XL, a.19.
[37] I *Sent.,* d. XLI, B. a.3.
[38] *Summa theol.,* Ia, tr. 16, q.63, m. 3, a.1.
[39] *Ibid.*
[40] *Com. in Iam,* q.23, a.5, no. 4.
[41] *Loc cit.,* q.1 ad 3um.
[42] *Ibid.,* q.2, ad 5um.

From these formulas enunciated in the foregoing texts we see that God gives grace either because of future merits, or for some other useful purpose. Thus St. Albert prepares the way for the much simpler formula which we read in the *Summa* of St. Thomas, which is: "God preordained to give grace to merit glory." [43]

St. Albert remains faithful to the principle of predilection, and he has given us a sufficiently clear formula of it. He says: "That is loved more which receives a greater good." [44] And again he says: "In all things God loves the good that is from Him." [45] No created being therefore would be better than another unless it were loved more by God. "What hast thou that thou hast not received?" [46] But, in any case, God never commands what is impossible and He makes it possible for all to keep His commandments.[47]

[43] *Summa theol.*, Ia, q.23, a.5.

[44] *Summa theol.*, Ia, tr. 16, q.64 ad quaest. 1.

[45] *Ibid.*, ad 3um.

[46] I Cor. 4: 7.

[47] *Ibid.*, Ia, tr. 20, q.79, a.1; see our article in the *Revue Thomiste*, March, 1931, pp. 371–86: "The will to save and predestination as St. Albert the Great views it."

CHAPTER II

The Doctrinal Principles of St. Thomas

St. Thomas Aquinas developed a higher, simpler, and more comprehensive theory concerning the great problem of the reconciliation of God's universal will to save with the mystery of predestination. The limits of this book do not permit us to trace St. Thomas' thought in his different works, examining them in chronological order. We have his interpretation of St. Paul's text on this subject.[1] He has also discussed this question from the speculative point of view.[2] In his theological treatise which he wrote toward the end of his life, he gave us his final decision on this question.[3]

We shall present his point of view in these pages, stressing the principle of this synthesis and how it applies, by way of inference, to God's universal will to save and to the principle of predilection.[4] As for the scriptural foundation for this teaching, so as to avoid repetitions, we shall examine this point in connection with the leading article of this treatise.[5] The point at issue is whether predestination depends upon the foreseeing of our merits. We shall see that St. Thomas, like St. Augustine, is of the opinion that the absolute gratuity of predestination to glory is affirmed by St. Paul. Later we shall see this exegesis adopted by St. Robert Bellarmine and Suarez.

[1] Cf. *Com. on Rom.*, chaps. 8, 9, 11; *Com. on Eph.*, chap. 1.
[2] Cf. *Com. on Sent.*, I, d. XL, XLI; *Contra Gentes*, Bk. III, chap. 164; *De verit.*, q.6.
[3] Cf. *Summa theol.*, Ia, q.23.
[4] *Ibid.*, q.23. All the articles of this question may be viewed as corollaries of these two principles.
[5] *Ibid.*, Ia, q.23, a.5.

We shall assign here a considerable number of pages to the teaching of St. Thomas on this subject which concerns us, and this for three reasons: (1) because he himself proposes it in explanation of the revealed doctrine transmitted to us by St. Paul, and such as St. Augustine understood it; (2) because, the authority of St. Thomas being admitted, almost all the theologians since his time, even the Molinists of our day, claim to follow him; (3) because, by so doing, we shall need to comment but briefly on it in the theoretical part of this work. It will suffice for us to recapitulate the principles of this teaching of St. Thomas, showing how superior they are to the proposed attempts at synthesis as recorded in later chapters.

THE PRINCIPLE OF THE THOMIST SYNTHESIS

St. Thomas had a grander conception than St. Albert the Great and preceding theologians ever had, of the sublimity and unlimited scope of the principle that *God's love is the cause of goodness in things*. He expressed this very forcibly in the following passage: "It has been shown above (q. 19, a. 4) that God's will is the cause of all things. It must needs be, therefore, that a thing has existence, or any kind of good, only inasmuch as it is willed by God. To every existing thing, then, God wills some good. Hence, since to love anything is nothing else than to will good to that thing, it is manifest that God loves everything that exists. Yet not as we love. Because since our will is not the cause of the goodness of things, but is moved by it as its object, our love, whereby we will good to anything, is not the cause of its goodness. . . . On the contrary, God's love infuses and creates goodness in things." [6] In substance St. Thomas had already said as much in two fundamental articles of preceding questions.[7]

[6] *Ibid.*, Ia, q.20, a.2.
[7] *Ibid.*, q.14, a.8: "Whether knowledge is the cause of things?"; q.19, a.4: "Whether God's will is the cause of things?" These two articles will be the source of all we have to say on this subject.

THE UNIVERSAL WILL TO SAVE

By the light of this principle, that God's love is the cause of goodness in things, St. Thomas clears up the two extreme and apparently contradictory aspects of the mystery that confronts us. On the one hand, we have the universal will to save, which St. John Damascene so strenuously defended, and on the other, we have the dogma of predestination, which was stressed by St. Augustine.

First of all, the universal will to save is conceived not only as a sign of God's will, like some oral or written precept, but it is also viewed as a will of good pleasure that really exists in God.[8] If, in truth, God's love is the cause of the goodness in things, then it is by reason of His will of good pleasure and His love that He gives to all men not only a human nature by which they can know and love Him in a natural way, but that He also makes it possible for them to observe the precepts of the natural law, and in this very way salvation is possible. God can never command what is impossible, for that indeed would be an injustice. Sin would then become inevitable, which, in such a case, would no longer be sin, and could not be justly punished either in this life or in the next. God, by reason of His love, therefore, makes it possible for all to observe His precepts, avoid sin, and thus be saved.[9] St. Thomas also says that even in those things that are due to one, God gives more than strict justice demands; for mercy or entirely gratuitous and superabundant kindness is at the root of all divine works of justice, which presuppose that intellectual

---

[8] *De verit.*, q.23, a.3.

[9] *Loc. cit.*, Ia, q.21, a.1 ad 3um, where it is stated that God gives to each thing what is due to it by its nature and condition; also Ia, q.23, a.5 ad 3um, where we read that God deprives nobody of his due; Ia IIae, q.106, a.2 ad 2um, in which he states that it (New Law) gives man sufficient help to avoid sin.

creatures from purely gratuitous love were created and destined for the supernatural life of eternity.[10]

This was the point St. John Damascene insisted upon; but he scarcely considered it but from the moral point of view, in its relation to the divine goodness and the malice of men. God, he said, by an act of His *antecedent* will, of His goodness wills to save all men; but, as some sin and remain in sin, by an act of His *consequent* will He punishes them eternally because He is just.

It remained for future theologians to probe this distinction more deeply, considering it not only from the moral point of view but also from the metaphysical, in its relation either to God's omnipotence or to the efficacy of His will and love. This is what St. Thomas did by the light of that principle which, in his opinion, completely dominates the problem, and from which a whole series of corollaries is deduced.

If God's will and love are the cause of the goodness of creatures,[11] this will, in so far as it is that of the omnipotent Being, produces infallibly the good that it wills unconditionally to be realized right at the moment,[12] even that good that has to be realized by our free act, and this without forcing the will. He is also powerful enough to produce in and with the will that its acts are freely performed. "Since the divine will is perfectly efficacious," says St. Thomas, "it follows not only that things are done which God wills to be done, but also that they are done in the way that He wills. Now God wills some things to be done necessarily, some contingently, to the right ordering of things, for the building up of the universe." [13] This free mode of our acts is still an entity and therefore is included in the adequate object of the omnipo-

10 *Ibid.*, Ia, q.21, a.4.
11 *Ibid.*, Ia, q.19, a.4.
12 *Ibid.*, *Ia*, q.19, a.6, ad 1um.
13 *Ibid.*, Ia, q.19, a.8.

tence and love of God, the Creator.[14] Only evil is excluded
from this adequate object, and therefore God cannot be the
cause of sin either directly or indirectly because of insufficient
help given.[15]

What metaphysical definition shall we give, then, of the
consequent and antecedent wills? St. Thomas gives us in substance the answer to this question. He points out that good is
the object of the will; now goodness, unlike truth, is formally
not in the mind but in things as they actually are. Hence we
will, truly and simply, what we will as having to be at once
realized, and this is called the consequent will, which in God
is always efficacious. As St. Thomas says: "The will is directed to things as they are in themselves, and in themselves
they exist under particular qualifications. Hence we will a
thing simply, inasmuch as we will it when all particular circumstances are considered; and this is what is meant by willing consequently. . . . Thus it is clear that whatever God
simply wills, takes place." [16] As we shall see later on, this
principle concerning the will is of supreme importance for
St. Thomas as constituting the foundation for the distinction
between efficacious and sufficient graces.

If, on the other hand, the will is drawn to what is good in
itself regardless of the circumstances, not to a thing as it actually is, then this is called the *antecedent will,* which of itself and as such is not efficacious, since good, whether natural
or supernatural, easy or difficult to acquire, is realized only
with its accompanying circumstances. As St. Thomas says: "A
thing taken in its primary sense, and absolutely considered,
may be good or evil, and yet when some additional circumstances are taken into account, by a consequent consideration
may be changed into the contrary. Thus that a man should

14 *Ibid.,* Ia, q.22, a.4 ad 3um.
15 *Ibid.,* Ia IIae, q.79, a.1, 2.
16 *Ibid.,* Ia, q.19, a.6 ad 1um.

live is good, . . . but if in a particular case we add that a man is a murderer . . . to kill him is a good." [17] Thus the merchant during a storm would will (conditionally) to retain his merchandise, but he wills to cast it into the sea so as to save his life.[18] Thus again, God wills antecedently that all the fruits of the earth become ripe, although for the sake of a greater good He permits this not to happen in all cases. He also wills antecedently that all men should be saved, although, in view of a greater good, of which He alone is the judge, He permits that some commit sin and are lost.

The conclusion, then, is that God never commands what is impossible, that by His will and His love He makes it possible for all to keep His commandments: "It (New Law) gives sufficient help to avoid sin." [19] God gives to each person even more than strict justice demands.[20] Thus St. Thomas explains metaphysically the notion of antecedent will by appealing to the definition of omnipotence, which should never be overlooked, and in virtue of which all that God wills simply is fulfilled.[21]

THE PRINCIPLE OF PREDILECTION AND WHAT IT PRESUPPOSES

On the other hand, as regards the consequent will, St. Thomas affirms, more clearly than anyone had done before his time, the principle of predilection, which is that one would not be better than another unless one were loved more by God. As he says: "Since God's love is the cause of goodness in things, as has been said, no one thing would be better than

[17] *Ibid.*, q.19, a.6 ad 1um.
[18] *Ibid.*, Ia IIae, q.6, a.6, c.
[19] *Ibid.*, q.106, a.2 ad 2um.
[20] *Ibid.*, Ia, q.21, a.4.
[21] *Ibid.*, q.19, a.6.

another if God did not will greater good for one than for another. . . . And the reason why some things are better than others, is that God wills them a greater good. Hence it follows that He loves more the better things." [22]

This principle of predilection is the corollary of the preceding one, that God's love is the cause of the goodness of created beings. It seems to follow in the philosophical order as a necessary consequence of the principle of causality, that what comes in addition to a thing in existence has an efficient and supreme cause in Him who is Being itself, the source of all being and all good. It follows also, as a consequence of the principle of finality, that every agent acts for an end, and the purpose of the action of the supreme agent is to manifest His goodness, by reproducing a likeness of Himself, which is a more or less perfect participation of His nature.

Not only is this principle of predilection a manifest truth of the philosophical order, but it is also a revealed principle, for it finds its special application in the order of grace which, by its very nature, is gratuitous and makes us pleasing in God's sight. This principle was enunciated by God to Moses, when He said: "I will have mercy on whom I will, and I will be merciful to whom it shall please Me." [23] St. Paul refers to this revealed truth when he writes concerning the divine election as follows: "Is there injustice with God? God forbid! For He saith to Moses: I will have mercy on whom I will have mercy. And I will show mercy to whom I will show mercy." [24] With this same principle always in mind, St. Paul also writes: "For who distinguisheth thee? or what hast thou that thou didst not receive?" [25] St. Thomas thus explains these words in his commentary on this epistle: "Who is it that distinguisheth thee from the mass of those who are lost? This is more

---

22 *Ibid.*, q.20, a.3, 4.
23 Exod. 33: 19.
24 Rom. 9: 14 f.
25 I Cor. 4: 7.

than thou canst do. Who is it that makes thee superior to another? Thou thyself canst not do this, and therefore why art thou proud of thyself?" [26] He says the same in commenting on the parable of the talents: "He who makes a greater effort, has more grace; but to make a greater effort, he needs to be moved by a higher cause." [27] Likewise, in asking whether grace is greater in one than in another, he replies: "We must not seek the first cause of this diversity in the subject (or in man), for man prepares himself, only inasmuch as his free will is prepared by God. Hence the first cause of this diversity is to be sought on the part of God, who disposes His gifts of grace variously, in order that the beauty and perfection of the Church may result from these various degrees; even as He instituted the various conditions of things, that the universe might be perfect. Hence after the Apostle had said (Eph. 4: 7): To every one of us is given grace according to the measure of the giving of Christ, having enumerated the various graces (v. 12), he adds: For the perfecting of the saints . . . for the edifying of the body of Christ.[28]

St. Thomas had come across this principle of predilection formulated in different ways in the writings of St. Augustine who, concerning the good and bad angels, says: "If both were created equally good, then, while some fell by their evil will, the others were more abundantly assisted, and reached that high degree of blessedness from which they became certain they would never fall." [29] The good angels would not be better than the rest unless they had been loved and helped more by God. This same thought, variously expressed, is constantly recurring in St. Augustine's writings on predestination against the Pelagians and Semipelagians.[30] This is also the meaning he gives to the famous Gospel text which St. Thomas often

[26] *Com. on Cor.* 4: 7.
[27] *Com. on Matt.* 25: 15.
[28] *Summa theol.,* Ia IIae, q.112, a.4.
[29] *De civitate Dei,* XII, 9.
[30] *De praedest, sanct.,* chap 8; *De dono persever.,* chap. 9.

quotes: "Why He draws this one and not that other, seek not to judge, if thou dost not wish to err." [31]

Having formulated this principle of predilection, that no created being would be better than another unless it were loved more by God,[32] St. Thomas makes it the keystone of his treatise on predestination.[33] To realize fully the importance of this principle, we must in the first place note more precisely what it presupposes as regards the efficacy of divine love, which is the cause of all kinds of created good. The principle of predilection presupposes, according to St. Thomas, that the decrees of the divine will with regard to our future salutary acts, are of themselves infallibly efficacious, and not because God foresees our consent. The same must be said of actual grace, by which we freely perform these salutary acts; it is of itself efficacious. St. Thomas spoke of these decrees as follows: "Determined effects proceed from His own infinite perfection, according to the determination of His will and intellect." [34] And again he says: "Even in us the cause of one and the same effect is knowledge as directing it, whereby the form of the work is conceived, and will as commanding it, since the form as it is in the intellect only is not determined to exist or not to exist in the effect, except by the will." [35] Similarly he remarks that: "God's knowledge is the cause of things, in so far as His will is joined to it." [36]

That these decrees of the divine will concerning our salutary acts are of themselves infallibly efficacious and not because God foresees our consent, is evidently the meaning of the famous eighth article of St. Thomas which we have already quoted. In it he says: "Since the divine will is perfectly efficacious, it follows not only that things are done which

[31] *Com. in Joan.*, tr. 26.
[32] *Loc. cit.*, Ia, q.20, a.3.
[33] *Ibid.*, Ia, q.23.
[34] *Ibid.*, Ia, q.19, a.4.
[35] *Ibid.*, ad 4um.
[36] *Ibid.*, Ia, q.14, a.8.

God wills to be done, but also that they are done in the way that He wills. Now God wills some things to be done necessarily, some contingently, to the right ordering of things, for the building up of the universe." [37] In this same article St. Thomas proposes this objection: "But the will of God cannot be hindered. Therefore the will of God imposes necessity on things willed." He replies as follows: "From the very fact that nothing resists the divine will, it follows that not only those things happen which God wills to happen, but that they happen necessarily or contingently according to His will." [38]

If, as all the Thomists without exception remark, these decrees and the grace that assures their execution were not of themselves efficacious, but only because our consent was foreseen by God, contrary to the principle of predilection, the result of this would be that of two men or two angels equally loved and helped by God, one would become better than another. He would become better either because of a first or final act, or of one easy or difficult to perform, without having been loved and helped more by God; and then it would follow, exclusive of God's intention, first as to conditionally free acts of the future, and then as to future acts, that of these two men equally loved and helped, and placed in the same circumstances, one of them would be more virtuous than the other.

St. Augustine, when writing about the efficacy of grace, had stated what is the foundation for the principle of predilection. He says: "And so this grace, which by divine liberality is secretly bestowed upon human beings, is spurned by no one hard of heart, for it is given for this very purpose that the hardness of heart may be taken away." [39]

---

[37] *Ibid.,* Ia, q. 19, a. 8.
[38] *Ibid.,* ad 2um.
[39] *De praedest, sanct.,* chap. 8; cf. *De dono persever.,* chap. 10; *De corrept. et gratia,* chap. 9; *De gratia Christi,* chap. 24.

THE ANTECEDENT AND CONSEQUENT WILLS

In no less clear terms than St. Augustine, St. Thomas expresses what is the foundation for the principle of predilection, in the fine distinction he draws between the antecedent will, which is the principle of sufficient grace, and the consequent will, which is the principle of efficacious grace. On this point he says: "Whatever God simply wills takes place; although what He wills antecedently may not take place." [40] God wills simply the good that must be accomplished right at the moment, as in the example of the good thief's conversion, who was loved and helped more than the other. However, God made the observance of the precepts really possible for this latter; if he was lost, it was truly his own fault, in that he resisted the sufficient grace which was offered and even given by Christ who was dying for him.

St. Thomas often distinguished between these two graces. He did so, for instance, in one of his commentaries in which he said concerning Christ as redeemer: "He is the propitiation for our sins, efficaciously for some, but sufficiently for all, because the price of His blood is sufficient for the salvation of all; but it has its effect only in the elect, because of the obstacle to it." [41] God often removes this obstacle, but not always. There is the mystery. "God deprives nobody of his due." [42] He also "gives man sufficient help to avoid sin." [43] As for efficacious grace, if it is given to this particular sinner, that is because of God's mercy; if it is refused to a certain other, that is because of His justice.[44]

A considerable number of texts could be quoted from St. Thomas in which he clearly shows that, in his opinion, grace is of itself efficacious, like the divine decrees, the execution of

[40] *Loc. cit.*, Ia, q.19, a.6 ad 1um.
[41] *Com. in ep. ad Tit.*, I, 2: 6.
[42] *Loc. cit.*, Ia, q.23, a.5 ad 3um.
[43] *Ibid.*, Ia IIae, q.106, a.2 ad 2um.
[44] *Ibid.*, IIa IIae, q.2, a.5 ad 1um.

which is assured by it. Thus, for instance, he writes: "The salutary work we perform is conferred upon us by God inasmuch as He operates in us, interiorly moving and urging us to good . . . inasmuch as His power operates in us to will and accomplish according to His good will." [45] Elsewhere he says: "No matter how perfect a corporeal or spiritual nature is supposed to be, it cannot proceed to its act unless it be moved by God." [46] "God's intention cannot fail, according to the saying of St. Augustine in his book on the Predestination of the Saints (*De dono persever,* XIV), that by God's gifts whoever is liberated, is most certainly liberated. Hence if God intends, while moving, that the one whose heart He moves should attain to grace, He will infallibly attain to it, according to John 6: 45: Everyone that hath heard of the Father and hath learned cometh to Me." [47] "If God moves the will to anything, it is incompossible with this supposition, that the will be not moved thereto. But it is not impossible simply. Consequently it does not follow that the will is moved by God necessarily." [48]

The necessity mentioned here is one of consequence, not of consequent. A good explanation of it had already been given by St. Albert the Great, and St. Thomas improved upon it when he showed that the divine will, by the very reason of its sovereign efficacy, reaches out mightily and sweetly, even to the free mode of our acts; it wills them to be performed freely, and so they are infallibly. Bossuet admirably expresses the mind of St. Thomas, writing as follows: "Thus God wills from eternity all the acts that will be performed by the free will of human beings, all the goodness and reality there is in them. What is more absurd than to say, that it is not because God wills, that a thing exists? Must we not say, on the contrary, that a thing exists because God wills it? And

---

[45] *Com. in ep. ad Eph.,* chap. 3, lect. 2.
[46] *Loc. cit.,* Ia IIae, q. 109, a. 1.
[47] *Ibid.,* q. 112, a. 3.
[48] *Ibid.,* q. 10, a. 4 ad 3um.

just as it happens that we are free in virtue of the decree that wills us to be free, so it happens that we act freely in this or that act, in virtue even of the decree which includes all this in detail." [49] St. Thomas had said the same: "God changes the will without forcing it. But He can change the will from the fact that He Himself operates in the will as He does in nature. . . . Hence as the will can change its act for another, much more so can God." [50] Farther on he says: "Only God can change the inclination of the will, which He gave it, according as He wills, from one thing to another." [51] Again St. Thomas says: "God moves the will immutably on account of the efficacy of the moving power which cannot fail; but on account of the nature of the will that is moved, which is indifferently disposed to various things, the will is not necessitated but remains free." [52] We shall see that the Thomists say just this and no more. This intrinsic efficacy of the divine decrees as regards our salutary acts is considered by St. Thomas as even a revealed truth. He quotes, in fact, well known scriptural texts in this sense.[53] "Lord, Thou hast wrought all our works for us." [54] "As the divisions of waters, so the heart of the king is in the hand of the Lord; whithersoever He will He shall turn it." [55] "For it is God who worketh in you, both to will and to accomplish, according to His good will." [56] In his theological treatise [57] he quotes the following passage: "O Lord, Lord almighty King, all things are in Thy power and there is none that can resist Thy will, if Thou determine to save Israel." [58] Another text quoted is as follows:

49 *Traité du libre arbitre*, chap. 8.
50 *De Verit.*, q.22, a.8.
51 *Ibid.*, a.9.
52 *De malo*, q.6, a.1 ad 3um.
53 *Contra Gentes*, Bk. III, chaps. 88–89.
54 Is. 26: 12.
55 Prov. 21: 1.
56 Phil. 2: 13.
57 *Summa theol.*, Ia, q.103, a.7.
58 Esth. 13: 9.

"And I will give you a new heart, and put a new spirit within you. And I will take away the stony heart out of your flesh and will give you a heart of flesh. And I will put My spirit in the midst of you; and I will cause you to walk in My commandments and to keep My judgments and do them." [59] St. Thomas sees the intrinsic efficacy of grace in these scriptural texts as well as in several canons of the Second Council of Orange.[60] Most of these texts of the Council of Orange are taken from the works of St. Augustine and St. Prosper. Now St. Augustine, as we have seen, held that grace is efficacious of itself. The five canons of the Council of Orange cited in the footnote express in different ways this truth that every good, whether natural or supernatural, comes from God. Now this is the very foundation of the principle of predilection.

Thus God willed efficaciously from all eternity that the Virgin Mary should give her free consent to the mystery of the incarnation. This had infallibly to be fulfilled; moved powerfully though very gently by a special grace, Mary infallibly uttered her fiat with complete freedom of will. Thus, too, Christ willed to die for us on the Cross at the hour irrevocably decreed. So also the good thief and the centurion were converted as God efficaciously willed. St. Thomas considers this the normal consequence of God's omnipotent will and love. The great mystery in this begins especially with sin. What is manifest for both St. Thomas and St. Augustine is this, that every good, even the free determination to perform a salutary act, comes from God, and entirely from Him as first cause, even though this determination comes entirely from us as secondary cause. As St. Thomas says: "There is no distinction between what flows from free will and what is of predestination; as there is no distinction between what flows from a secondary cause and from a first cause." [61]

[59] Ez. 36: 26 f.
[60] Cf. Denz., nos. 177, 182, 185, 189, 193.
[61] *Loc. cit.,* Ia, q.23, a.5.

Now if the divine decrees concerning our salutary acts, and if the actual grace which assures the execution of these decrees, were not of themselves efficacious, but only because our consent was foreseen, then God's knowledge and will would no longer be the cause in the free determinations of our salutary acts of the more intimate and better part. In that case there would be some good, and even the best part of our merits, which did not come from the source of all good. Moreover, with regard to this free determination of the salutary act, since God's knowledge and will are no longer the causes, these would be passive and dependent. We should have to admit a passivity in the pure Act. His knowledge with regard to certain determinations of the created order and even to the best of them, would be passive, measured by this created reality instead of measuring it.[62] This would mean the final rejection of the principle that no being would be better than another, unless it had been loved more by God.[63]

[62] *Ibid., Ia,* q.14, a.8; q.19, a.4, 8.
[63] *Ibid.,* Ia, q.20, a.3.

CHAPTER III

THE NATURE AND REASON OF PREDESTINATION ACCORDING TO ST. THOMAS

WITH this principle of predilection as his guiding star, St. Thomas wrote the whole question concerning predestination in which he gives us the mature reflection of his thought on this point. We may say that all the articles of this question are so many corollaries of this principle. Let us note carefully the conclusion and proof of each article. We shall again take up the discussion of these articles in the theoretical or synthetic part of this work.

1) The first article defines predestination as: "The plan of the direction of a rational creature towards the end, i. e., life eternal; for to destine is to direct or send." It is therefore the plan in God's mind of directing this particular man or that particular angel to the ultimate and supernatural end. It is this plan, once ordained and willed which, from all eternity, determines the efficacious means that will lead this particular man or that particular angel to his final end. In so defining predestination St. Thomas is faithful to the very letter to St. Augustine's definition, who states that it is: "the foreknowledge and preparation of the benefits by which most certainly are liberated whoever are liberated." [1] "By predestination God knew what He Himself will do." [2] The point at issue here is not a foreknowledge of our merits; for this would presuppose a passivity or dependence in God with regard to our conditionally future free determinations, and then to our future ones. The foreknowledge in question concerns what

[1] *De dono persever.*, chap. 14.
[2] *De praed. sanct.*, chap. 10.

God will do, what graces He will grant so as to lead this particular man or that particular angel to his final end. Thus predestination, by reason of its object, is to be considered as a part of providence. Note well that predestination so defined is predestination to glory; the formal wording of the text is: "towards the end, i. e., life eternal." Moreover, predestination merely to grace is not predestination in the true sense, since it is not the contrary of reprobation. This is admitted not only by Thomists but also by congruists of the Bellarminian and Suarezian type, and even by such Molinists as Father Billot.

2) The second article proves that predestination is in God who predestines and not in the one predestined; but its effects in the one predestined are calling, justification, and glorification.

3) The third article defines its contrary, which is reprobation. It is a part of Providence to permit certain ones to fall into and remain in sin (negative reprobation), and for this defection it inflicts upon them the penalty of damnation (positive reprobation). But whereas predestination is the cause of grace and of our salutary acts, reprobation is by no means the cause of sin.[3] Nowhere do we find in this article that negative reprobation consists, as some later Thomists thought, in a positive exclusion from glory on the grounds of an undue benefit. It is merely the non-election and the will to permit certain ones to fall into and remain in sin. We shall see that the motive for this reprobation is indicated by St. Thomas.[4]

4) The fourth article proves that the predestined are elected by God, so that predestination presupposes election, and this latter presupposes love. As St. Thomas says: "Predestination presupposes election in the order of reason; and election presupposes love."[5]

[3] *Summa theol.*, Ia, q.23, a.3 ad 2um.
[4] *Ibid.*, a.5 ad 3um.
[5] *Ibid.*, a.4, c.

Here we see the application of two principles ignored by some later theologians. First of all we have this principle that God, in this case as always, wills the end before the means, and therefore He wills the predestined glory before willing them grace by which they will merit it. Duns Scotus is not, therefore, as some recently maintained, the first one to apply this principle here. St. Thomas writes on this point as follows: "But nothing is directed towards an end unless the will for that end already exists. Whence the predestination of some to eternal salvation presupposes in the order of reason, that God wills their salvation, and to this belong both election and love—love inasmuch as He wills them this particular good of eternal salvation—since to love is to wish well to anyone, as stated above (q. 20, a. 2, 3); election inasmuch as He wills this good to some in preference to others, since He reprobates some, as stated above (a. 3)." [6]

The second principle applied here is that of predilection: no thing would be better than another, unless it were loved more by God. St. Thomas, without alluding at all to the foreseeing of our merits, whether conditionally future or future, excludes any idea of passivity or dependence from the divine knowledge. He writes as follows: "Election and love, however, are differently ordered in God and in ourselves: because in us the will in loving does not cause good, but we are incited to love by the good which already exists; and therefore we choose someone to love, and so election in us precedes love. In God, however, it is the reverse. For His will, by which in loving He wishes good to someone, is the cause of that good possessed by some in preference to others. Thus it is clear that love precedes election in the order of reason, and election precedes predestination. Whence all the predestinate are objects of election and love." [7] The Pelagians looked upon God as merely the spectator and not the author of the good

[6] *Ibid.,* a.4.
[7] *Ibid.,* a.4.

and salutary consent which distinguishes the just person from the sinner. Both St. Thomas and St. Augustine maintain that the better and more intimate part in the free determination of this good consent must come from the source of all good. No one has asserted this more positively than the Angelic Doctor.

We shall see that Molina departs from the teaching of St. Thomas in this fundamental article. In accordance with a definition of liberty which, in the opinion of the Thomists, cannot be reconciled with the principle of predilection, he affirms that: "Of two persons who receive an equal interior grace when called by God, it may happen that one of them, because of the freedom of his will, is converted and the other remains an infidel." [8] He even affirms [9] that of two sinners, the one who is converted is sometimes the one who received less help from God. Contrary to the principle of predilection formulated by St. Thomas and enunciated in various forms by many of his predecessors, this person thus becomes better than the other without having been loved more by God. This explains why Molina, in contradiction to St. Thomas, said that "election did not precede predestination." [10] He recognizes that St. Thomas seems to have held the contrary opinion; [11] but he adds: "I never approved, however, of this opinion." [12] He speaks in the same manner of the divine motion, regretting that St. Thomas and the majority of the Scholastics admitted with St. Augustine a predestination that did not have its foundation in the foreknowledge of merits. Here we detect the point about which, as we shall see, Thomists and Molinists differ. What they seek to know is this: whether the principle of predilection, which presupposes the

[8] *Concordia*, Paris ed., 1876, p. 51.
[9] *Ibid.*, p. 565.
[10] *Ibid.*, p. 429.
[11] *Summa theol.*, Ia, q.23, a.4.
[12] *Loc. cit.*, p. 429.

intrinsic efficacy of the divine decrees and of grace, is true or false.

5) In the fifth article, St. Thomas deduces other consequences from the principle of predilection, asking whether the foreknowledge of merits is the cause of predestination. He gives a negative answer to this question and explains it by a series of definite conclusions in the body of the article and in the reply to the third objection.

It is especially in connection with this principal point at issue that St. Thomas gives us his interpretation of the principal texts of St. Paul concerning predestination. It is of importance for us to insist on them.

CHAPTER IV

THE SCRIPTURAL BACKGROUND FOR THE TEACHING OF ST. THOMAS

EPISTLE TO THE EPHESIANS

LET us consider his exegesis on the two passages to the Ephesians. They are as follows: "Blessed be the God and Father of our Lord Jesus Christ, who hath blessed us with spiritual blessings in heavenly places, in Christ. As He chose us in Him before the foundation of the world, that we should be holy and unspotted in His sight in charity. Who hath predestinated us unto the adoption of children through Jesus Christ unto Himself, according to the purpose of His will, unto the praise of the glory of His grace. . . . In whom we are also called by lot, being predestinated according to the purpose of Him who worketh all things according to the counsel of His will that we may be unto the praise of His glory." [1]

In his commentary on this epistle, St. Thomas makes three important remarks, afterwards referred to by all the Thomists.

1) He notes that when the Apostle writes: "Who hath predestinated us unto the adoption of the children," though we may understand these words as referring to adoptive sonship realized here on earth by sanctifying grace, yet it is far better to say they refer to the perfect likeness to God that will be realized in our heavenly home, in accordance with what St. Paul himself said: "We who have the firstfruits of the Spirit, even we ourselves groan within ourselves, waiting for

[1] Eph. 1: 3–6, 11 f.

the adoption of the sons of God." [2] Grace, indeed, is given in view of future glory and, according to the teaching of St. Thomas,[3] God, all-wise as He is, wills the end before the means. Moreover, predestination only to the life of grace and not to glory, would be no more than predestination in name, since many of the reprobates are so predestined.

This remark of St. Thomas is retained in substance by several modern exegetes [4] who see in this text of St. Paul an immediate reference to the general election of Christians to a life of holiness, but in such a way that the principles declared on this subject apply as a consequence to the special election of this particular person rather than to a certain other. St. Thomas insists on these principles proclaimed by St. Paul.

2) He remarks that God has chosen us, not because we were saints but that we might become saints. His words are: "He chose us, not because we were saints, for we were not; but He chose us that we might become saints by leading a virtuous life and one free from vices."

3) St. Thomas observes that, for St. Paul, God's plan or His eternal decree is the reason why we are predestined, and not because He has foreseen our merits. Says St. Paul: "He predestinated us . . . according to the purpose of His will." [5] A beneficent design is this, which is the result of His most pure love. St. Thomas particularly stresses this in his commentary, for he says: "That anyone, however, is predestined to life eternal . . . this is a grace given that is purely gratuitous . . . for no merits preceded it." [6] It is not a question merely of predestination to grace, but also of predestination to glory, which is the only kind that cannot be shared in common between the elect and the reprobates.

The holy Doctor again insists on this in connection with

[2] Rom. 8: 23.
[3] *Summa theol.*, Ia, q.23, a.4.
[4] Cf. Lagrange, *Ep. aux Romains,* chap. 9; Vosté, *In ep. ad Eph.* 1: 11.
[5] Eph. 1: 5.
[6] *Com. in ep. ad Eph.* 1: 5.

verse eleven of this chapter: "In whom we are also called
. . . being predestinated according to the purpose of Him."
"Therefore the reason why we are predestined," says St.
Thomas, "is not because our merits were foreseen, but the
pure will of God is the reason for this; wherefore St. Paul
adds that it is according to the purpose of Him who worketh
all things according to the counsel of His will." These final
words, moreover, indicate that everything which happens depends upon God's will. There is nothing, therefore, in this
text of St. Paul that points to the foreseeing of our merits as
the reason for predestination.

EPISTLE TO THE ROMANS

St. Paul still more clearly expresses his mind, as St. Thomas
views it, in the Epistle to the Romans, which directly and explicitly treats of predestination with glorification as its effect:
"We know that to them that love God all things work together
unto good, to such as, according to His purpose, are called to
be saints. For whom He foreknew, He also predestinated to
be made conformable to the image of His Son, that He might
be the firstborn amongst many brethren. And whom He predestinated, them He also glorified." [7]

In explaining this text St. Thomas insists upon this, that
everything in this life contributes to the good of those who
persevere unto the end in God's love. This means in the life
of those predestined according to God's purpose. He refuses
to see in the words "whom He foreknew," any reference to
foreknowledge of merits, for, according to St. Paul, the merits
of the predestined are the effects of predestination. He recalls the texts so often quoted on this subject: "For who distinguisheth thee? Or what hast thou that thou hast not
received? It is God who worketh in you, both to will and to
accomplish, according to His good will." [8] St. Thomas holds,

[7] Rom. 8: 28–30.
[8] I Cor. 4: 7.

therefore, that according to this text of St. Paul quoted in the previous paragraph,[9] everything that directs the predestined to eternal salvation is the effect of predestination. It is definitely formulated by him as follows: "Whatsoever is in man disposing him towards salvation is all included under the effect of predestination," [10] even the free determination to perform a salutary act.

In addition to this, St. Thomas holds that Christ's predestination to divine sonship is prior to our Savior's foreseen merits, since these merits presuppose the Person of the Word made flesh and therefore His divine sonship. Now Christ's predestination, as St. Augustine said,[11] is the eminent exemplar of ours.

Concerning the ninth chapter of St. Paul's Epistle to the Romans, St. Thomas recognizes that he treats in the beginning of this chapter of the call of the Gentiles to the grace of the Christian faith. In contrast to this, he treats of the unbelief of the Jews; but St. Thomas recognizes that this chapter also contains principles applicable to individual cases. Father Lagrange [12] is in perfect agreement on this point, and says: "It is beyond dispute that this call of the Gentiles is at the same time a call to salvation. We cannot help thinking of the fate of each; we transpose the terms of the proposition, we apply St. Paul's principles to individual cases of salvation. It is purely a favor on God's part when He calls one to justification. . . . But God does not proceed in the same way toward those whom He calls and those who are not called. . . . According to St. Paul, man is truly the cause of his (positive) reprobation by reason of his sins: 'For they stumbled at the stumbling-stone.' " [13]

This brings St. Thomas to explain verse thirteen. Giving a

9 Rom. 8: 28.
10 *Summa theol.*, Ia, q.23, a.5.
11 *De praed. sanct.*, chap. 15.
12 *Epitre aux Romains*, p. 244.
13 Rom. 9: 32.

general scope to the words, "Jacob I loved," he formulates
the principle of predilection in these terms: "Election and
love are differently ordered in God and in man. In man election precedes love, for man is incited to love from a consideration of good in the object loved; for this reason he chooses in
preference this thing to the other and makes it the object of
his love." But whatever the Pelagians and Semipelagians may
have said about it, there can be no such dependence or passivity in God. St. Thomas continues in the same strain: "But
God's will is the cause of all good that is in the creature, and
therefore the good by reason of which one thing is preferred
to another by way of election is consequent to God's will,
which is concerned with His own good, and which has love
as its province." Therefore the conclusion of St. Thomas is:
"Foreknowledge of merits cannot be the reason of predestination, since foreseen merits are the effects of predestination."
On the contrary, demerits, of which God can by no means be
the cause, are the reason of damnation. St. Thomas finds this
thought expressed in the famous scriptural text: "Destruction
is thy own, O Israel: thy help is only in Me." [14]

Such is the mystery as St. Thomas, following St. Augustine,
finds it expressed in the epistles of St. Paul. He does not seek
to make it less obscure, for that would be to detract from its
sublimity. But he brings forward the objection raised by human reason, as foreseen by St. Paul, and he stresses the more
distinctive parts of the Apostle's reply.

The objection raised by the Pelagians and Semipelagians
against St. Augustine is not original, for it was already proposed by St. Paul when he asked: "What shall we say then?
Is there injustice with God?" [15] Is there injustice on God's
part in distributing so unequally His gifts to men who are
equal by nature?

St. Thomas remarks that St. Paul did not reply to this ob-

[14] Osee 13: 9.
[15] Rom. 9: 14.

jection by having recourse to the foreknowledge of merits as regards the elect, as if this were the reason for their predestination. He replied, maintaining it to be a mystery of revealed truth instead of representing it in an inferior light: "Is there injustice with God? God forbid! For He saith to Moses: I will have mercy on whom I will have mercy. And I will show mercy to whom I will show mercy. So then it is not of him that willeth, nor of him that runneth but of God that showeth mercy. . . . Therefore He hath mercy on whom He will, and whom He will He hardeneth." [16] St. Thomas remarks that St. Paul affirms the principle of predilection by presenting it in a new form, finding it revealed in these words of God to Moses: "I will have mercy on whom I will; and I will be merciful to whom it shall please Me." [17] Thus our election depends neither upon our will nor upon our efforts, but upon God who shows mercy.

Concerning verses fifteen and sixteen, St. Thomas says again that the effect of predestination cannot be the reason for this latter. Now the good use of grace or merit is the effect of predestination. Therefore foreseen merit cannot be the reason for predestination. There is no other reason for this but the will of God. Now, he goes on to say, we cannot speak of justice or injustice in cases of pure mercy; such as, for instance, on meeting two persons, if we give to one and not to the other; or, if two persons have equally offended us, we pardon one and demand reparation from the other. The same is to be said with regard to sinners. God is merciful toward the one whom He restores to grace, and just toward the one whom He leaves in sin. He is unjust to nobody. The conclusion therefore of St. Thomas is that, according to St. Paul, foreknowledge of merits cannot be the cause of predestination, and by this he understands predestination to glory, which is the only kind worthy of this name; for predestination only to grace is com-

16 *Ibid.,* 9: 14–16, 18.
17 Ex. 33: 19.

mon to the elect and many of the reprobates. Moreover, the merits that follow justification, since they are the effects of predestination that is peculiar to the elect, cannot be the cause of this latter. St. Thomas is among the clearest on this point, and we shall find him expressing himself still more clearly in that article of the *Summa*, the scriptural proofs of which we give in this chapter.

St. Thomas completes his commentary on the ninth chapter of the Epistle to the Romans by examining the last objection St. Paul proposes. "Thou wilt say therefore to me," he says, "Why doth He then find fault? For who resisteth His will?" [18] This is how St. Thomas understands the objection: Why reprove the sinner for not having done what he was incapable of doing? To quote his own words: "It is useless to ask anyone to do that which is not in one's power to do." This is the well-known objection of the *insufficiency of divine assistance*.

The way to reply to this difficulty is by saying that God never commands what is impossible, and that He makes the attainment of salvation really possible for all who have to observe His commandments. Taken in this sense, we may say that He wills to save all; [19] but, on the other hand, no one would be better than another, unless one were loved more by God. Affirming the principle of predilection and presenting it in a new form, St. Paul says: "O man, who art thou that repliest against God? Shall the thing formed say to him that formed it: Why hast thou made me thus? Or hath not the potter power over the clay of the same lump, to make one vessel unto honor and another unto dishonor? What if God, willing to show His wrath and to make His power known, endured with much patience vessels of wrath, fitted for destruction, that He might show the riches of His glory on the vessels of

[18] Rom. 9: 19.
[19] I Tim. 2: 4.

mercy which He hath prepared unto glory . . . where is the injustice?" [20]

St. Paul's reply to this objection confirms all that precedes, as also does what he adds farther on when he asks: "Hath God cast away His people? God forbid! . . . As in the time of Elias. . . . There is a remnant saved according to the election of grace. And if by grace, it is not by works; otherwise grace is no more grace." [21]

In his commentary on the concluding portion of this ninth chapter in the Epistle to the Romans, St. Thomas remarks once more as follows: "Whatever good a man has, must be ascribed to the divine goodness as principal agent. For we read in Isaias: 'And now, O Lord, Thou art our Father, and we are clay; and Thou art our maker and we are all the works of Thy hands.' [22] If God does not promote man to better things, but leaving him in his weakness, makes the meanest use of him, He does him no wrong, so that he can justly complain about it." Where is the injustice, if God permits the bad thief to die unrepentant, and if He pardons the other so as to declare in him the riches of His glory?

THE GRATUITY OF PREDESTINATION IN THE THEOLOGICAL *SUMMA*

In the *Theological Summa*,[23] St. Thomas only summarizes and systematically arranges what he said in his commentary on the ninth chapter of the Epistle to the Romans. The title of the article is: "Whether the foreknowledge of merits is the cause of predestination?" This means, as explained at the beginning of the argument in the article: Whether God preordained that He would give the effect of predestination to

20 Rom. 9: 20–23.
21 *Ibid.*, 11: 1–8.
22 Is. 64: 8.
23 *Loc. cit.*, Ia, q. 23, a. 5, c. et ad 3um.

anyone on account of any merits? We find the same doctrine as set forth in this article in other works of St. Thomas,[24] but it is expressed here in a simpler, sublimer, and more precise manner.

According to his accustomed way of procedure in the statement of the question, St. Thomas posits three difficulties, the principal one being the very same as that formulated by St. Paul when he asks: "Is there injustice in God?" [25] He gives at first, in the argument *on the contrary,* a general and negative answer. The Apostle wrote to Titus: "Not by the works of justice which we have done, but according to His mercy, He saved us." [26] Now, as it is a fact that He saves us, so He has predestined us to salvation. Foreknowledge of merits is therefore not the cause or reason of predestination which, as St. Thomas defined it in the first article, means predestination to glory. After having formulated this negative and general response on the authority of St. Paul, St. Thomas explains it, recalling and refuting Origen's error, the Pelagian and Semipelagian heresies, and an opinion held by some Scholastics. He formulates the following conclusions: (1) Pre-existing merits in a former life cannot be the reason for predestination; [27] (2) nor can it be because of merits acquired prior to justification; [28] (3) nor can it be because of merits acquired after justification.

To prove this third conclusion, St. Thomas has recourse to a principle, the force of which was not realized by many of the later theologians. Of those who held the contrary opinion he says: "But these seem to have drawn a distinction between that which flows from grace, and that which flows from free will, as if the same thing cannot come from both. It is, however, manifest that what is of grace in the life of the predes-

[24] *Com. in Sent.,* I, d. XLI, q.1, a.3; *De veritate,* q.6, a.2.
[25] Rom. 9: 14.
[26] Tit. 3: 5.
[27] Rom. 9: 2.
[28] II Cor. 3: 5.

tined is the effect of predestination; and this cannot be considered as the reason of predestination, since it is contained in the notion of predestination. Therefore, if anything else in us be the reason of predestination, it will be outside the effect of predestination. Now there is no distinction between what flows from a secondary cause and from a first cause. For the providence of God produces effects through the operation of secondary causes, as was shown above (q. 19, a. 8). Wherefore, that which flows from free will is also of predestination." [29] In other words, in the life of the predestined neither the good use of free will nor of grace can be given as the reason for predestination, for they are its effects. Why so? The reason is because we cannot distinguish between what is produced by the secondary cause and what is produced by the first cause; these are two total causes, not co-ordinated but subordinated. Not only does the whole effect come from both, as in the case of two horses drawing a heavy vehicle which one of them would not succeed in drawing alone; but, whereas one of these horses is not moved by the other, the secondary cause does not act except it be moved by the first Cause. On this point Molina very plainly separates from St. Thomas.[30] From this text just quoted we see that the Angelic Doctor considers even the free determination to perform a salutary act as coming entirely from us as a secondary cause, and entirely from God as first Cause, without which we would not determine ourselves to act. This is but the application of principles that have already been explained by him.[31] St. Thomas also writes farther on: "Whatsoever is in man disposing him towards salvation, is all included under the effect of predestination." [32]

In the continuation of this fifth article St. Thomas formulates a conclusion that to us seems accurately to express and

[29] *Summa theol.*, Ia, q.23, a.5.
[30] *Concordia*, disp. 26.
[31] *Loc. cit.*, Ia, q.19, a.8.
[32] *Ibid.*, Ia, q.23, a.5.

clinch several assertions of St. Albert and St. Bonaventure. He writes: "There is no reason why one effect of predestination should not be the reason or cause of another, a subsequent effect being the reason of a previous effect, as its final cause; and the previous effect being the reason of the subsequent as its meritorious cause, which is reduced to the disposition of the matter. Thus we might say that God preordained to give glory on account of merit, and that He preordained to give grace to merit glory." [33] How are we to understand this last statement? According to all that has been quoted so far, and taking especially into consideration the refutation of the third error recorded in the preceding paragraph, we must understand this statement to mean that God decided to give to a certain person, for instance, to the good thief in preference to the other, that grace which is of itself efficacious, so that he may merit eternal glory to which He predestined him. By this St. Thomas does not mean that God decided to give the good thief a grace that will become efficacious by reason of the good consent of this latter. This interpretation is excluded by what is said in the preceding paragraph: "there is no distinction between what flows from a secondary cause and from a first cause." It is also excluded by the final conclusion in the argumentative part of the article, which is as follows: "In another way, the effect of predestination may be considered in general. Thus, it is impossible that the whole of the effect of predestination in general should have any cause as coming from us; because whatever is in man disposing him towards salvation is all included under the effect of predestination, even the preparation for grace." [34]

Various theologians of a later date,[35] contrary to this, said that the free determination of the salutary act is neither the effect of the divine causality nor of predestination. Undoubt-

[33] *Ibid.*, q.23, a.5.
[34] *Ibid.*, q.23, a.5.
[35] Molina, *Concordia*, q.23, a.4–5, memb. ult., ed. 1876, p. 546.

edly they granted that complete predestination does not depend on foreseen merits, understood in this sense, that it includes the first grace which we cannot merit; but they do not accept the interpretation of St. Thomas, who declares that everything in man which directs him to salvation, even the free determination of the salutary act, is the effect of the divine causality and of predestination. Their opinion is about the same as the one held by those to whom St. Thomas replied when He said that "there is no distinction between what flows from free will and what is of predestination; as there is no distinction between what flows from a second cause and from a first cause." [36]

We see that these different conclusions from the argument of the fifth article, explain the general and negative reply of the argument *on the contrary,* which states that the foreknowledge of merits is not the cause or reason of predetermination. This applies to predestination to glory, which is the only predestination that answers the definition of it given in the first article; on the other hand, predestination to grace is set up in opposition to reprobation. We also see that this general answer and the conclusions explaining it are just so many corollaries of the principle of predilection, that one would not be better than another, unless one were loved more by God.

THE PRINCIPAL DIFFICULTY

In the reply to the third objection of this same fifth article there are two final conclusions that present still more prominently the scope of this great principle. The conclusion before the last is: "God willed to manifest His goodness in men, in respect to those whom He predestines, by means of His mercy, in sparing them; and with regard to others, whom He reprobates, by means of His justice, in punishing them. This is the reason why God elects some and rejects others." This

[36] *Ibid.,* q. 23, a. 5.

general reason has its foundation, says St. Thomas, in the words of revelation as expressed in the Epistle to the Romans: "What if God willing to show His wrath (that is the vengeance of His justice) and to make His power known, endured (that is permitted), with much patience, vessels of wrath, fitted for destruction, and that He might show the riches of His glory on the vessels of mercy which He hath prepared unto glory (where is the injustice?)." [37] Divine goodness, on the one hand, tends to communicate itself, and thus it is the principle of mercy; on the other hand, it has an inalienable right to be loved above all things, and is thus the principle of justice. It is fitting that this supreme Goodness be manifested in its two aspects, and that the splendor of infinite justice appear as the refulgence of infinite mercy. Evil is thus permitted by God only for a greater good, of which infinite justice is the judge, and which the elect are destined to contemplate in heaven.

Finally, in the last conclusion, St. Thomas visualizes no longer the good and bad in general, but each one in particular. He says: "Yet why He chooses some for glory and reprobates others, has no reason except the divine will." [38] St. Augustine had said: "Why He draws one, and another He draws not, seek not to judge, if thou dost not wish to err." [39] He has even shown how the foreknowledge of either future or conditionally future merits could not be the cause of predestination. This last conclusion, which is common to St. Augustine and St. Thomas, is a rigorous consequence of the principle of predilection. "Since God's love is the cause of the goodness of created things, no one thing would be better than another unless it were loved more by God." [40] The last conclusion of the synthesis is reunited to the principle of this latter. St. Thomas confirms it by an analogy taken from things in na-

[37] Rom. 9: 22 f.
[38] *Summa theol.,* Ia, q.23, a.5 ad 3um; cf. *De veritate,* q.6, a.2.
[39] Tr. 26 *in Joan.*
[40] *Loc. cit.,* Ia, q.20, a.3.

ture or from those made by human skill. It depends solely upon God's will that this particular part of matter should receive one of the lowest forms, and that other one of the noblest. It likewise depends solely upon the artist's will that, among several equal stones, this particular stone should be put in this part of the wall, and that in another. In the choice of the elect the sovereignty of the divine liberty is made manifest. If God, without any inconvenience to Himself, could have not created, not willed to raise us up to the supernatural order, not willed the incarnation, with far greater reason He could have not chosen Peter in preference to Judas. If He chose him, He did so most freely and because He loved him more. All this doctrine is included in the principle that one thing would not be better than another, unless it were loved more by God.

There remains the other aspect of the mystery, which St. Thomas most emphatically affirms in terminating his argument: "Neither on this account can there be said to be injustice in God, if He prepares unequal lots for not unequal things. . . . In things which are given gratuitously a person can give more or less, just as he pleases—provided he deprives nobody of his due—without any infringement of justice." [41] God does not take away what is due to anyone, for He never commands what is impossible; on the contrary, however, by reason of His love He makes it really possible for all to observe His commandments, and He even grants out of His goodness more than strict justice would demand; [42] for He often raises men many a time from the grave of sin, when He could leave them therein.

CONCLUSION

We will conclude this exposition of the Angelic Doctor's doctrine by saying that St. Thomas, better than any of his

[41] *Ibid.*, Ia, q.23, a.5 ad 3um.
[42] *Ibid.*, Ia, q.21, a.4.

predecessors, has set forth clearly the principles underlying the true extreme and apparently contradictory aspects of this great mystery. He perceives only the more clearly the sublimity of the mystery. He has brought out into very bold relief the contrast between this light and shade in theological matters. On the one hand, we have the shining light of the two principles enunciated by him, one of which declares against predestinarianism, God's infinite justice, that He never commands what is impossible and makes it possible for all to be saved. The other principle, directed against Pelagianism, declares the free intervention of God's mercy, that one thing would not be better than another unless it were loved more by God. But just as these two principles, viewed separately, are certain and clear, so is their reconciliation an impenetrable obscurity. Why is this? It is because infinite justice, infinite mercy, and sovereign liberty are reconciled only in the eminence of the Deity, in the intimate life of God, in which they are identified without destroying one another. Now St. Thomas has shown that we cannot have in this life any positive concept of the Deity as such.[43] We can know God only by what He has analogically in common with creatures; but what belongs *properly* to Him is known by us only negatively (as not finite being), or relatively (as supreme being). In this sense we say that the Deity is above being and above the one. Likewise, the divine paternity, filiation, and spiration are manifested to us only analogically by revelation. Hence the mystery, and especially the obscurity of the problem that confronts us. The intimate reconciliation of infinite justice, infinite mercy, and sovereign liberty is beyond the scope of speculative theology and its discursive method of procedure. By reason of its obscurity, it is the very object of faith (faith is of things unseen) and of contemplation, which is the result of faith enlightened by the gifts of understanding and wis-

[43] *Ibid.*, Ia, q. 13, a. 1.

dom: "O the depth of the riches of the knowledge and the wisdom of God!" [44]

Bossuet admirably expresses the Angelic Doctor's thought. Writing on this subject, he says: "I do not deny that God in His goodness is moved to compassion for all men, nor do I say that He does not provide the means for their eternal salvation in the general dispensation of His providence. . . . But however great may be His plans for all mankind, He shows a certain peculiar regard and preference for a number of them known to Him. All those whom He regards in this manner bewail their sins and are converted in due time. . . . This is the will of the Father who sent Me, that of all that He hath given Me, I should lose nothing. [45] And why does He introduce us to these sublime truths? Does He do this to trouble and alarm us? . . . Our Savior's plan is this, that by contemplating this glance He casts in secrecy upon those whom He knows, and whom His Father has given Him by a certain choice, and recognizing that He can lead them to their haven of eternal salvation by unfailing means, we should learn, first of all, to ask for these means, and uniting our prayer with His, say with Him: Deliver us from evil, [46] or else say with the Church: Permit us not to be separated from Thee; when our will seeks to be its own master, permit it not; hold it in Thy hand, change it and bring it back to Thee. . . . There is another thing which our Savior wishes to teach us, and it is this; that we abandon ourselves to His loving kindness; not that there is no more need of action and toil on our part. . . ; but in doing everything to the best of our ability, we must above all give ourselves up completely to God alone, now and forever. . . . Let no one say to me that this doctrine of grace and of preference is the despair of good souls. What! For my

44 Rom. 11: 33; cf. Com. of St. Thomas.
45 John 6: 39.
46 Matt. 6: 13.

greater assurance, they think of throwing me upon my own resources, and thus rid me of my inconstancy? No, my God, I do not consent to this. My only assurance is in abandoning myself to Thee. . . . Help me, and I shall be saved.[47] Heal me, O Lord, and I shall be healed.[48] Convert me, and I shall be converted." [49] All this is quite in agreement with the teaching of St. Thomas on the formal motive of hope, which relies not on our efforts, but upon God's power to help.

[47] Ps. 118: 117.
[48] Jer. 17: 14.
[49] *Ibid.*, 31: 18, cf. *Médiations sur l'Evangile,* La Cène, 2e. partie, 72e. jour.

CHAPTER V

PREDESTINATION AND THE VIEWS OF THE FIRST THOMISTS

THE first Thomists who wrote on predestination follow faithfully the teaching of St. Thomas as just presented by us. Especially is this the case with Capreolus, Cajetan, and Sylvester of Ferrara.

Before considering these authors we would point out that Aegidius Romanus of the Augustinian Hermits and a pupil of St. Thomas in Paris (1269-71), wrote on this subject as follows: "God wills all men to be saved by His *antecedent will*, when we consider the order as established, its nature and the common helps afforded; but He does not will all to be saved by His *consequent will*, when we consider the execution of the order, the individual and the special helps afforded." [1] Among the common helps he includes the precepts and the counsels; special helps are the conferring of grace, justification and conversion, and perseverance in doing good. In the same passage he makes the following observation: "The conferring of grace requires the movement of free will . . . although such willing on God's part is effected by Him in us through the intermediary of our free will.

1) Capreolus [2] emphasizes the seven conclusions quoted by us from the works of St. Thomas, and he is unmistakably clear in his defense of predestination to glory previous to foreseen merits, as Dr. John Ude points out. [3] In this same work he proves (pp. 149-217) that Capreolus taught the in-

---

[1] *In I Sent.*, d. XLVI, princ. 2, q.1.
[2] Cf. *In I Sent.*, d. XLI, a.3.
[3] Cf. *Doctrina Capreoli,* "de influxu Dei in actus voluntatis humanae."

trinsic efficacy of the divine decrees as regards our salutary acts, and also the intrinsic efficacy of grace which is explained as a physical but non-necessitating predetermination. His words are: "Although God's consequent will is always fulfilled, yet it does not generally impose a necessity upon the things willed." [4] Capreolus proves this conclusion from many texts of St. Thomas, especially from the following one: "The divine will does not exclude contingency nor impose absolute necessity on things. For God wills all that is requisite for the thing which He wills, as already stated. Now it is befitting some things, according to the mode of their nature, that they be contingent, and not necessary. . . . Therefore He wills certain things to be contingent. Now the efficacy of the divine will requires not only that what God wills to be should be, but also that it should be in the mode that God wills it to be. . . . Therefore the efficacy of the divine will does not remove contingency." [5] The divine consequent will is therefore always of itself efficacious. Capreolus also says: "No effect proceeds from the divine knowledge without the will as intermediary, and this latter determines the knowledge to realize the effect." [6] This means the decree without which the divine intellect cannot know infallibly the free acts of the future, whether these be conditional or absolute.[7]

2) Cajetan [8] defends, against Henry of Ghent, the teaching of St. Thomas such as we have presented it. Moreover, previous to this, in commenting on the divine will [9] he had positively affirmed the transcendent efficacy of the divine causality as follows: "Because that willing is most efficacious, the effects

[4] Loc. cit., d. XLV, q.1, concl. 5.
[5] Contra Gentes, I, 85.
[6] Loc. cit., d. XXV, q.2, a.2.
[7] Cf. Ude, loc. cit., pp. 222–45, where the principal texts from Capreolus are quoted, who admits, however, as all Thomists do, that one man would not be better than another, unless he were loved more by God. Cf. I Sent., d. XLI, q.1, a.2.
[8] In Iam, q.23, a.4–5.
[9] In q.19, a.8, no. 10.

follow not only as to the things willed, but also as to the mode of their being willed." Far from destroying the freedom of our acts, the divine causality, which is supremely efficacious, produces this effect in us and with us.[10] Cajetan, moreover, admits also the principle of predilection. On this he says: "For this reason some things are better, because God wills for them a greater good."[11] And again he says: "The reason why God chose us is because He loved us."[12] Similarly, in his commentary on the Epistle to the Romans, Cajetan wrote on the transcendency of the mystery of predestination a page that commands our admiration; a page in which certain assertions of his,[13] for which he had been criticized by Sylvester of Ferrara,[14] receive their finishing touch.

3) Sylvester of Ferrara, a contemporary of Cajetan, writes in defense of this same doctrine in his commentary as follows: "According as God preordained from eternity to direct some to their ultimate end, He is said to have predestined them. . . . But He is said to have reprobated those to whom He decided from eternity not to give the final grace. . . . Whatever there is in man ordaining him to salvation is included in this total effect of predestination."[15] Predestination to glory cannot therefore be because of foreseen merits.

Sylvester, like Cajetan, refutes here Henry of Ghent; like him, he also admits that the decrees of the divine will with regard to our salutary acts are of themselves efficacious.[16] From this he concludes the principle of predilection.[17] St. Thomas had affirmed this principle too clearly for it to be denied by any of his commentators. Now it presupposes, as we have seen, that the divine decrees with regard to our salutary acts

10 Cf. *In Iam*, q.105, a.4–5.
11 *Ibid.*, q.20, a.3–4.
12 *Ibid.*, q.23, a.4; cf. *in Iam*, q.14, a.13, no. 17.
13 *In Iam*, q.22, a.4, no. 8.
14 *Contra Gentes*, III, 94.
15 *Com. in Contra Gentes*, III, 163.
16 *Ibid.*, I, 85; II, 29 f.; III, 72 f., 90, 94.
17 *Ibid.*, I, 91; III, 150.

are of themselves efficacious, and not because our free consent was foreseen.

Almost all the old theologians, whether they are Augustinians, Thomists, or Scotists, agree on this principal point and on the intrinsic efficacy of grace; although they differ on a secondary issue, which concerns the divine motion that gives assurance of the execution of the divine decrees. The Thomists, following the teaching of their master,[18] maintain that this motion is not merely of the moral or objective order, by way of attraction, but that it is also physical or as regards the exercise of the act. They also maintain that it is not merely a general and indifferent premotion, but one which, without necessitating us, inclines us infallibly, though firmly and sweetly, to determine ourselves to perform this particular act rather than its contrary.

The Augustinians explain the intrinsic efficacy of the divine decrees and of grace by means of a motion of a moral or objective order, which they often called a *victorious delectation*. To this the Thomists reply that there is no such delectation in the case of salutary acts performed in a state of great aridity and with much difficulty. Moreover, they add, of moral motions by way of attraction, seeing God face to face is the only one that infallibly attracts.

Scotus, as we shall see, agrees with St. Thomas and the Thomists on the absolute gratuity of predestination to glory and on the intrinsic efficacy of the divine decrees and of grace; but for the physical predetermining and non-necessitating premotion, he substitutes a sort of sympathy that prevails between created and uncreated liberty, a sympathy that amounts to a moral motion by way of victorious attraction.

In the great problem that confronts us, these differences of opinion, as the Thomists have frequently pointed out, are of secondary importance. If, in fact, we agree in admitting that

---

[18] *Summa theol.*, Ia, q.19, a.8; q.105, a.4–5; Ia IIae, q.9, a.6; q.10, a.4 ad 3um.

the divine decrees and grace are of themselves efficacious, and not because our consent to them was foreseen, it is of much less importance for us to know by what kind of motion the execution of these decrees is assured. Likewise, if we agree that our will moves of its own accord our two arms, it is of much less importance for us to know by the intervention of what nerve centers the will does so.

CHAPTER VI

PREDESTINATION ACCORDING TO THE TEACHING OF DUNS SCOTUS

THE Subtle Doctor most clearly affirms the absolute gratuity of predestination to glory, as well as the intrinsic efficacy of the divine decrees and of grace. He writes: "It is only because God wills or preordains that one shall make good use of free will that He foresees this person will make good use of it; for, as stated in the thirty-ninth distinction (no. 1129), the certain foreseeing of future contingent things is due to the determination of these by the divine will. If, therefore, the occasion presents itself to the divine will of two persons equal in natural endowments, why, I ask, does He preordain that this one shall make good use of free will and the other not? There seems to be no reason to assign for this except the divine will." [1] Scotus writes this against Henry of Ghent, and on this point he is in agreement with St. Thomas.

In addition to this, he says: "In another way this can be expressed, by saying that there is no reason for predestination even on the part of the one predestined, such that it is in any way prior to this predestination. But there is some cause for (positive) reprobation.

a) This is proved first from the fact that one who wills methodically the end and those things which are means for attaining the end, first wills the end before willing any of those things which are means for attaining the end, because one wills other things in view of such end. Therefore, since the whole of this process by which the creature capable of eternal happiness is brought to the perfection of its end, the ulti-

---

[1] *Com. Oxon. in Ium Sent.,* d. XLI, no. 1153, p. 1256, ed. Quaracchi.

mate end of which is perfect happiness, God who wills to give anything in this order, first wills the end to this creature capable of eternal happiness, and afterwards, as it were, wills to it those things which are in the order of means pertaining to that end. But grace, faith, merits, and the good use of free will, all of these are directed to this end, although some refer more remotely and others more closely to it. Therefore God wills eternal happiness to the creature before any of these means; and He wills whatsoever of these means before He foresees that it will have any of them. Therefore He does not will eternal happiness to it because He foresaw any of these means.

b) In the second place this is proved from the fact that it is only because damnation is just that it is seen to be good. As St. Augustine says: [2] "God is not the avenger before one is a sinner." [3]

In all this Scotus agrees with St. Thomas. Someone wrote recently that Scotus is the one who first injected into this question the principle that the one who wills methodically the end and those things which are the means for attaining the end, first wills the end. St. Thomas had written equivalently in the following words: "Nothing is directed towards an end unless the will for that end already exists. Whence the predestination of some to eternal salvation presupposes in the order of reason that God wills their salvation; and to this belong both election and love." [4]

It is on the notion of merit and on the nature of the divine motion assuring the execution of the divine decrees that Scotus differs from St. Thomas. Instead of admitting a physical and non-indifferent premotion, he speaks, as we have seen, of a mysterious influx, called "sympathy" by several of his disciples. In virtue of this sympathy, created liberty in-

[2] *Super Gen.*, XI, 17.
[3] *Loc. cit.*, no. 1154.
[4] *Summa theol.*, Ia, q.23, a.4.

clines infallibly and freely to accept the decree of divine liberty, which virtually includes it.[5]

The Thomists reply to this, saying that this sympathy which subordinates the created will to God, either follows as a natural consequence of the necessary subordination of the creature to God, and in this case liberty is out of the question; or else it is a moral motion, of the objective order by way of attraction, and then only the vision of God face to face can so captivate the will as to attract it infallibly.[6]

But, let us repeat, this difference is of secondary importance in the question which confronts us, since Scotus admits, as St. Thomas and his disciples do, the absolute gratuity of predestination to glory as well as the intrinsic efficacy of the divine decrees with regard to our salutary acts and the grace by which we are enabled to put them into effect.[7]

[5] *Loc. cit.*, d. VIII, q.5; II, d. XXXVII, q.2, nos. 1 ff., no. 11.

[6] Cf. Joan. a S. Thoma, *Cursus Phil., Phil., Nat.,* q.12, a.3.

[7] If one wanted to write the history of the problem of predestination in the fourteenth century, it would be necessary to bear in mind that Occam held that the absolute autonomy of the divine willing makes God's liberty the sovereign arbiter of good and evil, and this to such an extent that there is no longer anything good or evil in it, so that God could have commanded us to hate it. Radical nominalism thus ends in absolute voluntarism and libertism, which is a sort of theological positivism.

It would also be necessary to take note of what Thomas Bradwardine taught about predestination in his *De causa Dei contra Pelagium et de virtute causarum* (1338–46), and in his commentaries on the *Sentences* and the *Summa theologica*. He was influenced in his writings, as several historians relate, by Duns Scotus and Occam, who were countrymen of his. He failed to avoid falling into certain errors that reappear in the writings of John Wyclif.

In his *De causa Dei* (1, 21, p. 233, ed. 1618), T. Bradwardine writes as Occam did: "That there is no reason or necessary law in God prior to His will." From this he deduced that the divine will is the necessitating cause, the antecedent necessity, of our volitions: "It suffices for man to be free as regards all things that do not concern God, and that He be only God's slave, of his own accord, I say, not forced." (*Ibid.*, III, p. 667, E. cf. p. 675, C.) This made him say that "God somehow wills sins as such." Cf. Dr. S. Hahn, "Thomas Bradwardinus und seine lehre v.d. menschlichen willensfreiheit" (*Beitr. Gesch. Phil. Mittelalt.*, V, 2).

Nicholas d'Autrecourt, John of Mircourt, and John Wyclif deduced disastrous consequences from Thomas Bradwardine's principles. Wyclif taught a necessitating predestination and went back to predestinationism. The most determined opponents of Bradwardine were Peter Plaoul and John of Rive. Cf. Du Plessis d'Argentré, *Collectio judiciorum de novis erroribus*, I, 328.

CONCLUSIONS

On these essential points, almost all the old theologians, whether Augustinians, Thomists, or Scotists, are in agreement. Almost all admit the principle of predilection, namely, that one man would not be better than another (by reason of an act either easy or difficult to perform, whether the first or final act), unless he were loved more and helped more by God. Now this principle, as we have seen, presupposes that the divine decrees with regard to our salutary acts are of themselves efficacious, and not because of our foreseen consent. At the same time this principle virtually includes the doctrine of the absolute gratuity of predestination to glory *previous to foreseen merits.* So speaks the Augustinian author of the *Imitation of Christ,* in the following extract: "I am to be praised in all My saints; I am to be blessed above all things and to be honored in all whom I have thus gloriously exalted and predestined without any merit of their own. . . . They glory not in their own merits, inasmuch as they ascribe no goodness to themselves but attribute all to Me who of Mine own infinite love have given them all things. . . . In Thee, therefore, O Lord God, I place my whole hope and refuge." [8] St. Thomas said the same when he wrote: "Since God's love is the cause of goodness in things, no one thing would be better than another, unless it were loved more by God." [9]

To this principle we must add one no less certain, which is that God never commands what is impossible, and wills to make it possible for all to be saved. We already stated that it is impossible for us, according to our present knowledge, to see how these two principles are perfectly reconciled. As long as we have not the light of the blessed in heaven, vivid faith enlightened by the gifts of the Holy Ghost must preserve the equilibrium between these two principles, and by their means

[8] *Imitation of Christ,* Bk. III, chaps. 58, nos. 4, 8; 59, no. 3.
[9] *Summa theol.,* Ia, q. 20, a. 4.

it senses the direction of the summit toward which it tends and which cannot be seen by anyone here on earth. Thus the two extreme aspects of the mystery are preserved intact, without compromising this latter.

This admirable harmony was unknown to Protestantism, which, in denying one of the two aspects of the mystery, gave an entirely false interpretation of the data of revelation.

SECTION II

Predestination According to the Tenets of Protestantism and Jansenism

Protestantism has given us a conception of predestination that is absolutely irreconcilable with God's universal will to save. On this point Jansenism differs but little from it. In the two chapters of this section, we will consider: (1) Protestantism; (2) Baianism and Jansenism.

CHAPTER I

Protestantism

1) Luther. Protestantism derived its notion of predestination from its preconceived theory of the consequences of original sin. According to its theory, man in a state of fallen nature no longer has the strength, even after justification, to resist temptation. We know that Luther was thus ensnared into the path of error. The observance of the divine law and resistance against unruly passions necessitated his making great efforts; as humble prayer was something unknown to him, he concluded that concupiscence, since the fall of man, cannot be overcome, and that the command, "thou shalt not covet," is impracticable, and that God has commanded what is impossible. Thus it is that, through lack of an interior justice, which seemed impossible to him, Luther set out in quest of an exterior justice; not recognizing the necessity of contrition and a firm purpose of amendment, he appealed from these to Christ and said in conclusion that man of himself is always

weak, always in a state of sin; but that Christ's justice covers the sins of sinners. Christ's justice covers them and is imputed to them.

Continuing on this path of error, Luther rejected free will. Free will is dead, so he said. In consequence of this, the Christian's faith is solely God's work. "He operates in us without our co-operation," and this faith is formal justification. "Faith is the formal justice, by reason of which we are justified. Faith is already the grace of justification." The nuptial robe is faith without good works. For salvation nothing more than faith is required.[1] This is how Luther came to conclude one of the fundamental principles of his doctrine, so that he taught not only that eternal predestination is previous to foreseen merits, but also that good works performed or merits acquired in this life are not necessary for salvation. In proof of this he appealed to St. Paul's epistles, falsely interpreting them, and to the teaching of St. Augustine, which he understood in a wrong sense.[2] It would be a mistake, however, for one to believe that all Lutherans preserved intact Luther's teaching on this point. Already in 1535, Melanchthon declared good works to be necessary for salvation. Something similar to this was taught by the *Interim* of Augsburg, and by that of Leipzig.[3]

2) Zwingli. A sort of pantheism and fatalism is what Zwingli concludes from this teaching, as Bauer points out.[4] According to his theory, creatures come from God by way of emanation. Man is not free, but is to God as the instrument is to the artist. God is the cause of everything, even of evil and of sin. Sin is truly a transgression of the law, but man commits it of necessity. Even God does not sin in forcing man to sin, because there is no law for God. Original sin is the inclination to evil, to self-love; it is a natural malady not re-

---

[1] Luther's works, ed. Weimar, I, 105, 30 f., 35; IV, 68, 75 ff.
[2] See his *Com. on Epistle to Romans*, chap. 9.
[3] Cf. *Dict. de théol. cath.*, art. "Merite," X, 716 ff.
[4] Cf. Zwingli's *Theologie, ihr Werden und ihr System*, Halle, 1885–86.

moved by baptism, as Luther had said. Instead of the Church, we have a democratic organization which includes only the elect.

3) Calvin. He surpasses Luther and Zwingli in the force of his logical conclusions.[5] The fundamental thesis of his doctrine is that some are freely predestined, and the rest are freely and positively damned. According to his theory, God urges man to sin, which is, however, freely committed, in the sense that there is no exterior influence compelling man to commit sin. There is no fatalism in this, says Calvin, but a mysterious and just will of God, although this is beyond man's comprehension. On this point he writes: "We say, therefore, as evidently attested by the Scripture, that once for all God has decreed by His eternal and immutable plan, whom He willed to accept for eternal salvation and whom He willed to consign to eternal perdition. We say that this counsel, as regards the elect, has its foundation in God's mercy, without any consideration of man's dignity. On the contrary, admittance to eternal life is foreclosed to all those whom He wills to deliver up to eternal damnation; and this is the result of His secret and incomprehensible judgment, although it is according to strict justice." [6] The corresponding Latin text does not differ from this except by the addition of "gratuitous" to the word "mercy." It reads as follows: "The plan, as regards the elect, has its foundation in His gratuitous mercy." [7] This doctrine admits, of course, a certain necessity of good works for the salvation of adults; but it does not acknowledge them to be meritorious.[8]

The antilapsarians, who were disciples of Calvin, said that even before Adam's sin was foreseen, God did not will to save all mankind. On the contrary, the infralapsarians said that, as

[5] Cf. *Institution chrétienne,* first ed., March, 1536; final ed., 1559.

[6] Cf. *ibid.,* Bk. III, chap. 21, no. 7, ed. Baum, Cunitz and Reuss, IV, 467.

[7] Cf. *ibid.,* II, 686.

[8] Cf. C. Friethoff, O.P., *Die Praedestinationslehre bei Tomas von Aquin und Calvin,* Friburg, Switz., 1926.

a consequence of this foreseen sin, God does not will to save all mankind. Calvin, following up the stand taken by Wyclif, added that those who come under the sentence of reprobation are purified only externally by baptism, not receiving the grace of this sacrament. In the sacrament of the Lord's Supper, the predestined do not receive the body of Christ, but merely a divine power that emanates from Christ's body present in heaven.[9] The Church is invisible, consisting of the assembly of the predestined.

This Calvinist doctrine on predestination was not accepted by those of moderate views. One of their distinguished leaders since 1588 was James Harmensz, who was called Arminius. He was appointed in 1602 a professor in the University of Leyden, where the stern Gomar already held the same position. Arminius attacked Calvin's and Beza's system, on certain points attracting the attention of several Catholic theologians. Arminius' theory of liberty aroused the anger of some, and he had to engage in a very spirited argument with Gomar, who defended the following thesis: God's free good pleasure alone is the impelling antecedent cause of reprobation from grace and glory to a just damnation.[10] This doctrine left no trace of the distinction between negative reprobation which permits sin, and positive reprobation which punishes it. This doctrine was imposed, however, by the Synod of Dordrecht. It maintained with the infralapsarians that at least after original sin God no longer wills the salvation of all mankind, and that Christ died only for the elect. This doctrine, which at first was optional among the Calvinists of the Low Countries, was later on made obligatory.

CONDEMNATION OF THE PROTESTANT THESES

In opposition to this, the Council of Trent had been more explicit on these questions in formulating the revealed doc-

[9] *Loc. cit.*, Bk. IV, chap. 17, no. 12.
[10] Gomar, *Op. theol.*, III, 34, 346.

trine such as always taught by the Church. The principal definitions relative to the point at issue are found in the following canons of the sixth session.

Can. 4: "If anyone saith that man's free will moved and excited by God, by assenting to God exciting and calling, no wise co-operates toward disposing and preparing itself for obtaining the grace of justification; that it cannot refuse its consent, if it would, but that, as something inanimate, it does nothing whatever and is merely passive, let him be anathema." [11]

Can. 5: "If anyone saith that, since Adam's sin, the free will of man is lost and is extinguished; or that it is a thing with only a name, yea, a name without a reality, a figment in fine, introduced into the Church by Satan, let him be anathema." [12]

Can. 6: "If anyone saith that it is not in man's power to make his ways evil, but that the works that are evil God worketh as well as those that are good, not permissibly only, but properly and of Himself, in such a wise that the treason of Judas is no less His own proper work than the vocation of Paul, let him be anathema." [13]

Can. 17: "If anyone saith that the grace of justification is attained only by those who are predestined unto life; but that all others who are called, are called, indeed, but receive not grace, as being by the divine power predestined unto evil; let him be anathema." [14]

Can. 18: "If anyone saith that the commandments of God are, even for one that is justified and constituted in grace, impossible to keep; let him be anathema." [15]

In the eleventh canon, which is the counterpart of this last quoted canon, the Council of Trent has in mind two propo-

[11] Denz., no. 814; cf. no. 797.
[12] Ibid., no. 815.
[13] Ibid., no. 816.
[14] Ibid., no. 827; cf. no. 200.
[15] Ibid., no. 828; cf. no. 804.

sitions of St. Augustine, whose doctrine the Protestants appealed to in the following passages, though interpreting him in a wrong sense: "God does not command what is impossible, but in commanding advises you to do what you can, and to ask for what you cannot do." [16] "God does not abandon those whom He has once justified by His grace, unless He is first abandoned by them." [17] In saying that God never commands what is impossible, St. Augustine had equivalently affirmed that in a certain way He wills all men to be saved, in this sense that He wills to make it really possible for all to keep the commandments, and that no one is lost except through his own fault.[18]

[16] *De natura et gratia,* chap. 43, no. 50.
[17] *Ibid.,* chap. 26, no. 29.
[18] On this possibility, read the statement of Pius IX, Denz., no. 1677.

CHAPTER II

Baianism and Jansenism

THREE years before the end of the Council of Trent, in 1560, the Sorbonne condemned eighteen propositions of Baius in which there were traces of the Protestant principles relative to grace and original sin. In 1567, a bull of St. Pius V condemned seventy-nine propositions of Baius, among which the following that more or less directly concern our subject must be noted: "Without the aid of God's grace, free will has power only to sin. All the actions of unbelievers are sins, and the virtues of philosophers vices. Only violence is repugnant to man's natural liberty. Man sins even meriting damnation, in what is done out of necessity. It is a Pelagian error to say that there is in free will the power to avoid any sin. The integrity in which man was created was not an exaltation of human nature to which it had no claim, but its natural condition. The elevation and exaltation of human nature to a participation in the divine nature was due to it because of its original state of integrity; hence it must be declared natural and not supernatural." [1]

We perceive the trend of thought since Luther's error and how this pseudosupernaturalism, which confounds the two orders of nature and grace, resulted from it. Viewed from this angle, it approaches Pelagian naturalism, although it differs very much from this latter in its notion of original sin and the consequences of the same.

Luther begins by saying that concupiscence is invincible,

---

[1] Denz., nos. 1021, 1025–28, 1066–67. For the exact meaning of these propositions, consult also *Dict. de théol. cath.*, art. "Baius," II, 64 ff.

and that certain commands, as a consequence of original sin, are impracticable. Moreover, without the help of divine grace, free will can do nothing but sin. Grace of itself efficacious, though it was not necessary for perseverance in good in the state of innocence, became so by reason of our infirmity, and man is powerless to resist it when it is offered to him. The subsequent outcome of this pessimistic conception of human nature, such as it is in the present state, was that original integrity came to be viewed as something due to human nature, and grace, which is a participation in the divine nature, as due to the state of natural integrity. This pessimistic view led to the confusion of the order of nature with that of grace, a confusion which the Pelagians reached by the inverse method. Pelagianism is a phase of naturalism which attached no importance to original sin. Baianism is another phase of naturalism which attached very much importance to the fall of the first man.

Finally, Jansenius on the subject of original justice revived the errors of Baius. This explains his false doctrine concerning original sin, grace, predestination, and reprobation. According to his theory, by the sin of the first man human nature became entirely corrupt, so that it was no longer capable of doing anything good. At the same time he denied the freedom of the human will, declaring it to be completely passive and determined by the *victorious delectation*. If this delectation is terrestrial, it begets sin; if it is celestial, it results in virtue and merit; and for this, freedom from external constraint suffices, but not necessarily freedom from interior compulsion.

The five propositions taken from his *Augustinus* and condemned by Rome, show that this doctrine differs from that of St. Augustine and St. Thomas, though it has been at times confused with their teaching. Whereas St. Augustine and St. Thomas always steadfastly maintained that God never commands what is impossible, but makes it really possible for all to keep His commandments, the following Jansenist propositions deny this; they say: (1) "For the justified, willing and trying to do what they can, according to the present powers they possess, some of God's commandments are impossible to keep. (2) In the state of fallen nature no one ever resists interior grace. (3) For meriting and demeriting in the state of fallen nature, freedom from internal compulsion is not required; it is sufficient to be free from external constraint. (4) It is a Semipelagian heresy to say that Christ died or shed His blood for all men without exception." [2] Moreover, to understand exactly in what sense this last proposition is condemned, it is absolutely necessary to give in addition the text of this condemnation, which reads as follows: "It is declared and condemned as false, temerarious, scandalous, and, understood in this sense that Christ died only for the salvation of the predestined, it is impious, blasphemous, contumelious, contrary to the divine compassion, and heretical."

Jansenism was thus led to adopt a teaching on grace and predestination that excludes God's universal will to save. In order to preserve intact one of the aspects of the mystery with which we are concerned, the other was completely rejected. Instead of a mystery of revealed truth, we have thus a cruel and absurd doctrine, for in this case sin is inevitable, which is no longer then a sin, and which cannot be punished, at least with eternal punishment, without manifest cruelty. God commanding what is impossible ceases to be God, and in vain would we seek to discover in Him not only mercy, but even justice.

[2] Denz., nos. 1092-94, 1096.

SECTION III

Predestination According to the Teaching of the Post-Tridentine Theologians

After the Council of Trent, whose especial concern was to counteract Protestantism, L. Molina proposed a theory of foreknowledge and predestination which was the occasion of long controversies on these subjects, which are keenly enough disputed even at the present day. We shall proceed to examine the following theories, taking them in this order: (1) Molinism; (2) the congruism of Bellarmine and Suarez; (3) the congruism of the Sorbonne; (4) the Augustinian doctrine subsequent to the Council of Trent; (5) the Thomist doctrine subsequent to the Council of Trent. In giving an account of the doctrines of these schools, we shall at the same time point out the difficulties presented by each.

CHAPTER I

Predestination According to the Theory Advocated by Molina and the Molinists

THAT we may bring out clearly the essential points of this theory, we shall summarize it in Molina's own words.[1] We shall stress the principles on which it rests and compare his teaching with that of St. Augustine and St. Thomas.

[1] *Concordia liberi arbitrii cum gratiae donis, divina praescientia, providentia, praedestinatione et reprobatione,* 1595. Cf. q.23, a.4–5, disp. I, membr. ult., Paris ed. 1876, pp. 546–49. Here Molina sums up his doctrine on this subject.

WHAT MOLINISM AFFIRMS

Molina states that St. Augustine satisfactorily proved against the Pelagians and Semipelagians that the *beginning of salvation* is the result of prevenient and excitant graces, which are given to us by Christ, according to God's good pleasure, and not according to the effort made by our free will. Then he adds: "But Augustine believed that, connected with what he had most correctly taught from the Scripture about grace against the Pelagian heresy, is the question of God's eternal predestination, which is not according to the merits and nature of the use of free will as foreseen by God, but only according to His election and good pleasure (and in this sense it is most true, as was explained in Member XII); and it was in this sense that he interpreted in many of his works the text of St. Paul's Epistle to the Romans (chap. 9), and he restricted to this meaning the text: 'He will have all men to be saved'; [2] so that this is not understood to refer absolutely to all men, but only to the predestined; (in fact St. Augustine says so, if it be a question of the efficacious will to save). This doctrine alarmingly disturbed the minds of many of the faithful, especially of those living in France, not only of the uneducated but even of the learned, and it was even the occasion that their eternal salvation was placed in jeopardy. . . . The divine-like Thomas, and subsequently many of the Scholastics, followed Augustine's opinion." [3]

On the question of true predestination, and this means predestination to glory, which alone can be said to apply both to the elect and the reprobates, Molina thus recognizes, precisely when summing up all his teaching on this subject, that St. Augustine, St. Thomas, and the majority of the Scholastics taught this proposition, that God's eternal predestination was not according to the merits and nature of the use of free will

[2] I Tim. 2: 4.
[3] *Concordia,* p. 546.

as foreseen by God, but solely according to God's election and good pleasure. In other words, he recognizes that St. Augustine, St. Thomas, and the majority of the Scholastics taught the absolute gratuity of predestination to glory, not because of foreseen merits, and Molina finds this very difficult to reconcile with the freedom of our will.

Then he adds: "In our humble opinion we declare that the whole question of reconciling the freedom of the will with divine grace, foreknowledge, and predestination, which we have taught throughout article thirteen of question fourteen, and in article six of question nineteen, and throughout question twenty-two, rests upon the following principles . . . ; and if these principles had always been given and explained, perhaps neither the Pelagian heresy would have sprung up, nor would the Lutherans have dared so impudently to deny the freedom of our will . . . , nor would so many of the faithful have been disturbed in their mind because of Augustine's opinion." [4]

This page from Molina's work has often been quoted in course of time by the Thomists as evidence that the author of the *Concordia* had it well in mind to propose a new theory, and one which he esteemed far superior to the teachings of St. Augustine, St. Thomas, and the majority of the Scholastics. According to this theory, predestination to glory is not absolutely gratuitous, but is on account of foreseen merits. What are the underlying principles of this theory?

PRINCIPLES OF MOLINISM

Molina [5] enunciates four that refer: (1) to the divine concurrence; (2) to final perseverance; (3) to foreknowledge (*scientia media*); (4) to the disposition of circumstances in the life of the predested. For greater accuracy, let us give a close translation of the words of the Latin text.

[4] *Op. cit.,* p. 548.
[5] *Ibid.,* p. 548.

1) The first and fundamental principle is the mode of the divine influence, both by the general concurrence in the natural acts of our free will and by the particular helps given for supernatural acts, as already explained.[6] In these passages Molina strove, in fact, to establish the sufficiency of a divine simultaneous concurrence and of a grace which is not of itself infallibly efficacious, but which moves one morally by way of attraction. It becomes efficacious *in actu secundo* (completed act) by means of our free consent. Thus it is that Molina affirmed: "The helps of prevenient and adjuvant graces, which in the ordinary course are given to people here below, and which may be either efficacious or inefficacious for conversion or justification, depend upon the free co-operation of our will with them, and so it is freely within our power either to make them efficacious by our consent . . . or inefficacious by withholding this consent." [7] In like manner, he says: "Predestination was not the result of foreordaining to confer helps of themselves efficacious." [8] Hence we have the following affirmation by Molina: "Wherefore it can happen that of two persons who are called by God, each receiving an equal interior grace, one of them of his own free will is converted, and the other remains an unbeliever. . . . It can even happen that one prevented and called by a far greater grace, of his own free will is not converted, and another with a far less grace is converted." [9] St. Thomas had written the contrary of this in formulating the principle of predilection, which is the keystone of his doctrine on predestination. He says: "Since God's love is the cause of the goodness of things, no one thing would be better than another, unless God willed a greater good for this than for the other." [10] We at once see that Molina starts out with a conception of the created will which at least does

6 *Ibid.*, q.14, a.13, disp. 7–25, 27.
7 *Ibid.*, q.14, a.13, disp. 40, pp. 230–31.
8 *Ibid.*, p. 355; cf. p. 459.
9 *Ibid.*, q.14, a.13, disp. 12, p. 51; cf. p. 565.
10 *Summa theol.*, Ia, q.20, a.3.

not seem able to be reconciled with the principle of predilection, namely, that no one thing would be better than another, unless it were loved more and helped more by God. This principle is for St. Thomas the equivalent of the text: "For who distinguisheth thee? Or what hast thou that thou hast not received?" [11] It presupposes, as we have seen, that the decrees of divine love and grace are of themselves efficacious, and not because of our foreseen consent. We at once perceive that these two doctrines are in opposition and we see why Molina separated from St. Thomas concerning the divine concurrence and predilection. He wrote, indeed, in the above quoted question, as follows: "I am confronted by two difficulties with regard to what St. Thomas teaches (Ia, q. 105, a. 5) about the divine motion. I do not see what is this motion and application, in secondary causes, by which God moves and applies these causes to act. . . . And I candidly confess that I have difficulty in understanding this motion and application which St. Thomas requires in secondary causes." [12]

Farther on, too, after stating the doctrine according to which divine election precedes predestination and the foreseeing of the merits of the elect, he writes: "And this seems to be the opinion of St. Thomas (Ia, q. 23, a. 4). . . . But I never found it acceptable." [13]

2) Second principle. No less striking is the difference between these two teachings when we consider Molina's second principle:

"The second principle is a lawful or rather orthodox one, which explains the way in which the gift of perseverance operates. We have, indeed, clearly shown that no adult at all can persevere long in the state of grace without God's help, and for this reason perseverance in grace is God's gift; but God denies no one the help sufficient for perseverance. Hence

[11] I Cor. 4: 7.
[12] *Ibid.*, q. 14, a. 13, disp. 26, p. 152.
[13] *Ibid.*, q. 22, a. 1–2, disp. 2, p. 429.

two things are necessary for the gift of perseverance. One is that God has decided to confer those helps by means of which He foresaw that the adult freely will persevere. The other is that the adult's free will is required as an indispensable condition; for without it the will to confer such helps would not imply the will to confer the gift of perseverance, which is such that the adult will, of course, freely co-operate with these helps so as to persevere; and it is in his power for him to do so." [14]

In other words, the actual grace of final perseverance for adults is not of itself efficacious, but only by reason of our foreseen consent, so that, as Molina says,[15] of two dying persons who are helped by equal graces, one dies a good death, and the other does not; sometimes even the one who dies a Christian death received a lesser grace. St. Thomas had written the contrary of this in formulating the principle of predilection: "He who makes a greater effort, has received a greater grace; but that he makes a greater effort, he needs to be moved by a higher cause, according to the text: 'Convert us, O Lord, to Thee, and we shall be converted. Lam. 5: 21.' " [16]

According to the Thomist opinion, this Molinist conception depreciates this grace which is reserved for the elect and which the Council of Trent calls the great and special gift of perseverance.[17] How can we possibly imagine this gift to be equal or even inferior to the assistance given to one who does not persevere?

3) The third principle to which Molina appeals as foundation for this theory on predestination concerns the *scientia media:*

"The third principle is that foreknowledge mediate be-

---

[14] *Ibid.*, q.23, a.4–5, disp. I, memb. ult., p. 548.

[15] *Ibid.*, pp. 51, 565.

[16] *In Matt.* 25: 15; cf. *Summa*, Ia, q.20, a.3–4: "No one thing would be better than another, unless it were loved more by God." Also Ia IIae, q.112, a.4.

[17] Denz., no. 806.

tween God's free knowledge and that which is merely natural. By this mediate foreknowledge, as explained (q. 14, a. 13, disp. 50 ff.), God knew, before any free act of His will, what ᵥin each particular case the created free will would do, if God decided to arrange the circumstances for these men or angels. If the created free will should decide upon an opposite course of action, as it can do, He would, nevertheless, know it by this same foreknowledge." [18]

This theory of the *scientia media,* which, together with the Molonist definition of created liberty, constitutes the keystone of Molinism, is proposed by Molina as a new way of viewing the question. He writes: "I do not know of anyone who has ever advanced this theory of ours for reconciling the freedom of the will with divine predestination." [19]

What this new theory states is this: Before any free decree of His will, God foresaw what a certain man would freely choose, if he were situated in certain circumstances and prompted by a certain grace. It is not in God's power to foresee by the *scientia media* any other thing, but He could do so if the created free will were to choose something different. This divine foresight depends upon the choice a person would make in these given circumstances.

This new way of viewing the question, rejected by all Thomists, Augustinians, Scotists, and other theologians as contrary to God's sovereign independence with regard to every determination of the created order, was thus formulated by Molina: "It was not in God's power to know by this knowledge (mediate) anything else than He actually knew. Then again it must not be called natural even in this sense, as if it were so innate in God that He could not know the contrary of what He knows by it. For, if the created free will had chosen to do the opposite, as it truly can do, this very same

[18] *Loc. cit.,* p. 549.
[19] *Ibid.,* p. 550.

thing He would have known by the same knowledge, but not that He actually knows it."[20]

According to this theory, God no longer determines what choice the creature would make in certain circumstances. His knowledge, said to be mediate in this case, is dependent upon this choice and is determined by it. Is not this a positing of passivity in pure Act, who is incapable of passivity or dependence upon anything whatsoever? The dilemma still remains to be solved, to wit: God determining or determined; there is no other alternative.

Molina, it is true, not only declares that his theory is a new one, but also that it seems to be contrary to the teaching of St. Thomas. After explaining it, deriving his inspiration from Origen, he adds: "Although, to tell the truth, St. Thomas seems to suggest the contrary (Ia, q. 14, a. 8 ad 1um), when he explains and attempts to interpret in the opposite sense the passage of Origen to which we shall immediately refer, in which he is clearly of the same opinion as we are."[21]

Origen, whose views on predestination are known to be very erroneous, had written: "A thing will happen not because God knows it as future; but, because it is future, it is on that account known by God before it exists."[22] If we were to interpret literally these words of Origen, God's knowledge, far from being like the artist's knowledge, the cause of things, would be caused, measured by the things, dependent upon them, and passive with regard to them. It would follow that creatures do not depend upon the divine knowledge and will, but that God's foreknowledge depends upon them.[23] That is why St. Thomas strove to give a more benign interpretation to these words of Origen. In this he was not followed by Molina.

20 *Ibid.*, q. 14, a. 13, disp. 52, pp. 317–18.
21 *Ibid.*, p. 325.
22 *Com. in Rom.* 8: 30.
23 *Summa theol.*, Ia, q. 14, a. 8 ad 1um.

4) The fourth principle to which Molina has recourse shows us clearly how predestination, according to his view of it, depends upon foreseen merits, and how the principle of predilection (that no one thing would be better than another, unless it were loved more by God) has thus charged against it, according to this theory, the note of relativity. We read, in fact, concerning this: "The fourth principle is that God willed to create this order of things preferably to any other, and in this order to confer these particular helps preferably to certain others, by means of which He foresaw these particular persons, and not certain others, will attain to eternal life, there being no cause or reason for this on the part of the adults, both predestined and reprobates. And so on this account we said that the use of free will on the part of the predestined and the reprobates is not the cause or reason of predestination; but this must be attributed to the free will of God." [24]

This means that God's good pleasure alone is the cause that this particular man is placed in these particular circumstances, in which He foresees that the man will save his soul. God could have placed him in certain different circumstances, in which by means of the *scientia media* He foresees that He would be lost. In other words, it is perfectly gratuitous that this particular man is predestined to live in these particular circumstances and with these particular helps in which God foresaw that he would be saved.

Molina also remarks: "That the divine will to place a certain man in a certain order of things and circumstances with certain helps, can be called predestination, is due solely to the fact that it is dependent upon merits foreseen by the *scientia media*. In this sense there is a reason for the predestination of the adults, in that God foresees their merits. And for this reason we said that there is a reason for the predestination of adults, in that the use of their free will was foreseen." [25]

[24] *Loc. cit.,* 549.
[25] *Ibid.,* p. 549.

As Father F. Cayré, A.A., says: "Without going so far as to make out almost the same case for the elect and the reprobates, as Vasquez does (*in Iam*, q. 23, disp. 89), Molina so stresses the part played by the intellect that Suarez feels obliged, by a discreet counterstroke, to modify his teaching and insist much more on the role of the will, thus coming nearer, in this delicate question, to the stand taken by Bannez." [26]

Father Billot, S.J.,[27] holds that Molina, like Suarez and Bellarmine, admitted predestination to glory *apart from foreseen merits*. Certain texts of the *Concordia* seem to say that it is not because of future foreseen merits; but those we have quoted and many others show that it is at least subsequent to conditionally future foreseen merits, or else that it presupposes the foreseeing by means of the *scientia media* the merits which a certain man would acquire, if he were placed in certain circumstances.

Moreover, the majority of Molinists, like Vasquez and Lessius, hold that for Molina predestination to glory is not only because of conditionally but also of absolutely future foreseen merits; so that it presupposes the foreseeing of the merits that will actually be acquired by a certain man placed in certain circumstances; for the divine will to place him in such circumstances can be called predestination, so said Molina, only because of its dependence upon the foreseeing of his future merits. Thus Lessius wrote: "The absolute and immediate election to glory does not take place before it is foreseen that one will persevere or die in a state of grace, just as absolute reprobation does not take place before it is foreseen that one will die in a state of sin." [28] Vasquez, Valentia, and the majority of the Molinists made similar statements.[29]

Such in substance is Molina's view of predestination. It has undergone slight variations of relative unimportance. Some,

26 *Précis de patrologie*, II, 1930, 768.
27 *De Deo uno*, 1926, pp. 290–92.
28 *De praedestinatione et reprobatione*, sect. II, no. 6.
29 Cf. *Dict. de théol. cath.*, art. "Molinisme," col. 2170.

as we have just said, interpret it in the sense that predestination is the result of future foreseen merits; others that it is the result of conditionally future foreseen merits. These latter, like Father Billot, strive to make their teaching on this point differ but little from that of St. Augustine and St. Thomas. St. Robert Bellarmine and Suarez almost succeed in accomplishing this, when they say that for God, as for every wise person, the choice of the means or of the graces follows logically the appointment of the end, or, in other words, predestination to glory, which, in this case, is conceived as *previous to foreseen merits*. Some Molinists also rejected Molina's theory of simultaneous concurrence, preferring to admit a divine premotion that is indifferent or non-determining. We shall return to a discussion of these variations, but let us first state precisely their common ground of support.

WHAT IS THE ESSENTIAL ELEMENT IN MOLINISM?

We can answer this question by stating what the Molinists are agreed upon in their defense of this doctrine. First of all, the essence of Molinism consists in a definition of created liberty which includes the denial of the intrinsic efficacy of the divine decrees and of grace, obliging one to admit the theory of the *scientia media*. All those theologians whose views are either closely or remotely connected with Molinism, are agreed on this point. Their opponents recognize also that such is the starting-point of the Molinist system, and they refuse to admit this definition which, in their opinion, is not at all the traditional teaching.

It is thus formulated by Molina at the beginning of his work: "That agent is said to be free, which, granted all the requisites for action, can either act or not act." [30] This definition, which is quoted eventually by all Molinists, does not

[30] *Loc. cit.*, pp. 51, 190, 225, 230–31, 304, 311 ff., 318, 356, 459 ff., 498, 502, 565.

seem at first sight to establish a precedent. But when we see that it is the underlying principle of all Molina's theses,[31] and that it necessarily implies the theory of the *scientia media* unknown to all theologians previous to his time,[32] we conclude that it is just as new as the theory which Molina told us had never been proposed before him.[33]

What exactly do the terms of this definition of free will mean for Molina and the Molinists, when it is declared to be "a faculty which, granted all that is required for action, can either act or not act?" These words, "granted all that is required," denote not only what is a prerequisite for the act to be free according to a priority of time, but also what is a prerequisite for it to be so according to a simple priority of nature and causality, like actual grace which is received at the very moment when the salutary act is performed. Moreover, according to its author, this definition does not mean that, under the influence of efficacious grace, the free will retains the power to resist, though it never does actually will to resist under the influence of this efficacious grace. It means that grace is not of itself efficacious, but only because of our foreseen consent. The nature of this grace is such that God could have foreseen not the good consent, but the actual resistance. This definition of free will is connected indeed with the two previously quoted propositions that concern the *scientia media*. They state: (1) That it was not in God's power to know by this knowledge anything else than He actually knew; (2) But if the created will were to do the opposite, as it truly can, God would have known even this by the same knowledge, but not that He actually knows it.[34] It was not in God's power to foresee anything else; but He would have foreseen something else, if the choice of the created free will had been different. The divine foreseeing thus depends upon the choice man

31 *Ibid.*, q. 14, a. 13, disp. 2, p. 10.
32 *Ibid.*, p. 318.
33 *Ibid.*, p. 550.
34 *Ibid.*, p. 318.

would and will make on the supposition that he is placed in certain circumstances.

This gave rise to all the controversies on this point since the Council of Trent. But we cannot really grasp the meaning of this definition and see all that it implies, unless we compare it with its opposite. In this way, by going back to what is the very point at issue in the controversy, it becomes clarified and simplified.

In the opinion of the Thomists, the Molinist definition of liberty is not formulated according to the true method of logical procedure, because it abstracts from the object that specifies the free act. It neglects the fundamental principle that faculties, habits, and acts are specified by their object. If, on the contrary, we consider the object to be the specifying principle, then we shall say with the Thomists: Liberty is the dominating indifference of the will as regards an object proposed by the reason as not being good in every respect. The essence of liberty consists in the dominating indifference of the will as regards every object proposed by the reason at the moment of consideration as good in one aspect, and not good in another; rightly so it is the indifference as to willing or not willing the object, an indifference that is potential on the part of the faculty, and actual on the part of the free act. For even when the will actually wills this object, when it is already determined to will the same, it still tends toward this object with an indifference that is no longer potential but actual. Liberty, therefore, results from the disproportion prevailing between the will that is specified by universal good and a certain finite good, this latter object being considered good in one aspect and not so in another. This is what St. Thomas says, for he remarks as follows: "If the will is offered an object that is not good from every point of view, it will not tend to this of necessity." [35] And in opposition to Suarez, the Thomists add: "Even by His absolute power, God cannot, by mov-

[35] *Summa theol.*, Ia IIae, q. 10, a. 2.

ing the will, necessitate it to will a certain object, when the indifference of judgment remains unchanged." Why so? Because it implies a contradiction for the will to wish *necessarily* the object proposed to it as indifferent by the intellect, or one that is absolutely out of proportion to the universality of its scope.[36] What are we to conclude about the subject in question that concerns us?

It was pointed out earlier in this work that the theologians of the twelfth and thirteenth centuries always use the same formula, stating that if God wills efficaciously a certain salutary act to be performed, such as the conversion of the good thief or of St. Paul, this act infallibly though freely is accomplished, according to a necessity not of consequent but of consequence "just as it is necessary for Socrates to sit whilst he is seated, though it is optional for him to be seated."[37] We have drawn particular attention to the following important text of St. Thomas: "If God moves the will to anything, it is incompossible with this suggestion, that the will be not moved thereto. But it is not impossible simply. Consequently it does not follow that the will is moved by God necessarily."[38] Similarly, St. Thomas says: "It is incompossible for anyone to sit and stand at the same time, but whilst one sits, one has the power to stand." To deny this is to say that he who sleeps is blind; he does not see, but he has the power to see.

In other words, according to the teaching of St. Thomas, under the influence of efficacious grace, the free will never wills in fact to resist and posit the contrary act (for then grace would cease to be efficacious), but it retains the power to do so. Does it follow then that efficacious grace is necessitating, as the Protestants and Jansenists thought, and that liberty strictly so called is destroyed, which consists in an indifference as regards the two opposites, and which is free not only from

36 Cf. *De veritate,* q.22, a.5.
37 Cf. Pohle-Preuss on *Grace,* p. 243, for a criticism of this distinction. (Tr.)
38 *Loc. cit.,* Ia IIae, q.10, a.4 ad 3um; cf. Ia, q.105, a.4; Ia IIae, q.112, a.3; *De veritate,* q.22, a.8–9; *De malo,* q.6, a.1 ad 3um.

compulsion but also from necessity? By no means. For St. Thomas, efficacious grace affects liberty by a sort of virginal contact, without violating it. Under the influence of efficacious grace, at the indivisible instant in which the salutary act is performed, in our will which already determines itself and is determined (for becoming and done are simultaneous in those things that are done instantaneously), there is undoubtedly no more any question of a passive or potential indifference on the part of the will in determining itself to either of two contraries; but there is an actual and active dominating indifference in the free act itself already determined which, proceeding from a faculty, the scope of which is universal, tends not from necessity but freely toward the chosen good, having really within itself the power not to will it. Certainly one cannot, in willing this thing, actually not will it, for that would be a contradiction; but in willing it, one has really the power not to will it, just as, according to the classical example, one cannot at the same time be standing and seated, but, when one is seated, it is really within one's power to rise. St. Thomas added that potential indifference is not of the essence of liberty, for it does not exist in God, who is simply pure Act, in no way potential, and sovereignly free, not only before but in choosing, and after having determined from eternity His choice, whom nothing created could infallibly attract or determine. Under the influence of the divine and efficacious motion, according to the teaching of St. Thomas, we still retain this dominating indifference, which is not potential but actual, and which is an image of the divine actuality. For Molina, on the contrary, it must of necessity be that, under the influence of this so-called efficacious grace (not taking into consideration the divine foreseeing of our consent), the free will retains not only the actual dominating indifference, which properly belongs to the free act that is already determined and that still tends freely toward its object; but he also will have it retain under the influence of this grace the potential indifference, and that it be within its power actually to resist.

To this the Thomists reply that when the will actually resists, the grace is no longer efficacious but merely sufficient. Now most assuredly, he who actually fulfils a precept is certainly better, other things being equal, than he who can and does not do so. Therefore, in virtue of the principle of predilection, he who fulfils a precept is loved more and helped more by God than he who does not do so. He receives from God not only the power to fulfil the precept, but actually and freely to do so. "What hast thou that thou hast not received?" [39]

Certainly Molina could not ignore this last mentioned principle. But did his theory finally lead him to respect its truth? St. Thomas wrote: "If God moves the will to anything, it is incompossible with this supposition, that the will be not moved thereto." [40] Molina, however, declared it to be at the same time possible, at least abstracting from the fact of the divine foreseeing of our consent, a foreseeing which St. Thomas does not mention. For St. Thomas, it is a case of two total and subordinated causes, the secondary determining itself for good only under the influence of the primary cause. For Molina, even without taking too seriously here the famous comparison of the barge drawn by two horses, it seems truly to be a case of two partial and co-ordinated causes. The free will induced to act by grace has a causality that is exclusively its own; it is not applied to its act by God. We see that the two rival doctrines start from very different principles.

St. Thomas and the great theologians who preceded him start from this supreme principle: the love of God is the cause of the goodness in things. From this they conclude that divine love is the cause of the better part in our salutary act, its free determination, and this cannot be withdrawn from its de-

[39] 1 Cor. 4: 7.
[40] *Loc. cit.*, Ia IIae, q. 10, a. 4 ad 3um.

pendence upon the divine causality. They say that this free determination is not exclusively ours, but that it is totally from God as primary cause, and totally from us as premoved secondary cause. "There is no distinction between what flows from a secondary cause and from a first cause," [41] says St. Thomas. Taken in this sense we have here the case of two total subordinated causes and not of two partial co-ordinated causes.

St. Thomas adds that God's transcendent causality "produces in us and with us even the free mode of our acts," [42] for this mode is still a being that is dependent upon the first Being. This free mode is the actual dominating indifference of our will, which tends actually toward some particular good that is incapable of irresistibly attracting it; for the will is specified by universal good, and it could not be irresistibly held captive except by the attraction of seeing God face to face. This dominating indifference of willing, which constitutes for the will its free mode, is a participation in one of God's absolute perfections, this being His liberty; but it is merely an analogical participation, for no perfection can be attributed univocally, that is, in the same sense, to God and to us. From this St. Thomas concludes that no thing would be better than another unless it were loved more by God.[43] Thus his entire doctrine on predestination is derived from this principle: "Since God's love is the cause of the goodness in things, no one thing would be better than another, if God did not will greater good for one than for another." [44] It is a corollary of the principles of causality and of the universal causality of the first Agent. Not for one moment does St. Thomas doubt that the laws governing free action are in harmony with those more general laws governing being and acting, and that they cannot contradict them.

[41] *Ibid.*, Ia, q.23, a.5.
[42] *Ibid.*, Ia, q.19, a.8.
[43] *Ibid.*, q.20, a.3.
[44] *Ibid.*, q.20, a.3.

Molina, contrary to this, starts off with a definition of free will that excludes the intrinsic efficacy of the divine decrees and of grace. Consequently the better part in our salutary acts, their free determination, which makes them efficacious, seems to be withdrawn from its dependence upon God's universal causality. Hence his denial of the principle of predilection as formulated by St. Thomas. In fact we read in the index to Molina's work, under the heading "free will," the following statement: "Free will is sufficient, so that in the case of two called and helped by an equal interior grace, one is converted and the other not." [45] Of two men equally helped by God, one occasionally becomes better than the other, better without having received more than the other. We shall see that the principal objections of the Thomists bear upon this point, and that at the end of the controversy we are confronted by the dilemma of either God determining or determined. There is no other alternative; for the divine foreknowledge, united to the divine will, is either the cause of our free determination or else is passive in their regard. God is either the author or merely the spectator of that which begins to distinguish the just from the impious. In other words, what does St. Paul mean when he says: "For who distinguisheth thee? Or what hast thou that thou hast not received?" [46]

The essence of Molinism is to be found in the aforesaid definition of free will and in the consequences it entails, which are the denial of the intrinsic efficacy of the divine decrees and of grace, for which are substituted the theory of the *scientia media* and of grace extrinsically efficacious by reason of our foreseen consent. On these points, notwithstanding their incidental differences, all Molinists are agreed.

It must be noted that in the Molinist system this definition of free will ought to be applicable to the impeccable free will of Christ, who, for all that, freely obeyed in such manner

45 *Loc. cit.*, p. 51.
46 I Cor. 4: 7.

that He not only never did disobey, but that He never could
do so. It is a most perfect image of God's sovereign and impeccable free will, in which there is no trace of any potential
dominating indifference, but only an actual dominating indifference as regards all created things. This, the Thomists
say, shows us that our free will persists even when, under the
influence of efficacious grace, there remains no longer the potential but only the actual dominating indifference, understood in this sense that God, far from forcing us, causes in us
and with us that our acts be performed freely.

THE PRINCIPAL OBJECTIONS RAISED AGAINST MOLINISM

It is easy to account for the objections raised against Molina's work after its publication by referring to those mentioned in the appendix of that work. [47] They are directed
principally against the three theses of Molinism, which are:
(1) its definition of free will; (2) its theory of the *scientia media* and of efficacious grace, especially in its relation to the
principle of predilection; (3) its theory of predestination after
foreseen merits.

1) Its definition of free will. The first opponents of Molinism, as can be seen from the writings of the Thomists of
this period, affirmed that it rests entirely upon a definition of
human liberty which cannot be proved either by experience
or *a priori,* and which is nothing but a begging of the question.[48] It cannot be shown from experience, they say, that the
free determination of our salutary acts is independent as such
of the divine causality, and that God does not cause this in us
and with us, even to the extent that our actions are performed
freely. This mysterious divine causality, which is more intimate to the free will than this latter is to itself, no more comes

---

[47] *Concordia,* pp. 575–606.
[48] Consult Bannez, Lemos, Alvarez, John of St. Thomas, Salmanticenses, in
their treatises on God and grace.

within the scope of our experience than does the divine conservation which keeps us in existence.

No more could reason, so these theologians teach, prove the validity of this definition. On the contrary, it is manifest to reason that the potential indifference between two decisions is not of the essence of liberty, since it could not exist in God, who is sovereignly free, and no more is it present in our free act that is already determined. As for the actual or active indifference, which is included in the free act already determined, this cannot be attributed univocally to God and to us, but only analogically or as of things proportionately alike, according to a participation which makes what is more intimate and better in the choice of our salutary free act depend upon God's choice. It would be, so the Thomists said, a begging of the question to deny this dependence, thus discarding one of the elements of the problem to be solved; and in the name of the principle of causality, and of the universal and transcendent pre-eminence of the divine causality, they protest against this.

Revelation, they went on to remark, could not be invoked in favor of this definition, since it speaks to us in the following terms: "Lord almighty King . . . there is none that can resist Thy will"; [49] "As the divisions of waters, so the heart of the king is in the hand of the Lord"; [50] "for it is God who worketh in you, both to will and to accomplish, according to His good will." [51]

The Council of Trent does not impose this definition when it declares against the Protestants who maintained that grace efficacious of itself destroyed free will: "If anyone saith that man's free will moved and excited by God, by assenting to God exciting and calling does in no wise co-operate towards disposing and preparing itself for obtaining the grace of jus-

[49] Esther 13: 9.
[50] Prov. 21: 1.
[51] Phil. 2: 13.

tification; that it cannot refuse its consent, if it would, but that, as something inanimate, it does nothing whatever and is merely passive; let him be anathema." [52] By this definition, in the preparation of which several Augustinians and Thomists took part, is excluded, so Molina's opponents say, the Protestant thesis according to which grace of itself efficacious is necessitating or irreconcilable with the principle of freedom from necessity. By this declaration of the council, it is affirmed that, under the influence of this grace, our will co-operates vitally and freely with the salutary act, and that it is within its power to resist, if it so wishes; but it does not say that under the influence of this efficacious grace, it happens that the will actually resists this grace and, if it were so, grace could no longer be said to be truly efficacious, but, on the contrary, it would be inefficacious, and through our own fault would be sterile.[53]

As these Thomists point out, the Protestants said that grace *of itself* efficacious is irreconcilable with freedom from necessity. Now, grace is of itself efficacious. Therefore there is no freedom from necessity. Molinism concedes the major of this syllogism and denies the minor. The Thomists, the Augustinians, and the Scotists deny the major, concede the minor, and deny the conclusion.

2) The *scientia media*. The difficulties encountered in this theory were as great as those presented by the Molinist definition of liberty which it presupposes. These objections of the Thomists and the Augustinians are fully discussed in their treatises on God.[54]

a) They say that the theory of the *scientia media* supposes that, if Peter and Judas were placed in the same circumstances and given equal graces, it could happen that one is converted

[52] Denz., no. 797. For an interpretation of this in favor of the Molinist theory, see Pohle-Preuss on *Grace*, pp. 243-44. (Tr.)

[53] Cf. A. Reginald, O.P., *De mente concilii Tridentini,* and A. Massoulié, O.P., *Divus Thomas sui interpres,* Vol. I, diss. 2, q.9.

[54] Cf. Billuart, *Cursus theol., De Deo,* diss. VI, a.6.

and the other not, or that entirely of his own accord the one distinguishes himself from the other. In fact, Molina said: "Given equal help, it can happen that of two persons called, one is converted and the other not." [55] And Lessius added: "Not that he who accepts, does so by his free will alone, but because the difference is the result of free will alone, so as not to be due to the diversity of prevenient grace." [56] Now, the Thomists, the Augustinians, and the Scotists say that, contrary to this, St. Paul wrote in one of his epistles as follows: "For what distinguisheth thee? Or what hast thou that thou hast not received? And if thou hast received, why dost thou glory as if thou hadst not received?" [57] This text is explained by St. Augustine and St. Thomas in a sense quite the opposite of that which the theory of the *scientia media* claims it to have.[58]

b) Moreover, the opponents of Molinism remark that this so-called *scientia media* cannot have any object; for, previous to any divine decree, there cannot be any conditionate future or any conditionate future that is determined. Previous to any decree, God can well foresee, as we too can, that if Peter is placed in certain circumstances and helped by a grace not necessarily efficacious, there are two possibilities: for he can be either faithful to his Master or betray Him; but He cannot foresee infallibly which of these two possibilities Peter will choose; for neither the scrutiny of Peter's will, which is of itself undetermined, nor a survey of the circumstances or of the grace not necessarily efficacious, admit of God infallibly foreseeing this, but merely of conjecturing it. The conditionate future, in fact, is more than a mere possible; it denotes a new determination in answer to the question: Which of these two possible alternatives would happen? To say that the conditionate future is infallibly known because of God's super-

[55] *Loc. cit.*, p. 51.
[56] *De gratia efficaci*, chap. 18, no. 7.
[57] I Cor. 4: 7.
[58] Cf. Salmanticenses, *Cursus theol., De gratia efficaci*, disp. 2, dub. 1.

comprehension in knowledge of the created will and circumstances, is, instead of saving free will, to fall into the error of determinism of circumstances, which is the denial of free will; and so we cannot assign any object to the *scientia media*, if we wish to avoid determinism.

St. Thomas had written: "Contingent futures, the truth of which is not determined, are not in themselves knowable." [59] In his opinion, that is true of conditionally free acts of the future as well as of absolutely free acts of the future. God cannot see them in His essence previous to any decree; for He would see them there *on the same grounds* as absolutely necessary truths, and this would thus be a reverting to the logical fatalism of the Stoics.

The Molinists tried hard to answer this objection, which is considered by their opponents to be incapable of solution. On this point Leibniz remarked: "It is amusing to see how they torment themselves to find a way out of a labyrinth when there is absolutely no way out." [60]

c) Again the Thomists object to the theory of the *scientia media*, stating that it leads to the denial of God's universal causality since it takes away from the latter the better part in our salutary acts, which is their free determination. Hence it is derogatory to God's omnipotence and supreme dominion, since it claims that God cannot be the cause in us and with us that we determine ourselves to act, and that we do so freely. It leads also to the admission of a passivity or a dependence of God's foreknowledge upon this free determination of the created order, which at first is a conditional future, and then a simple future. God is no longer the cause but the passive spectator of that which distinguishes the just from the impious, who are equally helped by Him in the same circumstances. God, no longer being the first who determines by His free determination or election, is Himself determined;

59 *Loc. cit.*, IIa IIae, q. 171, a. 3.
60 *Théodicée*, Part I, chap. 48.

His knowledge is passive with regard to one thing, a determination that does not come from Him. Now there is nothing more inadmissible than the positing of a passivity in the pure Act, or of a dependence in Him who is sovereignly independent and the cause of all good. The Thomists pointed out several other inconveniences that arise from the theory of the *scientia media*. It suffices to note here the principal ones.

All of them have said that the theory of the *scientia media* violates the principle of predilection as formulated by St. Thomas, which is: "Since God's love is the source of all good, no one thing would be better than another unless it were loved more by God." [61] In fact, among the most criticized of Molina's propositions, as the appendix to his work shows,[62] there is one that must be quoted here. It is as follows: "Of two that are called and equally aided by an interior grace, it can happen that one of them of his own free will is converted and the other remains an unbeliever." [63] It was objected that this was contrary to the principle of predilection as formulated even before St. Thomas, by St. Paul and St. Augustine. The principle of predilection, as we have seen, presupposes that the divine decrees and grace are efficacious of themselves and not because of our foreseen consent. For this reason Molina is incapable of recognizing this principle to be of universal and absolute validity, and he reduces it to this: It is because God loved Peter more than Judas that He decided to place him in a certain situation of circumstances in which He foresaw that Peter would be saved; and this is due solely to God's good pleasure. But nevertheless it remains true that such a one elected is saved, without having been helped more than a certain person who is lost. Molina even said: "That those who received more help were not predestined and saved, but that those who received less were predestined and saved, was

---

[61] *Loc. cit.*, Ia, q.20, a.3.
[62] *Loc. cit.*, pp. 592, 600, 605.
[63] *Ibid.*, p. 51.

due to no other reason than that the latter refused to make use of their native free will, so that of their own accord they might attain salvation; but the former most assuredly did so." [64] This proposition was one of those most criticized from the outset of the controversies.[65]

3) Predestination "because of foreseen merits." Finally, the opponents of Molinism raised a serious objection against the theory of predestination "because of foreseen merits." Regardless of St. Paul's texts to which they appealed in refutation of this theory, they brought up against it the principle that God, like every intelligent being, wills the end before the means, since the latter are willed only in view of the end, and hence He wills glory to His elect before He wills the grace by which they will merit this glory. This is what St. Thomas had said. [66]

Such are the principal objections that were raised against the Molinist theory of predestination, especially in the Congregation appointed in Rome by Clement VIII and known as *De Auxiliis.* The conferences lasted from January 2, 1598 until August 20, 1607. Beginning with the year 1602, the sovereign pontiffs themselves took charge of the debates. Eighty-five papal congregations were held, sixty-eight under Clement VIII, and seventeen under Paul V. Under Clement VIII what particularly came up for examination was the Molinist doctrine concerning the natural power of free will, the *scientia media,* predestination, and the good use of the divine assistance. Especially so was Molina's doctrine compared with that of St. Augustine. The principal defenders of Thomism were Didacus Alvarez, Thomas de Lemos, and Michael a Ripa; the leading theologians in the Society of Jesus were Michael Vasquez, Gregory of Valentia, Peter Arrubal, and de Bastida, who in general recognized that the congruism

---

[64] *Ibid.,* p. 526.
[65] *Ibid.,* appendix, p. 605.
[66] *Loc. cit.,* Ia, q.23, a.4.

proposed by St. Bellarmine and Suarez was more in conformity with the teachings of St. Augustine and St. Thomas than Molinism was. On the whole, under Clement VIII, the opinions were unfavorable to the author of the *Concordia*. However, no sentence of condemnation was issued by Clement VIII, who died in 1605. At the end of that year Paul V resumed the discussions and authorized even an examination of the question of physical predetermination; but most of the censors declared themselves to be in favor of Thomism. The commission upheld its censures against forty-two of Molina's propositions. Neither Molina (†1600), nor Bannez (†1604) saw the end of this strife. On August 28, 1607, Paul V consulted for the last time the cardinals then present, who were very divided in their opinions. The Pope then adjourned the congregation, and ordered both parties not to indulge in mutual condemnations.

It is of particular importance here to quote the conclusion given by Paul V on August 28, 1607, after consulting various cardinals. This is to be found in the work of P. G. Schneeman, S.J.[67] It reads as follows: "By the grace of God the council defined it to be necessary for the free will to be moved by God. The difficulty consists in this, as to whether it is moved physically or morally; and although it would be desirable that there should be no strife of this kind in the Church, for disagreements often are the cause of the sudden rise of errors, it therefore is a good thing for these disputes to be finally settled. Nevertheless, we do not see the necessity for this at present, in that the opinion of the Dominican fathers differs very much from Calvin's; for the Dominicans say that grace does not destroy but perfects free will, and its power is such that man acts in his own way, which is freely. But the Jesuits differ from the Pelagians, who declared the beginning of salvation originated from us, whereas the former hold quite the

---

[67] Cf. *Controversiarum de divinae gratiae liberique arbitrii concordia initia et progressus,* Freiburg-Breisgau, 1881, p. 291.

contrary. Since there is therefore no urgent need of a definition on our part, the question can be deferred until in course
of time we are better informed about it."

This decision was afterward confirmed by a decree of
Benedict XIV, issued on July 13, 1748.

CHAPTER II

PREDESTINATION AS EXPLAINED BY THE CONGRUISM OF ST. ROBERT BELLARMINE AND SUAREZ

THESE theologians admit, as the Molinists do, the *scientia media,* and deny, as they do, the intrinsic efficacy of the divine decrees and of grace; but they agree with the Thomists, the Augustinians, and the Scotists in this sense, that they recognize the absolute gratuity of predestination to glory, which they declare to be previous to foreseen merits not only as they are future, but even as they are conditionally future. In accordance with this congruism, God makes use of the *scientia media* only after He has predestined one to glory, for a distribution of the so-called congruous grace and so as to assure Himself that it will be efficacious in certain determined circumstances. In this way the principle is saved that God wills the end before the means, and a greater effort is made in this system than in Molina's to recognize the validity and universality of the principle of predilection.

EXPOSITION OF THIS DOCTRINE

Let us see just what congruism teaches: (1) on the absolute gratuity of predestination to glory; (2) on congruent grace; (3) on the *scientia media.*

1) The absolute gratuity of predestination to glory is distinctly the teaching of St. Bellarmine.[1] His purpose is to prove, like the Thomists and Augustinians, by means of Scripture, tradition, and theological reasoning, the proposi-

[1] Cf. *De gratia et libero arbitrio,* Bk. II, chaps. 9–15.

tion that no reason can be assigned on our part for divine predestination, which means that predestination to glory is absolutely gratuitous, or previous to any foreseen merits. St. Bellarmine excludes as a reason for predestination to glory, not only all merit in the strict sense, but also all congruous merit, whatsoever use of free will or of grace, and every indispensable condition.[2]

He proves [3] this doctrine from Scripture, which teaches that God has elected certain persons,[4] and efficaciously so, that they may infallibly get to heaven.[5] Texts in proof of this are: "This is the will of the Father . . . that of all that He hath given Me, I should lose nothing"; [6] "No man shall pluck them out of My hand . . . no one can snatch them out of the hand of My Father"; [7] "Whom He predestined, them He also called . . . and justified . . . and glorified." [8] He also proves that God's choice of the elect was entirely gratuitous and previous to any foreseeing of their merits. Texts in support of this are: "It hath pleased your Father to give you a kingdom"; [9] "You have not chosen Me, but I have chosen you, that you should go, and should bring forth fruit"; [10] "There is a remnant saved according to the election of grace. And if by grace, it is not now by works: otherwise grace is no more grace." [11]

St. Bellarmine also interprets like St. Thomas and the Thomists the following text of St. Paul: "As He chose us . . . that we should be holy, . . . according to the purpose of His will." [12] "In whom we also are called by lot, being predestinated according to the purpose of Him who worketh all things

2 *Ibid.*, chap. 9.
3 *Ibid.*, chap. 13.
4 Matt. 20: 16; 24: 31; Luke 12: 32; Rom. 8: 33; Eph. 1: 4.
5 Matt. 24: 24.
6 John 6: 39.
7 *Ibid.*, 10: 28 f.
8 Rom. 8: 30.
9 Luke 12: 32.
10 John 15: 16.
11 Rom. 11: 5 f.
12 Eph. 1: 4 f.

according to the counsel of His will." [13] Finally he adds [14] that
the elect were chosen gratuitously but independently of any
foreseeing of their good works, according to the teaching of
St. Paul, who says: "For when the children were not yet born,
nor had done any good or evil, that the purpose of God, according to election might stand . . . there is a remnant saved
according to the election of grace." [15] St. Bellarmine shows [16]
that these principles of St. Paul apply not only to the election
of nations, but also to individuals chosen for eternal life. To
those who object that in St. Paul's text [17] foreknowledge precedes predestination, for he says: "Whom He foreknew, He
also predestinated," St. Bellarmine replies that it is not a
question here of the foreknowledge of merits, for which there
would be no foundation in St. Paul's epistles, and which
would be in contradiction to several of his texts, but the
meaning is: "whom He foreknew by the knowledge of approbation, whom He loved, whom He willed, those He predestined. . . . For to know and to foreknow in the Scripture are
frequently taken to mean the knowledge of approbation, as
is evident from the following text: 'God hath not cast away
His people, which He foreknew' " (Rom. 11: 2).[18] This is the
exegesis of St. Augustine and St. Thomas, and is retained at
the present day by Fathers Lagrange, Allo, Zahn, Julicher,
and others.

Finally, St. Bellarmine proves that, according to the teaching of St. Augustine, St. Prosper, and St. Fulgentius, no reason
can be assigned on our part for predestination to glory. He
writes: "No reason can be assigned on our part that God
should predestine us to glory. . . . Not only do these holy

---

[13] *Ibid.,* 1: 11.
[14] *Loc. cit.,* chap. 13.
[15] Rom. 9: 11; 11: 5.
[16] *Loc. cit.,* chap. 13.
[17] Rom. 8: 29.
[18] *Loc. cit.,* chap. 13; cf. Matt. 7: 23; Gal. 4: 9; 1 Cor. 8: 3; 13: 12; II Tim.
2: 19; Ps. 1: 6.

Fathers (Augustine, Prosper, and Fulgentius) affirm this, but also the more learned of their predecessors, whom the rest subsequently followed, record this opinion as pertaining to the Catholic faith, and they reject the contrary opinion held by the Pelagians. I shall mention some of their works, so that if any perchance are of the opposite opinion, they may realize, from the judgment of these most holy Fathers, how manifestly they err on this point." [19] He mentions in particular two works, one by St. Augustine,[20] and the other by St. Prosper.[21] In addition to this he remarks,[22] as St. Augustine does, that the Fathers who lived previous to the rise of the Pelagian heresy touched but incidentally upon this question of predestination. He quotes, however, St. John Chrysostom who, on the words: "For who distinguisheth thee?" comments as follows: "Therefore thou hast received what thou hast, neither this only or that, but whatever thou hast. For these are not thy merits, but God's gifts." [23] Finally, he points out that the fathers previous to the time of St. Augustine, especially the Greek Fathers, often took predestination as meaning the will to give glory after this life, and that they scarcely spoke of it except by way of exhortation, and therefore they had in mind the *order of execution,* in which merits precede glorification; whereas in the order of intention the case is the reverse. God, in the order of intention, wills the end before the means, glory before grace and merits; but in the order of execution He wills glory as the reward of merits. God wills to give glory gratuitously in the order of intention; but in the order of execution He does not will to give it gratuitously, and this is contrary to what the Protestants say. In this Bellarmine speaks exactly as the Thomists do, and like them he remarks that after the rise of the Pelagian heresy it was necessary to con-

[19] *Ibid.,* chap. 11.
[20] *De dono persever.,* chaps. 18, 23.
[21] *Prima responsio ad objectiones Gallorum.*
[22] *Loc. cit.,* chap. 14.
[23] *In I Cor.* 4: 7, hom. 12.

sider predestination no longer merely in the order of execution, but also in that of intention, so that everything in the affair of salvation may be attributed to God, as the Fathers previous to the time of Bellarmine had said when commenting on St. Paul's words: "For who distinguisheth thee?"

Thus St. Robert Bellarmine saw in the absolute gratuity of predestination the very teaching of Scripture and its great interpreters. This accounts for the fact of his admitting St. Augustine's definition of predestination, which states that it is "the foreknowledge and preparation of those gifts of God whereby they who are liberated are most certainly liberated." [24] In support of this definition, in which the foreknowledge refers not to merits but to the divine gifts, Bellarmine appeals to the scriptural text: "No man shall pluck them out of My hand." [25]

Suarez says the same. He writes as follows: "I say first: On the part of the one predestined, there is no cause for predestination inasmuch as this refers to eternal predestination to glory or to perseverance or to sanctifying grace or to supernaturally good acts, although for such effects, in that they are bestowed in time, in the order of execution, some cause or reason can be assigned on man's part, as in the case of glory which, in the order of execution, is given on account of merits. This is the opinion of St. Thomas, (Ia, q. 23, a. 5), with which Cajetan and other modern Thomists agree. Undoubtedly it is Augustine's opinion." [26] Since election to glory is previous to foreseen merits, it follows for Suarez as for the Thomists, that non-election, or negative reprobation, is also previous to foreseen demerits.

We see that on this point of the absolute gratuity of predestination to glory there is a considerable difference between the congruism of Suarez and of Bellarmine, and the Molinism

24 De dono persever., chap. 14, no. 35.
25 John 10: 28.
26 De auxiliis, Bk. III, chaps. 16–17; De causa praedest., Bk. II, chap. 23.

such as especially Vasquez, Lessius, and the majority of Molinists understood it to mean. The Thomists always took care to note this difference.[27] Billuart adds that among the theologians of the Society of Jesus, several agree with Bellarmine and Suarez on this point, such as Toletus, Henriquez, Ruiz, Typhanus.

In recent times Father Billot,[28] although he disagrees with Suarez on the question of negative reprobation, also admits the absolute gratuity of predestination to glory, this being the only kind—and he says so with good reason—that merits the name of predestination; for predestination to grace is common to the elect and to many reprobates.

The difference between congruism and Molinism is less, as we shall see, when it is a question of congruous grace; and still less is this difference when it is a question of the *scientia media*.

2) Congruous grace. The nature of this grace is well explained in a decree made famous by the general of the Jesuits, Father Aquaviva. By it, six years after the meetings of the *Congregatio de Auxiliis,* in December, 1613, he ordered the theologians of the Society to teach congruism, "an exposition and defense of which was given," he said, "in the controversy entered into by the *Congregatio de Auxiliis,* as being more in agreement with the teachings of St. Augustine and St. Thomas." "Henceforth let our fathers," says this decree, "always teach that efficacious and sufficient graces do not differ merely *in actu secundo* (completed act), because the one obtains its effect by the co-operation of the free will and not the other; but they differ also *in actu primo* (first movement), in this sense, that, the *scientia media* presupposed, God Himself, with the fixed intention of producing good, designedly chooses those determinate means and employs them in the manner

---

[27] Cf. Billuart, *De Deo,* diss. IX, a.4, sec. 2; and more recently del Prado, O.P., *De gratia et libero arbitrio,* 1911, III, 347.

[28] *De Deo uno,* 1926, pp. 289, 291.

and at the moment when he knows that the effect will be infallibly produced; so that, if He had foreseen the inefficacy of these means, God would have made use of other means. That is why, morally speaking, and considering it as a favor, there is something more in efficacious than in sufficient grace even *in actu primo*. It is in this way that God causes us to perform the act instead of giving us the grace which enables us to act. The same kind of reasoning applies to perseverance, which undoubtedly is God's gift."

From this we see the difference between Molinism and this type of congruism. In Molinism, God gives the grace which He *knows to be efficacious;* in this type of congruism, God gives the grace *because He knows it will be efficacious.* Hence even congruous grace becomes infallibly efficacious only by the consent of the human will, and this is foreseen by means of the *scientia media.* Therefore the Thomists asked whether the principle of predilection is truly safeguarded.[29]

3) The *scientia media* as viewed by Suarez. Whereas Bellarmine[30] explains the *scientia media* as Molina does, by having recourse to the supercomprehension of causes, Suarez in opposition to Molina writes as follows: "That God knows our future free acts in their proximate causes because of His perfect comprehension of our free will . . . this we must reject . . . for this simply means the end of freedom . . . and is repugnant to it."[31] In other words, the *scientia media* explained as Molina wants it to be, by the theory of the supercomprehension of our free will if placed in certain circumstances, makes Suarez say, as the Thomists do, that it leads to determinism of the circumstances.

But does Suarez have better success in explaining this *scientia media,* which he wishes to retain in substance? God, he says, previous to any decree, infallibly foresees condition-

[29] Consult Pohle-Preuss, *Grace,* pp. 260–66, for a critical estimate of this congruism. (Tr.)

[30] *Loc. cit., Bk.* IV, chap. 15.

[31] *De scientia futurorum contingentium,* chap. 7.

ate futures in their objective or formal truth. Of two conditional contradictory propositions, such as: "If Peter were placed in these circumstances, he would sin and he would not sin," the one is definitely true and the other is definitely false. It is impossible, indeed, for both to be true or both to be false. Therefore the infinite intelligence that penetrates all truth, sees certainly which of the two is true and which is false.

Suarez, the Thomists reply, forgets that Aristotle [32] has shown that of two contradictory propositions which are particular ones and which concern a contingent future event, neither is positively true or false. If it were otherwise, as Aristotle remarks, the truth would be in determinism or fatalism, and our choice would not be a free one. The Stoics, as Cicero relates,[33] intended to prove determinism precisely by the argument that, of two contradictory propositions, one is necessarily true. Therefore, between the two propositions, A will be, A will not be, the necessity of one of them, at the moment I am uttering it, excludes the possibility of the other. From all eternity is the flow of imperishable truth. From this it would follow that creation is no longer a free act, and the divine will would be subjected to the logical fatalism of the Stoics.

THE INHERENT DIFFICULTIES OF THE CONGRUISM
OF BELLARMINE AND OF SUAREZ

In this theory the principle of predilection is certainly much better safeguarded than in Molinism. Concerning the question of the absolute gratuity of predestination to glory, it follows faithfully St. Paul's interpretation given by St. Augustine and St. Thomas. But, in the opinion of the Thomists, this theory still limits the universal validity of the principle of predilection and stamps it with the seal of relativity, in that

[32] *Perihermenias*, Bk. I, chap. 9. See St. Thomas, commentary, lect. 13.
[33] *De divin.*, I, 55.

it retains the main structure of Molinism, which is the *scientia media* or the denial of the intrinsic efficacy of the divine decrees and of grace. It remains true, then, according to this conception of the *scientia media,* that human effort makes grace efficacious instead of being the result of the efficacy of this grace; so that if two men or two angels are equally helped by God, it may happen that one of them becomes better than the other, though this one was not helped more, and did not receive more than the other. Undoubtedly congruism is right in saying that congruous grace is from the moral point of view a greater gift than the other, but it is none the less true that its actual efficacy is due solely to the subsequent consent of the human will, as foreseen by the *scientia media.* And then we have a recrudescence of all the difficulties of Molinism, which seems to posit a dependence in the divine foreknowledge as regards the creature, a passivity in pure Act, and leads on our part to determinism of circumstances.[34] Neither can it be said that previous to any decree God foresees a certain conditionate future, for instance, Peter's infidelity, in so far as this conditionate future is present to Him from all eternity; for it is not independently of God's decree that this conditionate future rather than its contrary is present to Him from all eternity; otherwise it would be present to Him as a necessary truth, and thus we have again determinism.

As for what directly concerns predestination, the Thomists as a rule point out that congruous grace, since it is not infallibly efficacious of itself, is not an infallible means of leading the elect to glory, as St. Augustine's definition would demand, which states that it is "the foreknowledge and preparation of those gifts of God, whereby they who are liberated are most certainly liberated." [35] Congruous grace, since it is infallibly efficacious, not because God wills it but because man wills it, does not express adequately—as Bellarmine himself

---

[34] Cf. del Prado, O.P., *De gratia et libero arbitrio,* 1911, III, 362–68.
[35] *Loc. cit.,* chap. 14, no. 35.

admits—the meaning of the scriptural text: "No one can snatch them out of the hand of My Father." [36] No more does congruous grace, since it is not infallibly efficacious of itself, seem to express adequately the meaning of St. Augustine in the following text: "God effects with the very wills of men what He wills and when He wills. Undoubtedly the human heart is inclined as it pleases His omnipotent will. . . . The wills of human beings are more in God's power than in their own." [37] And again when he says that efficacious "grace is not spurned by the hard of heart; for this very purpose it is bestowed, that the hardness of heart may first be taken away." [38]

Certainly St. Augustine [39] called efficacious grace *congruous;* but his later works just quoted by us, show that at least he came finally to the conclusion that it is a question here not of extrinsic but of intrinsic congruousness, and this latter is grace infallibly efficacious of itself.

These difficulties in the congruism of St. Robert Bellarmine and of Suarez made other congruists admit the necessity of grace intrinsically efficacious at least for difficult acts. This was the stand taken in the eighteenth century by the congruists of the Sorbonne.

[36] John 10: 29.
[37] *De correptione et gratia,* chap. 14.
[38] *De praed, sanct.,* chap. 8.
[39] *Ad Simplicianum,* Bk. I, q.2, no. 13.

CHAPTER III

THE CONGRUISM OF THE SORBONNE

WE come across this theory, though expressed with slight differences of meaning, in the works of several theologians of the eighteenth century, such as those of Tournely, Habert, Ysambert, Frassen, Thomassinus, and Duhamel. St. Alphonse is inclined to accept it. In the nineteenth century we find Father John Hermann, C.SS.R., still admitting it, though the way he sums it up is according to its essential principles, which are: (1) "Grace is intrinsically efficacious, and in this we follow the Thomists and the Augustinians as against the Molinists. (2) Contrary to the Thomists, we say this intrinsically efficacious grace is not physical but merely a moral motion. (3) Intrinsically efficacious grace is required only for difficult salutary acts; for the easy acts, especially for prayer, sufficient grace, which is commonly granted to all, is the only grace that is required." [1]

Thus a middle system is established, which is in opposition to the others, and which adopts the good points of the others. It is an eclectic system, which lays claim to the general rejection of the *scientia media* of the Molinists, and to the admission of a grace not extrinsically congruous, as Suarez does, but to one that is intrinsically congruous.

Father John Hermann writes: "According to the congruists of the Suarezian and Bellarminian type, the infallible effect of grace depends not upon its intrinsic power, but upon the consent of the will or the circumstances in which a man is placed. God cannot infallibly know what effect grace will have, unless He has first found out by means of the *scientia*

[1] Cf. *Tractatus de divina gratia*, no. 509.

media whether the will, situated in these or those particular circumstances is or is not going to accept the grace. We, however, say that it is a case of intrinsic congruousness, which is given by God Himself to the grace, and it consists not in any absolute entity that is superadded to the grace (and thus we reject physical premotion), but it consists in the special mode of the divine call, in its perfect adjustment, namely, to the will of the one called. . . . Wherefore, in our opinion, the congruousness of the grace reacts upon the will, and God has no need at all of the *scientia media* so that He may know what effect the grace will have." [2]

We see the consequence of this as regards predestination and the relations of this latter to salutary acts easy to perform, especially to the case of prayer. This same author adds: "Whereas Molinism and Thomism have their foundations in indemonstrable philosophical arguments (the former in the *scientia media,* the latter in physical premotion), our congruism has no special philosophic foundation, but rests solely on the truths of faith." [3] Yet this same Father Hermann said elsewhere: "The Thomist system has for its foundation the metaphysical principle that God is the first Cause and universal Mover from whom all being and action must originate." [4] Does not this principle transcend the limits of opinion and belong to the *preambles of the faith?* From this point of view, even eclecticism cannot afford to overlook it. We may ask ourselves whether this congruism does not violate this principle, by denying to salutary acts easy to perform the necessity of grace that is infallibly efficacious of itself.

THE DIFFICULTIES IN THE CONGRUISM OF THE SORBONNE

This new theory may seem more acceptable than Thomism and also than Molinism to those who scarcely consider things

[2] *Ibid.,* no. 561.
[3] *Ibid.,* no. 748.
[4] *Ibid.,* no. 399.

otherwise than from the practical point of view. It tells us, indeed, that intrinsically efficacious grace is required only for salutary acts difficult to perform, but not for easier ones, such as for prayer to obtain the efficacious help. By this theory the obscurity in the mystery seems to a great extent to be eliminated. But if things are regarded from the speculative point of view, this new theory has, in the opinion of the Thomists, all the difficulties of Molinism for easy acts, and, in the opinion of the Molinists, all the obscurities of Thomism for difficult acts. In other words, from the theoretical point of view, this congruism accumulates to itself all the difficulties of the other systems, and, furthermore, the principles it admits for difficult acts have not the least metaphysical validity, since they no longer apply to other acts.

In their criticism of this theory, the Thomists and Molinists are agreed in saying that this congruism cannot help having recourse to the *scientia media* so that salutary acts easy to perform may be foreseen. Among Thomists of modern times, Father del Prado writes: "The congruism of the Sorbonne rejects the *scientia media* in name, but retains it in fact. Knowledge of simple intelligence is the name it gives to its knowledge, but in reality it is the same as the *scientia media,* because it precedes the decree of the divine will." [5] The essence of the *scientia media* consists, as a matter of fact, in the foreseeing of free conditionate futures previous to any divine determining decree. Now such is exactly the stand taken by the Sorbonne congruism in the case of salutary acts easy to perform, since in this theory these acts do not demand either divine determining decrees or grace that is infallibly efficacious of itself. Of two persons equally helped by God, it would happen, then, that one of them prays and the other does not, and the former would become better without having been loved more by God. Once more this is a violation, so the Thomists say, of the principle of predilection, that no one

[5] *De gratia et libero arbitrio,* 1911, III, 390.

thing would be better than another, unless it were loved more by God.

It will be said that at least man without a help that is efficacious of itself sometimes avoids resisting grace. Father del Prado replies to this, pointing out that for St. Thomas, "the very fact that one does not place an obstacle to grace, is due to grace." [6] Not to resist grace is a good thing which must originate from the source of all good things, that is, from God's love. Therefore he who does not resist is loved more by God than he who, situated in the same circumstances, does resist. God mercifully preserves him in the state of goodness, whereas he justly permits the other to commit sin, often as a punishment for previous sin. Thus we find ourselves confronted by two mysteries, the one of grace and the other of iniquity. This congruist theory of salutary acts easy to perform forgets this saying of St. Augustine: "Because all good things, great, mediocre, and least, come from God, it follows that even the good use of free will comes from God." [7] In every salutary act, however trifling, there is to be found the mystery of grace. [8]

In the criticism of this congruism, Thomists and Molinists agree in saying with Schiffini: "The intrinsic and infallible efficacy of the divine decrees and of grace either is or is not in harmony with our liberty. If it is, why restrict it to difficult acts? If it is not, why admit it for them? The question here is one of salutary acts, considered as acts and as supernaturally free acts, whether they are easy or difficult to perform; because the greater or less difficulty in performing these acts does not change their species. Finally, prayer is not always an easy act, especially perseverance in prayer." [9]

[6] *In ep. ad Hebr.*, XII, lect. 3.

[7] *Retract.*, I, 9.

[8] Cf. del Prado, *loc. cit.*, III, 404 ff.

[9] *De efficaci gratia*, disp. IV, sect. 6. On this point consult the first appendix in which a more recent opinion is examined by us concerning efficacious grace and salutary acts easy to perform (pp. 341-52).

We might speak here of a congruism of later date, that of cardinals Satolli, Pecci, and Lorenzelli and of bishops Paquet and Janssens, O.S.B., who, rejecting outright the *scientia media* and predetermining decrees, endeavor to take an intermediate stand. They hold that God knows conditionally free acts of the future by means of His knowledge of simple intelligence, before any decree of His divine will.

To this the Thomists reply that it is a confounding of the *possible* with the *conditionate future*. This latter, even if it will never become a reality, is more than a mere possibility. It implies a new determination in answer to the question as to which of two possible contradictories Peter would choose if placed in certain circumstances. Would he or would he not be faithful to his Master? One does not have to be omniscient to see that there would be two possible choices here for Peter. But previous to any determining decree, God, by His knowledge of simple intelligence, cannot foresee what decision Peter would make, which of the two possibles he would choose.[10] In the third part of this book and in the second appendix we shall resume the discussion of the view on the divine motion held by cardinals Satolli, Pecci, Lorenzelli, and also by Father Billot, S.J.

We see that the outstanding difficulty of these different forms of congruism, whether that of Suarez or of Tournely or of Satolli, is the difficulty that is raised against the theory of the *scientia media,* which truly seems to posit a dependence or passivity in God's foreknowledge toward a determination that is independent of His action. Chiefly on this account the Augustinians and Thomists who wrote subsequent to the Council of Trent attack the *scientia media.* It remains for us now to give an account of their teaching.

10 Cf. del Prado, *loc. cit.,* III, 497, 504, 506.

CHAPTER IV

PREDESTINATION ACCORDING TO THE TEACHING OF THE POST-TRIDENTINE AUGUSTINIANS

AUGUSTINIANISM is the name given in particular to the doctrine proposed in the seventeenth century by Cardinal Noris (1631–1704) and defended later on by the theologian Lawrence Berti (1696–1766), both of them being Augustinians. They were accused of Jansenism, though they were never condemned. Far from this being the case, their doctrine, as a matter of fact, differs essentially from Jansenism, in that it sincerely affirms liberty (freedom from necessity) and sufficient grace.

Though fully admitting for the present state of man intrinsically and infallibly efficacious grace, they differ from Thomism in their manner of conceiving the influence of the divine action on free will. For them it is a determining influence that is not physical, but merely moral. Grace acts on the soul by way of delectation. Man in his present state is determined to act either by reason of an evil delectation (concupiscence) or by reason of a good and spiritual delectation (charity). This latter is a sufficient grace when it gives the power to overcome concupiscence; it is an efficacious grace when it actually gains the victory over concupiscence, not necessitating but infallibly moving the will.

This explains the conclusions relative to predestination enunciated by L. Berti.[1] In these conclusions they draw a much finer distinction than the Thomists do, between the present state and that of original justice, and these conclusions

[1] *De theologicis disciplinis,* Vol. I, Bk. IV, chaps. 6, 11; Bk. VI, chaps. 1–5.

presuppose that grace intrinsically and infallibly efficacious is required in the present condition of man, not because the created free will, whether of angel or man, depends upon God, but because of the weakness of our free will since the fall. These conclusions appear at the beginning of Berti's work,[2] and are enunciated as follows: "Prop. LXXXVIII: God does not predetermine naturally free actions, and consequently He does not foresee them in the efficacious preordination of His will (p. 175). Prop. XCII: The creature in the state of innocence did not need the help of predetermining grace, and consequently God in the efficacious decree of His will had not the least knowledge of the perseverance of the angels (p. 186). Prop. XCVIII: God sees future free acts of the supernatural order, which acts refer to the state of fallen nature, and His seeing them is dependent upon the decree of His efficacious will (p. 197). Prop. XCIX: Human liberty is in no way affected by the divine preordinations (p. 208). Prop. C: By His antecedent will God wills all men to be saved, without a single exception (p. 215). Prop. CVI: In the dogma of predestination and grace there must be no departure from the teaching of St. Augustine (p. 228). Prop. CXIII: Morally virtuous acts, which are foreseen by God, by no means are the cause of our predestination (p. 235). Prop. CXIV: Predestination to glory precedes predestination to grace (p. 237). Prop. CXV: It is proved from Sacred Scripture that in the state of fallen nature predestination to glory is gratuitous (p. 239). Prop. CXVI: Our Holy Father Augustine most plainly taught that this same predestination to glory is gratuitous (p. 242). Prop. CXXXIII: On the part of the reprobate, original sin, of course, is partly the cause of negative reprobation (p. 289)."

The principal objection raised by the Thomists against these theses of seventeenth and eighteenth century Augustinianism is that the principle of predilection formulated by St. Augustine and St. Thomas is of absolute universality, and

2 *Ibid.*, I, xii.

that it applies therefore not only to man in the present state, but also to man in the state of innocence and even to the angels. In speaking of the angels and their predestination, St. Augustine [3] said that if the good and the bad were created equally good, the former, since they received more help, attained eternal happiness, whereas the latter fell through their own fault, and this, moreover, was permitted by God for a greater good. St. Thomas gave a most universal scope to the principle of predilection, so that it applies not only to fallen man, but to every created being, and this not only because of the infirmity of their nature, but also because of their dependence upon God: "Since God's love is the cause of the goodness of things, no one thing would be better than another, unless God willed a greater good for this thing than for the other." [4] No one angel or man, in whatever state he may be, would be better than another, unless he were loved more by God. The principle is of absolute universality.[5]

Moreover, in addition to this, the Thomists say that every salutary act, particularly if it is performed in a state of aridity, is not due to the victorious delectation. Finally, when this latter is present, since it is only a moral motion, operating by way of an objective attraction, and is not a physical motion, emanating from it and moving the will to act, it cannot be intrinsically and infallibly efficacious. God seen face to face certainly would infallibly attract our will; but the case is not the same with the pleasure we experience at the thought of God known in the obscurity of faith.

[3] *De Civitate Dei,* XII, 9.
[4] *Summa theol.,* Ia, q.20, a.3.
[5] Cf. Billuart, *Cursus theol., De gratia,* diss. II, a.4.

CHAPTER V

Predestination According to the Teaching of the Post-Tridentine Thomists

PRINCIPLES ON WHICH THEY AGREE

ABSOLUTELY all the Thomists who wrote after Molina's time are opposed to his theory of the *scientia media*. In their opinion it posits a dependence or passivity in God's foreknowledge with regard to a determination that is independent of His action. The whole controversy brings us back to the dilemma: "God determining or determined, there is no other alternative." We cannot admit, say the Thomists, any dependence or passivity in pure Act. Hence they maintain that the only way in which God can know conditionally free acts of the future is in an objectively conditionate decree, and free acts of the future only in a conditionate decree that is positive in the case of good acts, and permissive in the case of sin. They add that the determining decree with regard to our salutary acts is intrinsically and infallibly efficacious, but that it is not necessitating, for it extends even to the *free mode* of our acts which God wills and produces in us and with us. God willed efficaciously from all eternity that the good thief should be converted of his own free will on Calvary, and this divine efficacious will, far from destroying the freedom of this act of conversion, produces this in him because God, who preserves our will in existence, is more intimate to it than it is to itself.

Thus all Thomists defend the intrinsic and infallible efficacy of the divine decrees. It is a question of the decrees that concern our salutary acts and of the grace by which these acts are performed, whether these salutary acts are easy or difficult to perform. There is no exception to the absolute universality of these principles, since they are indeed of the metaphysical order. They concern the creature's act considered as a free act, and not as a difficult act. From this point of view, intrinsically and infallibly efficacious grace was required for the salutary act as well in the state of innocence for men and angels, as in the present state. In other words, it is required not only on the ground of infirmity, but also on the ground of dependence, by reason of the creature's dependence in each of its acts upon God, who is the most universal cause of all things that come into existence, as to whatever reality and goodness is in them.

St. Thomas had affirmed this intrinsic efficacy of the divine decrees when he said that the divine consequent or efficacious will concerns the good that happens or will happen at the present moment, and that everything that God wills by this will happens infallibly, whether it is a question of acts easy or difficult to perform: "Whatever God simply wills takes place; although what He wills antecedently may not take place." [1]

This intrinsic and infallible efficacy of grace is to be understood, according to the teaching of the Thomists, not as a moral motion that influences the will by way of objective attraction (for only God seen face to face could infallibly attract our will), but it is to be understood as a motion that applies our will to posit its act vitally and freely,[2] and for this reason in opposition to moral motion, it is called *physical premotion*.[3] The Thomists even say that this motion is predetermining, in so far as it infallibly guarantees the execution

---

[1] *Summa theol.*, Ia, q. 19, a. 6 ad 1um. The eighth article of this question completes the doctrine of this article as regards the transcendent efficacy of the divine will, which extends even to the free mode of our acts.

[2] *Ibid.*, Ia, q. 105, a. 4, 5.

[3] Consult *God, His Existence and His Nature*, II, 152, no. 85, for the meaning given by Father Sertillanges, O.P., to these two words, "physical premotion." (Tr.)

of the predetermining eternal decree. It is not a formal but a causal determination, which means that it infallibly moves the will to determine itself in such a way that the result of the deliberation is a salutary act. Then the determination of the will is no longer causal, but formal and completed. What would be a contradiction, would be to say that the will is formally determined before it is formally determined.[4]

On these points all the Thomists are agreed, from the strictest, such as Bannez, Lemos, and Alvarez, to the mildest among them, such as Gonzalez de Albeda, who defended a special theory about sufficient grace.[5] We can inform ourselves of their views by reading their commentaries on St. Thomas.[6] Of more recent date are the articles on sufficient grace by Father Guillermin, O.P.,[7] who, with Gonzalez de Albeda and Massoulié, goes as far as he can in eliminating the difference between sufficient grace and efficient grace, maintaining, however, that only this latter infallibly removes the obstacles to the good consent of the will.[8]

THE PRINCIPLE OF PREDILECTION

All the Thomists, even Gonzalez, Massoulié, and Father Guillermin, defend most firmly and as a necessary consequence the principle of predilection, that "no one thing would be better than another unless it were loved more and helped more by God." All admit the absolute universality of this principle both for the state of innocence and for the present state, and this whether it be a question of acts easy or difficult to perform, of the initial or final act, or whether

---

[4] On this point see the third part of this book, chap. 8.

[5] See Appendix I (pp. 341 ff.).

[6] Consult in particular John of St. Thomas, Gonet, Contenson, Massoulié, Salmanticenses, Gotti, Goudin, and Billuart on the *Summa theologica*, Ia, q.14, a.8, 13; q.19, a.6, 8; q.23, a.4, 5; Ia IIae, q.109 ff.

[7] Cf. *Revue Thomiste* (1901–03).

[8] See also Father V. Carro, O.P., "De Soto a Bannez" in the *Ciencia Tomista*, 1928, pp. 145–78. Dr. Fred. Stegmüller: "Francisco de Victoria y la doctrina de la gracia en la escuela salmantina," Barcelona, pp. 227–44.

it be for the beginning or continuation of the act. We cannot dwell longer here on this point, which we have discussed at length elsewhere.[9]

THE GRATUITY OF PREDESTINATION

It is by the light of the foregoing principles that the Thomists who wrote after the Council of Trent explain the articles of St. Thomas on predestination.[10] They defend the interpretation given by St. Augustine and St. Thomas of St. Paul's teaching on this question, as St. Robert Bellarmine did in his works, but they insist more than he does on the words of St. Paul, who says: "It is God who worketh in you both to will and to accomplish." [11] And again when he says: "For who distinguisheth thee? Or what hast thou that thou hast not received?" [12] Thus they consider the doctrine of the absolute gratuity of predestination to glory as directly founded on the Scripture.

In the explanation of this doctrine they all agree in admitting that predestination to glory is prior to the foreseeing of merits, as the willing of the end is prior to the choice of the means; but that in the order of execution God gives glory as the reward of merits, and in this they combat the opinion of the Protestants and the Jansenists. God freely wills to give glory to His elect, but He does not will to give it gratuitously. They all hold, too, that negative reprobation, by which God wills to permit sin that deprives one of glory, is prior to the foreseeing of demerits. Furthermore, several of them say that original sin fails to explain it in the case of those in whom this sin is remitted. On the contrary, positive reprobation,

---

[9] Cf. "La grace infailliblement efficace par elle-même et les actes salutaires faciles," *Revue Thomiste* (Nov.–Dec., 1925, and March–April, 1926). See Appendix I at the end of this book.
[10] Cf. *Summa theol.*, Ia, q.23.
[11] Phil. 2: 13.
[12] I Cor. 4: 7.

which inflicts the penalty of damnation, is subsequent to the foreseeing of sin, which the penalty presupposes.

The Thomists therefore generally arrange the divine decrees in the following order: (1) God wills by His antecedent will to save all men, even after original sin was committed; and He puts at their disposal graces that are truly sufficient, so that they may keep the commandments; for He never commands what is impossible.[13] (2) God has a special love for and chooses a certain number of angels and men whom He wills efficaciously to save.[14] Predestination to glory thus precedes in the order of intention the foreseeing of merits.[15] (3) God puts at the disposal of the elect intrinsically and infallibly efficacious graces whereby infallibly, although freely, they will merit eternal life and attain it. (4) God, foreseeing in His decrees that His elect will persevere until the end, decides in the order of execution preconceived by Him to grant them glory as a reward of their merits. (5) But as He also foresees in His permissive decrees that others will complete their time of probation in a state of mortal sin, He positively casts them off as reprobates on account of their sins. This order of decrees is founded on the following principles that are admitted not only by the Thomists, but also by Scotus, Bellarmine, and Suarez: that the wise person wills the end before the means, and that if the end is first in the order of intention, it is last in the order of execution.

POINT ON WHICH THE THOMISTS DIFFER

The Thomists agree on these principal theses, and it is only on the notion of negative reprobation that there is a slight difference between them.

Alvarez, the Carmelites of Salamanca, John of St. Thomas,

---

[13] *Loc. cit.*, Ia, q. 19, a.6 ad 1um.
[14] *Ibid.*, Ia, q.23, a.4.
[15] *Ibid.*, a.5.

Gonet, and Contenson admitted that *negative reprobation*, which applies both to angels and to men and which is prior to the foreseeing of merits, consists in the positive exclusion from glory, in this sense that God would have refused them glory as a gift not due to them; then He would have permitted their sins and decided finally to inflict on them the penalty of damnation on account of their sins, which is positive reprobation.[16] We still have in this, in contradistinction to the Protestants, a certain difference between positive and negative reprobation, in that the former is a penalty and the latter is not, but merely the refusal of a pure gift.

However, many Thomists, such as Goudin, Graveson, Billuart, and nearly all at the present day, reject this interpretation of it, and they give three principal reasons for this: (1) because it is too harsh a view and can only with difficulty be reconciled with the divine antecedent will to save all men; (2) because it establishes an extreme parallelism between the two orders of good and evil: God first wills glory to the elect as a pure gift; then, in the order of execution preconceived by Him, He wills it as a reward of their merits; but He cannot will to exclude the others from glory before He foresaw their demerits; for this exclusion cannot be in itself a good and can be willed by God only as a punishment after He foresaw their demerits; (3) this theory of the positive exclusion from glory as being a gift not due, is not to be found in the works of St. Thomas or in those of Capreolus, Cajetan, and Sylvester of Ferrara, who were his first commentators. St. Thomas wrote: "It is part of that providence to permit some to fall away from the end (glory), and this is called reprobation." Toward the end of the argument in this article he says: "Reprobation includes the will to permit a person to fall into sin (negative reprobation), and to impose the punish-

---

[16] See Pohle-Preuss, *Grace*, pp. 217–20, for a criticism of this view especially as regards Gonet. (Tr.)

ment of damnation on account of that sin (positive reproba-
bation)." [17]

Also these last mentioned Thomists and nearly all at the
present day make negative reprobation to consist in the divine
will to permit sin, which merits exclusion from the glory of
heaven. God is not bound, indeed, to conduct effectively all
angels and men to the glory of heaven and to prevent a creature, of itself defectible, from sometimes failing. He can
permit this evil of which He is by no means the cause, and
He permits it in view of a greater good, as being a manifestation of His infinite justice.

THE CLEAR AND OBSCURE POINTS IN THOMISM

The Thomists deduce their doctrine on predestination entirely from the principle of predilection: "Since God's love is
the cause of all good, no one thing would be better than another unless it were loved more by God." [18] This principle
seems in the philosophical order to be an evident corollary
from the principles of causality and of the universal causality
of God who is the author of all good. This same principle is
found variously expressed in the revelation of both the Old
and New Testaments, as for instance: "I will have mercy on
whom I will, and I will be merciful to whom it shall please
Me. . . . For who distinguisheth thee? Or what hast thou
that thou hast not received?" [19]

Thus Thomism remains absolutely faithful to St. Augustine's interpretation of St. Paul's texts. It represents the luminous side of this doctrine, which fully safeguards the truth,
and the absolute universality of the principle of causality in
its relations to the transcendent causality of God who is the

---

[17] *Loc. cit.,* Ia, q. 23, a. 3.
[18] *Ibid.,* Ia, q. 20, a. 3.
[19] Ex. 33: 19; I Cor. 4: 7.

author of nature, grace, and salvation. Thomism absolutely refuses to violate these principles by a conception of human liberty that cannot be proved either by experience or *a priori*. It vigorously refuses to deny or limit the universal laws of being and action which clarify the whole doctrinal synthesis of philosophy and theology, inasmuch as the proper object of theology is God Himself, and it must therefore consider all things, our liberty included, guided by the true concept of God and not by one the reverse of this.

The obscurity in this doctrine is to be found when we consider the mystery from the other angle. This presents itself when it is a question of explaining God's universal will to save, the real possibility for those not elected to keep the commandments, and God's permission of sin, especially of the sin of final impenitence.

To this the Thomists reply that God most certainly wills to save all men, in the sense that He wills to make it really possible for them to fulfil His precepts; but this real possibility or this real power remains obscure for two reasons:

1) Everything is knowable according as it is actual. In every doctrine that admits the principle of potency and act, the act or determination is knowable in itself, although it may not always be easily knowable for us, because of its elevation or spirituality, which escapes our sense perception. On the contrary, undetermined potency, like an undeveloped germ, is not knowable in itself, but only in its relation to act. That is true of prime matter in its relation to form, of the essence of things in its relation to existence, of the intellect not yet informed by the knowable object, of the created free will that can choose this or that, of the real power of doing good which, however real it may be, does not pass over into act. We have fully discussed elsewhere [20] the reason for the obscurity in everything that remains potential.

[20] Cf. *Le sens commun, la philosophie de l'être et les formules dogmatiques*, 4th ed. Paris, 1935, pp. 149–53.

2) This real power of doing good, which does not pass over into act, remains obscure because it includes the divine permission to sin, and sin is a mystery of iniquity more obscure in itself than the mysteries of grace. Whereas these latter are in themselves light, truth, and goodness, the evil of sin is a privation of being, truth, and good.

Nevertheless we see that God, who is the sovereign Good and omnipotent, is by no means the cause of moral evil. As St. Thomas shows,[21] God cannot directly incite us to it without this being a denial of Himself, and neither can it be said that He is indirectly responsible for not having given us sufficient help. He does give this help, but the sinner resists it, and so merits to be deprived of efficacious help, as implied by the prophet Osee speaking in God's name, when he says: "Destruction is thy own, O Israel: thy help is only in Me." [22] Even if, by supposing an impossibility, God willed to be the direct or indirect cause of sin, He could not do so, for deficiency and disorder are not included in the adequate object of His omnipotence. As the eye cannot see sounds, nor the ear hear colors, still more so sovereign Goodness and Omnipotence cannot be the direct or indirect cause of moral evil. God can only permit it, let it happen, and this for a greater good, which we often fail to perceive.

Undoubtedly there is a very great obscurity in the mystery of God permitting the sin of final impenitence. But no one can prove that God by reason of His universal providence is bound to prevent the failure and the irrevocable failure of a creature that is by its nature defectible. God in His justice gives the very real power to avoid this irrevocable failure, but He does not give to all the power to avoid it *de facto*. It is not impossible for Him to permit, especially after many previous sins, that one should resist the final sufficient grace, a resistance whereby the sinner merits to be deprived of the last

[21] *Loc. cit.*, Ia IIae, q.79, a.1, 2.
[22] Osee 13: 9.

efficacious help. This is the great mystery in which is involved the whole obscurity of non-actuated real potency, of free potency, and the whole obscurity of the evil of sin, which is by its nature darkness, privation of light, truth, and goodness.

The solution to the problem of evil is to be found in the following words of St. Augustine: "Since God is supremely good, by no means would He permit any evil in His works unless He were powerful enough and good enough to bring good out of evil." [23] God can permit evil only for a greater good. The manifestation of the splendor of God's infinite justice and mercy is such a greater good that in many respects is beyond our power of comprehension. This is certainly an obscurity, but it is the very one of Christian faith, the obscurity that results from the light being too strong for our weak eyes, "the light inaccessible which God inhabits." [24]

The objections raised against the Thomist doctrine of predestination state in equivalent words that this doctrine destroys human liberty, that it is discouraging, and that it makes God out to be an accepter of persons, which is a kind of injustice. These objections were raised by the Semipelagians against St. Augustine. St. Paul puts the same question in one of his epistles, when he says: "Is there injustice with God? . . . O man, who art thou that repliest against God? . . . Hath not the potter power to make one vessel unto honor, and another unto dishonor?" [25]

Contrary to what the Protestants and the Jansenists say, the Thomists reply that the transcendent efficacy of the divine decrees and grace, far from destroying our liberty or our dominating indifference, actualizes it by causing in us and with us that our acts be performed freely; for this latter is an entity and a good, which comes as a necessary consequence from the source of all reality and good.[26]

[23] Enchir., XI, 24.
[24] I Tim. 6: 16.
[25] Rom. 9: 14, 20, 21.
[26] *Loc. cit.*, Ia, q. 19, a.8; also Bossuet, *Traité du libre arbitre*, chap. 8.

To the second objection the Thomists reply that the doctrine of St. Thomas, far from being discouraging, brings out into bold relief the formal motive of hope, which is not human effort but God's infinite power to help. The formal motive of a theological virtue cannot indeed be something created; and the supernatural effort we make, aroused to this by the efficacy of grace, cannot make this latter efficacious. It is better, therefore, as St. Augustine said, to trust in God, who is sovereignly good and omnipotent, rather than in ourselves, and in our inconstancy and weakness; for, notwithstanding the obscurity in the mystery, we are far surer of the rectitude of the omnipotent God's intentions than of our own. Bossuet laid special stress on this point.[27]

Let no one, therefore, say: If I am predestined, whatever I do I shall be saved; if not, whatever I do I shall be damned. To speak thus is as false and absurd as it is for a farmer to say: If the time for harvest is bound to come, whether I work and sow the seed or not, it will come. The reason for this is that predestination, like providence, concerns not only the end but also the means that will enable us to obtain the end. The Augustinian and Thomist doctrines, far from turning us away from good works, as the Protestant doctrine does, urges us to labor and strive so as to merit eternal life, telling us to put our trust above all things in God, who alone can give us the grace to persevere until the end, as the Council of Trent says.

There would be acceptation of persons and therefore injustice on God's part, if He gave to one more help than to the other, and refused what is due to the latter. But it is not so. Grace is a gratuitous gift and God grants sufficient grace to all those who have the obligation to keep His commandments. If they resist it, they merit thus to be deprived of the efficacious help which was virtually offered to them in the pre-

27 Cf. *Méditations sur l'Fvangile*, II*e* part., 72*e* jour: La prédestination des saints.

ceding grace. Thus, as St. Augustine said, if efficacious grace is granted to a certain one, it is because of God's mercy; if it is refused to a certain other, it is because of His justice.[28]

It remains for us to consider the impenetrable mystery of the intimate reconciliation of the two principles that clarify all these problems. On the one hand, we have the principle of predilection: no one thing would be better than another, unless it were loved more by God; on the other hand, is the principle that God never commands what is impossible, but wills to make it possible for all to keep His commandments.

How are these two principles intimately reconciled? This is beyond the natural powers of either the human or the angelic intellect. It would be necessary for the intellect to have received the light of glory so as to see how infinite justice, mercy, and sovereign liberty are really identified, without being destructive of one another, in the eminence of the Deity, or in the intimate life of God.

The exposition we gave in the beginning of this work [29] of the different theological opinions and their difficulties will enable us the better to understand their classification and comparison. It remains for us to combine the results of those researches, and in this we shall be guided by the light of revelation and the definitions of the Church.

[28] *Loc. cit.*, IIa IIae, q.2, a.5 ad 1um.
[29] See part I, chap. 4.

SYNTHESIS

By way of synthesis we shall combine here the notions, principles, and leading conclusions relative to predestination. In formulating them we shall follow the terminology of St. Thomas [1] and consider as he did: (1) the definition of predestination; (2) its cause; (3) its certainty.

For reprobation we shall also follow his example. With great insight he discusses it not in a question apart, as often was done since his time, but in the very question on predestination. One would destroy the harmonious blend of colors in a picture, and the picture itself, by seeking to separate the black from the white, the light from the shade.

CHAPTER I

How Shall We Define Predestination?

To destine means to ordain a thing or a person to something determinate. In this sense we say that a certain object is destined for the service of the altar and that soldiers about to give up their lives for the safety of an army are destined for death. In this sense the Third Council of Valencia (855), in its third canon, spoke of the predestination of the wicked to death in the following terms: "We unhesitatingly admit the predestination of the elect to life and of the wicked to death." Then it immediately adds: "But God foreknew the malice of the wicked, and because it was their own and He was not the cause of it, He did not predestine it. The punishment, of course, following their demerit, this He foreknew

---

[1] *Summa theol.,* Ia, q.23.

and predestined." [1] This means that God decided from all eternity to inflict the penalty of damnation upon the wicked for their sins, of which He is by no means the cause.

But the Scripture, the Church Fathers, and the theologians generally understand by predestination: the divine preordination of the elect to glory and the means by which they will infallibly obtain it. It is thus St. Augustine defined predestination, when he declared it to be: "The foreknowledge and preparation of those gifts whereby whoever are liberated are most certainly liberated." [2] The first word of this definition, "foreknowledge," was previously explained by St. Augustine in a work of his written about the same time, when he said that: "By predestination God foreknew those things which He was going to do." [3] It is not a question of a purely speculative knowledge that is previous to the divine decree, but of a practical knowledge that is subsequent to this decree.

Hence it follows that the certainty of which St. Augustine speaks is a certainty not only of foreknowledge but also of causality: "He foreknew those things which He was going to do." St. Augustine had already said on this point: "Therefore aid was brought to the infirmity of the human will, so that it might be unchangeably and invincibly influenced by divine grace." [4] And he applied this definition to the predestination of the good angels who received more help than the others. [5]

St. Thomas in like manner defines predestination thus: "The type of the ordering of some persons towards eternal salvation, existing in the divine mind." [6] And he states precisely that the certainty of this preordination is a certainty not only of foreknowledge but also of causality; he says: "The

---

[1] Denz., no. 322.
[2] *De dono persever.*, chap. 14.
[3] *De praed. sanct.*, chap. 10.
[4] *De corrept. et gratia*, XII, 38.
[5] *De civ. Dei*, XII, 9.
[6] *Summa theol.*, Ia, q.23, a.2.

number of the predestined is certain to God, not only by way of knowledge, but also by way of principal preordination."[7] St. Thomas develops this point in another of his works.[8]

From this it follows that predestination, since it is the efficacious ordination of the means of salvation to the end, is an act of the divine intellect which presupposes an act of the will. According to St. Thomas and the Thomists, it is a command that presupposes divine love and election.[9] God, indeed, ordains for Peter in preference to Judas the efficacious means of salvation, because He wills efficaciously to save him, because He loved him with a love of predilection and chose him. St. Thomas expressly says: "Predestination presupposes election in the order of reason; and election presupposes love. The reason of this is that predestination, as stated above (a. 1), is a part of providence. Now providence, as also prudence, is the plan existing in the intellect directing the ordering of some things towards an end. But nothing is directed towards an end unless the will for that end already exists. Whence the predestination of some to eternal salvation presupposes, in the order of reason, that God wills their salvation; and to this belong both election and love: love, inasmuch as He wills them this particular good of eternal salvation . . . ; election, inasmuch as He wills this good to some in preference to others, since He reprobates some, as stated above (a. 3). Election and love, however, are differently ordained in God and in ourselves: because in us the will in loving does not cause good, but we are incited to love by the good that already exists; and therefore we choose someone to love, and so election in us precedes love. In God, however, it is the reverse. For His will, by which in loving He wishes good to someone, is the cause of that good possessed

---

[7] *Ibid.*, a.7.
[8] *De veritate*, q.6, a.3.
[9] *Loc. cit.*, Ia, q.23, a.4; *De veritate*, q.6, a.1.

by some in preference to others. Thus it is clear that love precedes election in the order of reason, and election precedes predestination. Whence all the predestinate are objects of election and love." [10]

This text, which ranks among the most important ones of St. Thomas, proves especially three things: (1) That a predestination only to grace has but the name of true predestination, for it is common both to the elect and to many reprobates who, having once been justified, were afterwards estranged forever from God. (2) To speak of a predestination to grace that would not presuppose predestination to glory, is to forget that God wills the means only for the end, although on His part there are not two successive acts, the one referring to the end, and the other to the means. (3) If in us love follows election, in the sense that we cherish those whom we choose as lovable, which quality we did not cause but found in them; in God, on the contrary, election, since it is prior to predestination, follows love; for His creative and conservative love, far from presupposing lovableness in us, posits this in us, when He grants and preserves in us His natural and supernatural gifts.

This is an application in the highest degree of the principle of predilection: "Since God's love is the cause of goodness in things, no one thing would be better than another, if God did not will greater good for one than for another." [11] That is why in the Scripture and Church Fathers, the predestined are often called the elect and beloved.[12] The following text is worthy of notice: "Come, ye blessed of My Father, possess you the kingdom prepared from the foundation of the world." [13]

It follows, in fine, from the definition of predestination,

10 *Ibid.*, Ia, q.23, a.4.
11 *Ibid.*, Ia, q.20, a.3.
12 Matt. 20: 16; 22: 14; 24: 22; Mark 13: 20, 22; Rom. 8: 33; Col. 3: 12; II Tim. 2: 10.
13 Matt. 25: 34.

as St. Thomas says, that it is, "as regards its object, a part of providence." [14] Providence, indeed, concerns the three orders of grace, nature, and the hypostatic union, all of which are ordained to the same supreme end, which is the manifestation of God's goodness. But, whereas God's general providence does not always attain certain particular ends, for these are not always efficaciously but only antecedently and inefficaciously willed by Him, predestination, to be sure, always and infallibly leads the elect to eternal life, which God efficaciously wills for them.

IS THIS CONCEPTION OF PREDESTINATION THE KIND WHICH SCRIPTURE SPEAKS OF?

This predestination by which God directs infallibly certain persons rather than others to eternal life is affirmed by revelation, whatever the Pelagians and Semipelagians may say about it. Our Lord Jesus Christ said to those who murmured at what He was saying to them, that "no man can come to Me, except the Father, who hath sent Me, draw him; and I will raise him up in the last day." [15] On several occasions He speaks of the elect,[16] and He says that no one will be able to snatch them out of His Father's hand. "My sheep hear My voice. . . . And I give them life everlasting; and they shall not perish for ever, and no man shall pluck them out of My hand. That which My Father hath given Me is greater than all: and no one can snatch them out of the hand of My Father." [17] This shows that God not only knows beforehand who are the elect, but that He also loved them, chose them in preference to others, and that He keeps them infallibly in His hand, which means that they are protected by His omnipotence.

14 *Loc. cit.*, Ia, q.23, a.1.
15 John 6: 44.
16 Matt. 20: 16; 22: 14; 24: 22; Mark 13: 20, 22.
17 John 10: 27–29.

This is precisely St. Paul's point of view, for he says: "And we know that to them that love God, all things work together unto good, to such as, according to His purpose, are called to be saints. For whom He foreknew, He also predestinated. . . . And whom He predestinated, them He also called. And whom He called, them He also justified. And whom He justified, them He also glorified." [18] These are the infallible effects of eternal predestination. Let us note concerning the words "whom He foreknew" in the text just quoted that it is not said: at least those whose conditional merits He foreknew, and that this same expression, "whom He foreknew," means "whom He knew beforehand with a look of benevolence," and it applies not only to adults but also to the children who will die soon after baptism, so as to be unable to merit their reward. St. Augustine said on this subject: "By predestination God foreknew those things which He was going to do." [19] Later on St. Thomas understood this text to mean: "Those whom He benevolently foresaw, He chose and predestined," and he saw the normal sequence in these acts, in which the final practical judgment is first; then comes election, and afterward command followed by its execution: in other words, vocation, justification, glorification.[20] These acts, in St. Paul's judgment, presuppose a divine intention expressed by him in the passage just quoted, for he says: "Whom He foreknew, He also predestinated to be made conformable to the image of His Son; that He might be the first-born amongst many brethren." [21]

Such is the divine intention that inspires all these acts; it is in conjunction with that of God's glory and the manifestation of His goodness as stated by St. Paul: "That He might show the riches of His glory on the vessels of mercy, which

18 Rom. 8: 28–30.
19 *De praed. sanct.*, chap. 10, no. 19; cf. *De dono persever.*, chap. 18, no. 47.
20 *Loc. cit.*, Ia, q.23, a.1, 4.
21 Rom. 8: 29.

He hath prepared unto glory." [22] Just as plainly did St. Paul refer to election, for he writes: "He (God) chose us in Him (Christ) before the foundation of the world, that we should be holy. . . ." [23] He insisted on the sovereignly free character of this election, saying: "In whom we also are called by lot, being predestinated according to the purpose of Him who worketh all things according to the counsel of His will." [24] St. Augustine, too, was able to write against the Semipelagians as follows: "No one who sought to avoid falling into error, could argue against this predestination which we defend in accordance with Holy Scripture." [25]

Moreover, evidently there is not anything done by God in time which was not preordained by Him from all eternity; otherwise He would begin to will something in time, or something would happen by chance apart from any intention or permission on His part, which is absurd. Now, it is God who, in time, brings certain persons to eternal happiness, which is beyond the natural powers of any created being to attain. He therefore preordained from all eternity to bring them to it, and this is predestination. It is therefore an established fact that predestination is beyond the possibility of any doubt. Furthermore, without predestination no one would attain eternal happiness; because every good comes from God, especially salvation and the culmination of this, which is eternal happiness; for this is of the supernatural order, and is absolutely beyond the natural powers of any created or creatable being.

The Semipelagians raised the following objection: if there is an infallible predestination, then I am either predestined or not. If I am, whatever I do I shall infallibly be saved; if I am not, whatever I do I shall infallibly be damned. I can

22 *Ibid.,* 9: 23; cf. Eph. 1: 12.
23 Eph. 1: 4.
24 *Ibid.,* 1: 11.
25 *De dono persever.,* chap. 19.

therefore do whatever I please. St. Augustine replied at once to the Semipelagians, pointing out that if this reasoning were of any value, it would prevent us from admitting not only the fact of predestination, but also that of God's foreknowledge, which is admitted, however, by the Semipelagians.[26] The Thomists replied in the same way to a similar objection raised against them by the Molinists.

Several saints went on further to remark that if there were any foundation for this Semipelagian dilemma, the demons by the natural vigor of their intellect would grasp the truth of this far better than we do and would no longer take the trouble to tempt us. There are even some saints who replied to the demon by turning against him this sophism, whereby he intended to plunge them into despair, and saying: "If I am not predestined, even without your efforts to have me lose my soul, I shall be lost; and if I am predestined, whatever you do, I shall be saved."

The decisive reply to this objection is given by St. Thomas. He states that providence, of which predestination is a part, does not suppress the secondary causes and concerns not only the final effect, but also the means or the secondary causes that must produce this effect. God does not predestine, there-fore, the adults to the end, that is, to glory, without predestining them to the means, that is, to salutary and meritorious good works whereby this end can and must be obtained by them.[27]

The Semipelagian sophism is as false as that of the plow-man who would say: If God has foreseen that next summer I shall have wheat, whether I sow the seed or not, I shall have it. "Let us not deny what is very clear," says St. Augustine, "because we do not understand what is hidden."[28] In

---

[26] *Ibid.*, chap. 15.
[27] *Loc. cit.*, Ia, q.23, a.8.
[28] *De dono persever.*, chap. 14.

truth, according to the dispensation of Providence that concerns the end and the means, without violating liberty, as wheat is obtained only by the sowing of the seed, so adults obtain eternal life only by the performance of good works. It is in this sense that Peter says: "Labor the more, that by good works you may make sure your calling and election." [29] Although election is eternal on God's part, yet in the order of execution, it is in time and by means of good works that this is effected in us. We must not confuse the two vistas of time and eternity. By God's eternal predestination grace is given to the elect, not that they may let themselves get into a state of spiritual torpor, but it is given precisely for the purpose that they may work out their salvation. As St. Augustine says, it is given for them to act, not for them to remain inactive. Such are the principal consequences deduced from the definition and existence of predestination.

HOW SHALL WE DEFINE REPROBATION?

The term reprobation is commonly used in reference to our rejection of an error of judgment by the intellect, and in reference to the moral disorder which we reject by a judgment of the intellect and by an aversion of the will. In this sense the Scripture speaks of those whom God reprobated from all eternity. Thus St. Paul writes: "I chastise my body . . . lest perhaps, when I have preached to others, I myself should become a castaway." [30] The Scripture also makes use of equivalent words and expressions, such as: "cursed," [31] "vessels of wrath and dishonor," [32] "child of hell," [33] "son of

29 II Pet. 1: 10.
30 I Cor. 9: 27.
31 Matt. 25: 41.
32 Rom. 9: 21 f.
33 Matt. 23: 15.

perdition." [34] The fact that certain persons are reprobated has therefore the certainty of faith.

St. Thomas explains it by remarking that it belongs to God's universal providence to permit for the general good of the universe the failure or deficiency of certain defectible creatures, otherwise spoken of as physical and moral evil. Thus Providence permits the death of the gazelle for the life of the lion, and the crime of persecutors for the heroic patience of the martyrs. Now intellectual creatures, since they are by nature defectible, are ordained to eternal life by divine providence. It pertains, therefore, to this latter to permit, for a greater good, that certain persons fail and do not attain this end. This is called negative reprobation, quite distinct from positive reprobation that inflicts the penalty of damnation for the sin of final impenitence. [35]

Nothing, however, happens that God from all eternity has not either willed, if it is a good, or has not permitted, if it is an evil. Now, according to revelation, certain persons are lost through their own fault and are eternally punished. [36] This would not happen, therefore, unless God from all eternity had permitted their failure to do their duty—of which, moreover, He is by no means the cause—and if He had not decided to punish them for it.

Is reprobation simply the denial of predestination? It implies the divine permission of the sin of final impenitence (negative reprobation), and the divine will to inflict the penalty of damnation for this sin (positive reprobation). If reprobation were simply the denial of predestination, it would not be an act of providence, and the penalty of damnation would not be inflicted by God. St. Thomas says: "As predestination includes the will to confer grace and glory; so also reprobation includes the will to permit a person to

---

[34] John 17: 12.
[35] *Loc. cit.*, Ia, q.23, a.3.
[36] Matt. 25: 41.

fall into sin, and to impose the punishment of damnation on account of that sin." [37]

Having defined predestination and reprobation, we must now seek their cause.

[37] *Loc. cit.,* Ia, q.23, a.3.

CHAPTER II

The Cause of Predestination

What is the cause of the predestination and of the election whereby God chose certain persons in preference to others for the purpose of bringing them to eternal life?

The liberty of the divine election in the Old Testament comes to our mind. Seth was elected, and not Cain; then Noe, also Sem in preference to his two brothers; after this, Abraham, Isaac in preference to Ismael, and finally Jacob (Israel) was chosen. How does the case stand now as regards each of the elect?

We saw from the definitions of the Church in the councils of Carthage (418) and Orange (529), directed against the Pelagians and Semipelagians, that the cause of predestination cannot be the naturally good works of certain persons which are foreseen by God, or the naturally good beginning of the will in performing a salutary act (*initium salutis*), or the perseverance in good works until death without a special grace.[1]

According to the same definitions of the councils of Orange [2] and Trent,[3] which refer to the special grace of final perseverance, it is also beyond doubt that the cause of predestination to glory cannot be because God foresees that certain persons without a special grace would retain their supernatural merits until death: "If anyone saith that one justified is able to persevere without the special help of God in the

[1] Denz., no. 183.
[2] *Ibid.*
[3] *Ibid.*, nos. 806, 826, 832.

justice received; or that with this help is not able; let him be anathema." [4] St. Thomas, moreover, proves inadmissible the opinion of those who say that God chose these particular persons in preference to others because He foreknew that they would make good use of the grace received (at least at the moment of death), just as the king gives a fine horse to a rider because he foresees the good use he will make of it. St. Thomas points out that this opinion cannot be admitted; for we cannot eliminate from our salutary acts a part of the good as not coming from the primary cause that is the source of all good; therefore the good use of grace in the elect is itself an effect of predestination, and cannot therefore be its cause or motive. Furthermore, St. Thomas even says: "Whatsoever is in man disposing him towards salvation, is all included under the effect of predestination," [5] and therefore this includes even the free determination of his salutary acts.

Is this reply of St. Thomas a cogent reply to the Molinist opinion that maintains the cause of our predestination to glory to be because God foresaw our merits? We leave this for our readers to judge.

Let us recall that, according to the principle of predilection, the cause of predestination and election whereby God chose certain persons in preference to others so as to bring them to eternal life, is not the fact of their foreseen merits but pure mercy, as all the Thomists, Augustinians, Scotists, Bellarmine, too, and Suarez say, who on this point are in agreement with St. Augustine and St. Thomas.

The foundation of the principle of predilection is not only an established fact of the natural order, but it is also a revealed truth. The Old and New Testaments make use of most varying expressions to tell us that without exception all good comes from God, from God's love: that there is no

---

[4] *Ibid.*, no. 832; cf. nos. 804, 806.
[5] *Summa theol.*, Ia, q.23, a.5.

good which God by His love has not efficaciously willed: that everything which God wills effectively comes to pass: that no evil, either physical or moral, happens and happens in this particular place rather than that without God's permission. These are the most universal of principles, and they dominate the whole question. Reference was made to them at the opening of the Council of Thuzey (860) in the following terms: "Whatsoever the Lord pleased He hath done, in heaven and in earth,[6] the final perseverance of Peter, for instance, in preference to that of Judas. For nothing is done in heaven or in earth, except what it has pleased Him to do if it is a good or what He has justly permitted to happen if it is an evil." [7]

We find this fundamental truth expressed in very many texts both of the Old and New Testaments. Thus we have: "Lord, Thou hast wrought all our works for us"; [8] "Thou art Lord of all and there is none that can resist Thy majesty"; [9] "O Lord, king of gods, and of all power . . . turn his (king's) heart to the hatred of our enemy"; [10] "And God changed the king's spirit into mildness"; [11] "As the division of waters, so the heart of the king is in the hand of the Lord: whithersoever He will He shall turn it"; [12] "As the potter's clay is in his hand . . . so man is in the hand of Him that made him"; [13] "I will cause you to walk in My commandments"; [14] "For it is God who worketh in you, both to will and to accomplish." [15] Several of these texts and similar ones are quoted by the Council of Orange [16] to show that every

[6] Ps. 134: 6.
[7] *PL*, CXXVI, 123.
[8] Is. 26: 12.
[9] Esther 13: 11.
[10] *Ibid.*, 14: 12 f.
[11] *Ibid.*, 15: 11.
[12] Prov. 21: 1.
[13] Eccli. 33: 13.
[14] Ezech. 36: 27.
[15] Phil. 2: 13.
[16] Denz., nos. 176–200.

good comes from God and that nothing good happens without His having efficaciously willed it.

This foundation for the principle of predilection, to which the Council of Thuzey refers, is not only often expressed in Scripture, but the very principle itself is formulated in equivalent words by St. Paul, when he says: "For what distinguisheth thee? Or what hast thou that thou hast not received?" [17] "Not that we are sufficient to think anything of ourselves, as of ourselves: but our sufficiency is from God." [18] St. Paul even finds that the principle of predilection is expressed in the Book of Exodus,[19] for he writes: "What shall we say then? Is there injustice with God? God forbid! For He saith to Moses: I will have mercy on whom I will have mercy. And I will show mercy, to whom I will show mercy. So then it is not of him that willeth, nor of him that runneth, but of God that showeth mercy." [20] We read, too, in the Book of Psalms: "He saved me because He was well pleased with me"; [21] "The salvation of the just is from the Lord"; [22] "The mercies of the Lord that we are not consumed." [23] Temporal salvation is the image of eternal salvation. We read, too, in the Book of Tobias these admirable words announcing what will be explicitly made known to us in the fulness of revelation: "He hath chastised us for our iniquities, and He shall save us for His own mercy." [24]

Our Lord Himself spoke in the same sense: "I confess to Thee, O Father . . . because Thou hast hid these things from the wise and prudent and hast revealed them to little ones. Yea, Father: for so hath it seemed good in Thy sight." [25]

[17] I Cor. 4: 7.
[18] II Cor. 3: 5.
[19] Ex. 33: 19.
[20] Rom. 9: 14–16.
[21] Ps. 17: 20.
[22] *Ibid.*, 36: 39.
[23] Lam. 3: 22.
[24] Tob. 13: 5.
[25] Matt. 11: 25.

According to this text, the little ones received more light and help because such was God's good pleasure, who loved them more. In like manner, our Lord said to His disciples: "Fear not, little flock, for it hath pleased your Father to give you a kingdom." [26] Of the elect our Lord said again that no one can snatch them from His Father's hand,[27] which means, without reference to the foreseen merits of the elect, the Father's special love for them and the infallibly efficacious help which He will grant them, so as to have them merit until death and save them. "None of them is lost but the son of perdition." [28]

Finally, in St. Paul's epistles the notions of election and predestination are more clearly defined, and this throws new light on the motive of predestination, as in the following text: "Blessed be the God and Father of our Lord Jesus Christ, who hath blessed us with spiritual blessings in heavenly places, in Christ. As He chose us in Him before the foundation of the world, that we should be holy and un-spotted in His sight in charity. Who hath predestinated us unto the adoption of children through Jesus Christ unto Himself, according to the purpose of His will, unto the praise of the glory of His grace. . . . In whom we also are called by lot, being predestinated according to the purpose of Him who worketh all things according to the counsel of His will." [29]

This text, as many theologians, like Bellarmine and Suarez, have remarked along with the Thomists, contains three principal assertions: (1) God chose us, not because He fore-saw that, if we were placed in certain circumstances, with a certain sufficient grace, we would become holy rather than others who were equally helped; but He chose us that we may be holy. (2) God thus chose us and consequently pre-

26 Luke 12: 32.
27 John 10: 28 ff.
28 *Ibid.*, 17: 12.
29 Eph. 1: 3–6, 11.

destined us, according to the purpose or decree of His will, according to His good pleasure, which is again pointed out in verse eleven. That denotes the order of intention, in which the end precedes the means. (3) Unto the praise and glory of His grace, so as to bring into prominence in the order of execution, not the power of the created free will but the glory of His divine grace, in accordance with the following text: "It is not of him that willeth, nor of him that runneth, but of God that showeth mercy." [30]

Moreover, it cannot be merely predestination to grace that is implied in these texts, since this latter is common both to the elect and to the reprobates. It is a question of true predestination that includes the decree to grant not only the grace of justification, but the special gift of final perseverance, which, strictly speaking, cannot be merited by us. On this point the Council of Trent, quoting St. Paul,[31] says: "God is able to establish him who standeth that he stand perseveringly, and to restore him who falleth." [32] It also recalls to mind these words of the Apostle: "Wherefore, my dearly beloved . . . with fear and trembling work out your salvation. For it is God who worketh in you, both to will and to accomplish, according to His good will." [33]

Finally, almost all theologians who admitted the absolute gratuity of predestination to salvation appealed in support of this doctrine to St. Paul's Epistle to the Romans [34] in which, speaking of the predestination of the Gentiles and the reprobation of the Jews, he formulates general principles that are evidently applicable, as Father Lagrange remarks,[35] to individuals, in accordance with the principle that "God works in us [in each of us] both to will and to accomplish,

[30] Rom. 9: 16.
[31] *Ibid.*, 14: 4.
[32] Denz., 806.
[33] Phil. 2: 12 f.
[34] See chaps. 8, 9, 11.
[35] *Com. sur l'épître aux Rom.*, chap. 9.

according to His good will." [36] Moreover, St. Paul even says: "That He might show the riches of His glory on the vessels of mercy which He hath prepared unto glory. Whom also He hath called, not only of the Jews but also of the Gentiles." [37] From this we see that he has in mind not only nations but also individuals who will become, as he expressed it, vessels of glory or of ignominy. In like manner, when he says: "Whom He predestined, them He also called . . . justified . . . and glorified," [38] this refers to individuals.

We saw that in the words of the preceding verse, "Whom He foreknew and predestined to be made conformable to the image of His Son," the expression "whom He foreknew" refers to those whom He previously looked upon with benevolence, which is applicable even to children who died so soon after baptism so as not to have had time for meriting. The expression "whom He foreknew" does not mean therefore "whose merits He foreknew."

What then are the general principles formulated here by St. Paul on the question of predestination? He defined it as "purpose of God," [39] "Purpose of God according to election," [40] "according to the election of grace," [41] which means a purpose or resolution according to a gratuitous election, for he adds: "And if by grace, it is not now by works, otherwise grace is no more grace." [42]

St. Paul explains, too, in this epistle the properties and effects of predestination, for he says: "All things work together unto good, to such as according to His purpose, are called to be saints." [43] And immediately afterward he enumerates the three effects of predestination: vocation, justifica-

36 Phil. 2: 13.
37 Rom. 9: 23 f.
38 *Ibid.*, 8: 30.
39 *Ibid.*, 8: 28.
40 *Ibid.*, 9: 11.
41 *Ibid.*, 11: 5.
42 *Ibid.*, 11: 6.
43 *Ibid.*, 8: 28.

tion, and glorification, which, strictly speaking, apply to individuals. Finally, he points out its infallible efficacy, which he attributes not to the effort made by our will, but to God's omnipotence, saying: "If God be for us who is against us?" [44] As for the cause of predestination, he does not ascribe this to the foreknowledge of our merits, but to God's special mercy, saying with Moses: "I will have mercy on whom I will have mercy. And I will show mercy, to whom I will show mercy." [45] Hence it follows that "it is not of him that willeth, nor of him that runneth, but of God that showeth mercy." [46]

Finally, he proves this last assertion by an irrefutable principle which is the principle of predilection in a new form, for he writes: "Who hath first given to Him, and recompense shall be made Him. For of Him and by Him and in Him, are all things." [47] It is always to this supreme principle that he appeals, as when he asks: "For who distinguisheth thee? Or what hast thou that thou hast not received?" [48]

What St. Paul means in all these texts, finds its confirmation in his answer to the objections which he puts to himself, and which were taken up later on by the Pelagians and Semipelagians: "Hath not the potter power over the clay, of the same lump, to make one vessel unto honor and another unto dishonor? What if God, willing to show His wrath, His avenging justice, and to make His power known, endured with much patience vessels of wrath, fitted for destruction, that He might show the riches of His glory on the vessels of mercy which He hath prepared unto glory, where is the injustice?" [49]

St. Augustine and St. Thomas saw in all these texts of

---

[44] *Ibid.,* 8: 31.
[45] *Ibid.,* 9: 15.
[46] *Ibid.,* 9: 16.
[47] *Ibid.,* 11: 35 f.
[48] I Cor. 4: 7.
[49] Rom. 9: 21-23.

St. Paul the gratuity of predestination to eternal life. In other words, they perceived the motive of this to be a special mercy. St. Augustine often said that if God grants final perseverance to this particular person, it is by reason of His mercy; if He does not grant it to that other person, it is because of just punishment of sins, in the generality of cases repeated, and which have estranged the soul from God.[50] St. Thomas [51] and St. Prosper declared the same in these words retained by the Council of Quierzy: "That certain persons are saved, is the gift of Him who saves; but that certain persons are lost, is the fault of those who are lost." [52]

This explains the attitude of theologians such as Tanquerey who, after giving us an analysis of what St. Paul said on predestination, writes as follows: "Moreover, all these utterances are nothing else but the very thesis of the Thomists; for they presuppose that God of His good pleasure elects us to glory, and that all good things are the result of this election, even our merits." [53]

In addition to these reasons which are taken from Holy Scripture and which constitute the foundation of St. Thomas' doctrine on the cause of predestination,[54] we have the argument of theological reasoning which the holy Doctor gives as follows: "Predestination is a part of providence. Now providence, as also prudence, is the plan existing in the intellect directing the ordering of some things towards an end. But nothing is directed towards an end unless the will for that end already exists. Whence the predestination of some to eternal salvation presupposes, in the order of reason, that God wills their salvation; and to this belong both election and love." [55]

50 *De praed. sanct.*, VIII.
51 *Summa theol.*, Ia, q.23, a.5 ad 3um; IIa IIae, q.2, a.5 ad 1um.
52 Denz., no. 318.
53 *Synopsis theol. dogmat.*, Vol. II, De Deo uno, p. 325, ed. 1926.
54 *Loc. cit.*, Ia, q.23, a.5.
55 *Ibid.*, Ia, q.23, a.4.

In other words, whoever acts wisely, wills the end before the means. Now God acts with sovereign wisdom, and grace is the means with reference to glory or salvation. Therefore God first wills glory to His elect, and then the grace so as to have them attain it. St. Thomas, as we see, was in advance of Scotus in the presentation of this theological argument, and on this point Bellarmine and Suarez are in agreement with him.

This is one of the points that illustrate most clearly how St. Thomas and the greatest theologians along with him fear neither logic nor mystery. It is logic itself that leads them to the transcendence of the mystery, which is an object of contemplation far above reasoning.

Thus the motive of predestination becomes clear and, at the same time, that of negative reprobation as explained by St. Thomas in the following words: "The reason for the predestination of some, and reprobation of others, must be sought for in the goodness of God. Thus He is said to have made all things through His goodness, so that the divine goodness might be represented in things. Now it is necessary that God's goodness, which in itself is one and undivided, should be manifested in many ways in His creation; because creatures in themselves cannot attain to the simplicity of God. Thus it is that for the completion of the universe, there are required different grades of being; some of which hold a high and some a low place in the universe. That this multiformity of grades may be preserved in things, God allows some evils, lest many good things should never happen. Let us then consider the whole of the human race, as we consider the whole universe. God wills to manifest His goodness in men; in respect to those whom He predestines, by means of His mercy, in sparing them; and in respect of others, whom He reprobates, by means of His justice, in punishing them. This is the reason why God elects some and rejects others. To this the Apostle refers, saying (Rom. 9: 22–23): 'What if God, willing to show His wrath, that is, the vengeance of His justice, and to make His power known, endured, that is, permitted with much patience vessels of wrath, fitted for destruction; that He might show the riches of His glory on the vessels of mercy, which He hath prepared unto glory.' And elsewhere the same Apostle wrote (II Tim. 2: 20): 'But in a great house there are not only vessels of gold and silver, but also of wood and earth; and some, indeed, unto honour, but some unto dishonour.' Yet why He chooses some for glory, and reprobates others has no reason except the divine will. Whence Augustine says (Tract. XXVI in Joan.): 'Why He draws one, and another He draws not, seek not to judge if thou dost not wish to err.' Thus, too, in the things of nature, a reason can be assigned, since primary matter is altogether uniform, why one part of it was fashioned by God from the beginning under the form of fire, another under the form of earth, that there might be a diversity of species in things of nature. Yet why this particular part of matter is under this particular form, and that under another, depends upon the simple will of God; as from the simple will of the artificer it depends that this stone is in this part of the wall and that in another; although the plan requires that some stones should be in this place and some in that place. Neither on this account can there be said to be injustice in God, if He prepares unequal lots for not unequal things. This would be altogether contrary to the notion of justice, if the effect of predestination were granted as a debt, and not gratuitously. In things which are given gratuitously a person can give more or less, just as he pleases provided he deprives nobody of his due, without any infringement of justice. This is what the master of the house said: 'Take what is thine and go thy way. Is it not lawful for me to do what I will?' " (Matt. 20: 14–15.) [56]

What is due to each one, what God refuses to nobody, is

[56] *Ibid.*, Ia, q. 23, a.5 ad 3um.

sufficient grace for salvation, which makes it really possible to keep the commandments, for God never commands what is impossible. As for efficacious grace, especially the grace of final perseverance, this He grants by reason of His mercy. But of the adults, only those are deprived of it who through their own fault refuse to accept it. The doctors of the Church often pointed this out in the comparison they drew between the death of the good thief and that of Judas who resisted the final appeal of grace.

The general motive for predestination is, therefore, the manifestation of God's goodness that assumes the form of mercy in pardoning; and the motive for the predestination of this particular person rather than a certain other, is God's good pleasure. If it be so, how shall we formulate in exact terms the motive for either positive or negative reprobation?

CHAPTER III

The Motive for Reprobation

First of all it is clear that the positive reprobation of angels and men presupposes that their demerits were foreseen; for God can will to inflict the penalty of damnation only for failure in doing one's duty. In this all Catholics agree that God wills not the death of the sinner, but that he be converted and live.[1] The theologians often quote these words of God uttered by the prophet: "Destruction is thy own, O Israel: thy help is only in Me." [2]

Moreover, it is evident that God can will a thing only in so far as it is good; and for punishment to be good and just, this presupposes a sin. In this it differs from reward, which is good in itself, regardless of merits. Reward, in virtue of its being an excellent gift, can be willed in the order of intention before foreseen merits, although in the order of execution and in virtue of its being a reward, it depends upon them. We cannot say as much about punishment, nor look for an absolute parallelism between good and evil.

The motive for negative reprobation, taken absolutely or in a general way, is not the foreseen demerits of the reprobates; for this negative reprobation is nothing else but the divine permission of these demerits, and therefore it logically precedes instead of following the foreseeing of them. Without this divine permission, these demerits would not happen in time, and from all eternity they would remain unforeseen. We must say, in accordance with the text just quoted

1 Ezech. 33: 11; II Pet. 3: 9.
2 Osee 13: 9.

from St. Thomas,[3] that the motive for negative reprobation is that God willed to manifest His goodness not only by means of His mercy, but also by means of His justice, and that it belongs to Providence to permit certain defectible beings to fail and certain evils to happen, without which there would be no good things of a higher order.

If we ask why God chose this person and not that other, there is, as we have seen from St. Thomas, no reason for this but simply the divine will which is thus the motive both for individual predestination and the negative reprobation of this particular person rather than that other. In other words, among equally defectible rational creatures, why the defection of this particular person is permitted rather than of a certain other, there is no reason for this but the divine will. And somehow all Catholic theologians admit it, for all of them must admit at least that God could have preserved intact those who are lost, and permitted the fall of those who are saved.

The principal difficulty that confronts us here is this: the will to manifest the splendor of avenging justice before having foreseen the defection, is to will the punishment before the defection, and this is an injustice. Now, such would be the case according to the preceding explanation. Therefore it is inadmissible.

The Thomists reply by denying the major, because it confounds infinite justice with the punishment that is a manifestation of this justice. As a matter of fact, God does not will to permit the defection because of His love to chastise, for that would be repugnant to justice. But He permits it as a manifestation of His infinite justice and of the right of sovereign Good to be loved above all things, and He afterward inflicts the punishment on account of the defection.

In this way the punishment is but a finite means of manifesting infinite justice, and it is a means that is not an inter-

3 *Summa theol.*, Ia, q.23, a.5 ad 3um.

mediate end willed before the permission of the defection, for it is good and just to punish only for a defection. Therefore, most certainly God wills to permit sin, not from love of imposing a finite chastisement, but from love of His infinite justice, or from love of His sovereign goodness that has a right to be loved above all things. Finally, when God wills to manifest His avenging justice, this truly presupposes the possibility of sin, but not as yet that He permits or foresees it. The case is quite different when He wills to inflict the punishment of damnation.

Still the objection is raised that "God forsakes not those who have been justified, unless He be first forsaken by them," as the Council of Trent says.[4] Now this would be so if He willed to permit the defection or the sin before He foresaw it.

To this we must reply: (1) This text of the Council is taken from St. Augustine,[5] who admitted, however, that negative reprobation or the permission of sin is logically prior to the foreseeing of the same; (2) this text refers not to all men, but to the just, and it means that God does not deprive them of habitual or sanctifying grace except for mortal sin; (3) it means again in a more general way that nobody is deprived of an efficacious grace that is necessary for salvation except through his own fault, for God never commands what is impossible; (4) but this defect, on account of which God refuses efficacious grace, would not happen without God's permission, which is certainly not its cause but its indispensable condition. We must therefore distinguish between God's mere permission of sin, which is evidently prior to the sin permitted, and His refusal of efficacious grace on account of this sin. This refusal is a punishment that presupposes the defect, whereas the defect presupposes the divine permission.

4 Denz., no. 804.
5 *De natura et gratia*, XXVI, 29.

God's permission of sin, which is good in view of the end (for a greater good), implies certainly the non-continuance of the created will in the performance of good at that particular time. This non-continuance, not being something real, is not a good; but neither is it an evil, for it is not the privation of a good that is due to one; it is merely the negation of a good that is not due to one. Undoubtedly God is bound to maintain in existence a spiritual and created will, but He is not bound to maintain in the performance of good this will which by its nature is defectible. If God were bound to do so, sin would never happen, and the sinlessness of Mary would not be a privilege. The non-continuance of our will in the performance of good is not an evil, either of sin or of punishment; it is a non-good: just as nescience is not ignorance, but a negation and not a privation. On the contrary, God's withdrawal of efficacious grace is a punishment, and it is a punishment that presupposes at least a first defection.

We may still say with St. Thomas [6] that, after a first sin, the divine permission of a second and a third sin is already a punishment for the first. But we could not say this for God's permission of the first sin, and the Council of Trent just quoted cannot be applied to it.

It is certain that God's permission of the first sin is not subsequent to the foreseeing of it; for He can foresee a defect only in so far as He permits it; and without His permission it would never happen.

As a final objection, we may say that we understand, moreover, God permitting any sin whatever, especially in the life of the elect; for this sin is permitted only for a greater good that concerns them personally, which is to make them more truly humble. But how are we to explain God permitting the sin of final impenitence?

In reply to this we must say that as a rule the sin of final impenitence is permitted by God only as a punishment for

6 *Loc. cit.,* Ia IIae, q.79, a.3.

many other defects and for finally resisting His last appeal. St. Thomas writes: "The cause of grace being withheld is not only the man who raises an obstacle to grace; but God who, of His own accord, withholds His grace." [7]

Certainly there is a very great mystery in this, the most obscure of all those that concern us here; for the mysteries of iniquity are obscure in themselves, whereas the mysteries of grace are supremely luminous in themselves and obscure only for us. There is something that surpasses understanding in this, that God permits the final impenitence of some, for instance, of the bad thief rather than of the other, as a punishment for previous grave defects and for a greater good, which includes the manifestation of the splendor of infinite justice.

We must acknowledge that this proposition is the most obscure of all those formulated by us. But to show that no believer can deny it, we must take into direct consideration the contradictory proposition, and we shall see that no intellect can succeed in proving it. No one can establish the truth of this assertion, namely: God cannot permit the final impenitence of a sinner, of the bad thief, for instance, as a punishment for his preceding defects and in manifestation of the divine infinite justice. This assertion cannot be proved. Moreover, to deny the possibility of God's permission of sin, would be to deny the possibility of sin: *contra factum non valet ratio.*

On the splendor of divine justice, it is worth noting what St. Thomas says, when asking whether angels grieve for the ills of those whom they guard. He replies in the negative, and the reason He gives is: "because their will cleaves entirely to the ordering of divine justice; while nothing happens in the world save what is effected or permitted by divine justice." [8] The author of the Imitation sets forth this splen-

[7] *Ibid.,* q.79, a.3.
[8] *Ibid.,* Ia, q.113, a.7.

dor of divine justice when he says: "Be now solicitous and sorrowful because of thy sins, that at the day of judgment thou mayest be secure with the blessed. . . . Then shall he stand to judge them, who doth now humbly submit himself to the censures of men. Then shall the poor and humble have great confidence, but the proud man shall be compassed with fear on every side." [9]

The question has been raised whether original sin is a sufficient motive for reprobation. Evidently not so, if it is a question of reprobates who have been freed from original sin, although the effects of this sin remain in them, such as concupiscence that inclines one to evil. But the case is not the same for unbaptized children who die before the age of reason. Because of original sin they are deprived of the beatific vision, though they do not have to suffer the punishment of the senses.[10]

Included among the effects of reprobation are: (1) The permission of sins that will not be forgiven; (2) God's refusal of grace; (3) blinding of the intellect; (4) hardening of the heart; (5) the punishment of damnation. Sin itself is not the effect of reprobation, for God is in no way the cause of sin, either directly or indirectly, through lack of help. This lack of help would be neglect on God's part, and this is an absurdity.

As for moral defection that is permitted by God, this serves to show by way of contrast the value and power of divine grace that makes one faithful. It is in this sense that St. Paul said: "God . . . endured with much patience vessels of wrath, fitted for destruction, that He might show the riches of His glory on the vessels of mercy which He hath prepared unto glory." [11] And again, when he says: "Who hath pre-

---

[9] *Imitation*, Bk. I, chap. 24, no. 4.
[10] Denz., nos. 410, 1526.
[11] Rom. 9: 22 f.

destinated us . . . according to the purpose of His will, unto the praise of the glory of His grace." [12]

Having discussed the motives for predestination and reprobation, it remains for us to consider the certainty of these.

[12] Eph. 1: 5 f.

CHAPTER IV

ON THE CERTAINTY OF PREDESTINATION

THIS question can be viewed in two ways: (1) Is predestination a certainty so that its effect will infallibly come to pass? (2) Can we be certain in this life of being predestined?

THE INFALLIBILITY OF PREDESTINATION

Predestination is absolutely certain as regards the infallible positing of its effects, which are vocation, justification, and glorification. Revelation affirms this by the words of our Lord in the texts already quoted, which are: "Now this is the will of the Father who sent Me: that of all that He hath given Me, I should lose nothing. . . . My sheep hear My voice . . . and they shall not perish for ever. And no man shall pluck them out of My hand." [1]

This infallible certainty of predestination is indicated in the definition given by St. Augustine, who says that it is "the foreknowledge and the preparation of those gifts of God whereby they who are liberated are most certainly liberated." [2] This infallibility has on various occasions been affirmed by the councils. [3]

But the question is whether this certainty of predestination is merely a certainty of foreknowledge or also one of causality. There is no doubt that the certainty of God's foreknowledge of sin is merely a certainty of foreknowledge and

---

[1] John 6: 39; 10: 27–28.
[2] *De dono persever.*, chap. 14, no. 35.
[3] Denz., nos. 300, 316, 321, 1,784.

213

not of causality, since God cannot be either directly or indirectly the cause of sin, and so the foreknown are distinguished from the predestined. The Council of Valencia held in 855 said: "God foreknew the malice of the wicked because it was their own doing; He did not predestinate it, because He was not the cause of it." [4] What is the certainty of predestination as regards the free determination of the salutary acts of the elect? If we take the view that God does not cause in us and with us this determination and the free mode of the same, we shall see in this but a certainty of foreknowledge. If we are of the opinion, on the contrary, that God causes infallibly, powerfully, and suavely, this salutary determination and its free mode, we shall see in this not only a certainty of foreknowledge but also of casuality.

Is not this last point expressly stated by our Lord when He says: "No man shall pluck them out of My hand"? [5] We have the confirmation of this, too, in St. Augustine's definition just quoted. St. Augustine has even clearly affirmed both these certainties in the following words: "If any of these [the elect] perishes, God is deceived; but none of them perishes because God is not deceived. If any of these perishes, God is conquered by human vice; but none of them perishes, because God is invincible." [6]

St. Thomas speaks in still clearer terms: "Since predestination includes the divine will as stated above [q. 19, a. 3, 8], the fact that God wills any created thing is necessary on the supposition that He so wills, on account of the immutability of the divine will, but it is not necessary absolutely; so the same must be said of predestination." [7] Predestination includes the consequent or efficacious will of saving the elect, and St. Thomas pointed out that "whatever God simply wills

[4] *Ibid.*, no. 322.
[5] John 10: 28.
[6] *De corrept. et gratia*, chap. 7.
[7] *Summa theol.*, Ia, q.23, a.6 ad 3um.

takes place; although what He wills antecedently may not take place." [8]

In another of his works, St. Thomas states the case still more clearly: "It cannot be said that certainty of foreknowledge is the only thing superadded to providence by predestination; this is tantamount to saying that God ordains the one predestined to salvation as He does anyone else, but that in the case of the one predestined He knows that he will not fail to be saved. In such a case, to be sure, there would be no difference between the one predestined and the one not predestined as regards the order of cause to effect, but only as regards the foreknowledge of the event. Thus foreknowledge would be the cause of predestination, and predestination would not be because of the choice of the one predestinating, which is contrary to the authority of the Scripture and the sayings of the saints. Hence in addition to the certainty of foreknowledge, there is infallible certainty in this order of predestination as regards the effect. Yet the proximate cause of salvation, namely, the free will, is not necessarily but contingently directed to this end." [9]

The above passage is a commentary on the following words of Jesus: "This is the will of the Father who sent Me, that of all He hath given Me, I should lose nothing." [10] But just as the divine causality, far from suppressing the activity of secondary causes, applies them to their act, so the prayers of the saints help the elect to advance on the way to eternity; and our good works merit for us eternal life and we shall in fact obtain it, if we do not lose our merits, and die in the state of grace. It is in this sense that St. Peter says: "By good works make sure your calling and election." [11]

Is the number of the elect certain? God knows infallibly

[8] *Ibid.*, Ia, q.19, a.6 ad 1um.
[9] *De veritate*, q.6, a.3.
[10] John 6: 39.
[11] II Pet. 1: 10; see St. Thomas, Ia, q.23, a.8.

the number of those who will be saved and of those who will be lost. If it were not so, there would be no certainty about predestination. Jesus said: "I know whom I have chosen"; [12] and St. Paul wrote: "The Lord knoweth who are His." [13]

Can we be certain in this life that we are predestined? In answer to this question the Council of Trent says: "No one, so long as he is in this mortal life, ought so far to presume as regards the secret mystery of divine predestination as to determine for certain that he is assuredly in the number of the predestinate; as if it were true that he who is justified either cannot sin any more, or, if he do sin, that he ought to promise himself an assured repentance. For, except by special revelation, it cannot be known whom God hath chosen unto Himself." [14] The reason for this is because, without a special revelation, we cannot know for certain what depends solely upon God's free will. Not one of the just, unless it is specially revealed, knows whether he will persevere in the performance of good works and in prayer. We shall be, says St. Paul, "heirs indeed of God and joint heirs with Christ; yet so, if we suffer [perseveringly] with Him, that we may be also glorified with Him." [15]

Are there, however, any signs of predestination such as to give one a sort of moral certainty of perseverance? The Fathers, especially John Chrysostom, Augustine, Gregory the Great, Bernard, and Anselm, according to certain statements of Holy Scripture, pointed out several signs of predestination often enumerated by the theologians as follows: (1) a good life; (2) the testimony of a conscience that is free from

12 John 13: 18.
13 II Tim. 2: 19.
14 Denz., no. 805; cf. no. 826.
15 Rom. 8: 17.

serious sins and prepared rather to die than offend God grievously; (3) patience in adversities endured for the love of God; (4) readiness to hear the word of God; (5) compassion for the poor; (6) love of one's enemies; (7) humility; (8) a special devotion to the Blessed Virgin whom we ask every day to pray for us at the hour of our death.

Among these signs, certain ones, such as Christian patience in adversity, are proof that the inequality of natural conditions is at times more than compensated by divine grace. This is borne out by the beatitudes as recorded in the Gospel: "Blessed are the poor in spirit, the meek, they that mourn, they that hunger and thirst after justice, the merciful, the clean of heart, the peacemakers, they that suffer persecution for justice' sake: for theirs is the kingdom of heaven." [16] These are the predestined. St. Thomas points out especially in his teaching that to bear patiently a heavy cross and for a long time is a sign of predestination.

IS THERE A GREAT NUMBER OF PREDESTINED?

From the Apocalypse we gather that the number of the elect is very great, for we read: "And I heard the number of them that were signed, an hundred forty-four thousand were signed of every tribe of the children of Israel. . . . After this, I saw a great multitude, which no man could number, of all nations and tribes and peoples and tongues, standing before the throne and in sight of the lamb, clothed with white robes and palms in their hands." [17]

Are there not so many elect as reprobates? St. Augustine and St. Thomas think so, especially on account of what our Lord said, that "many are called but few chosen." [18] And again when He said: "Enter ye in at the narrow gate; for

[16] Matt. 5: 3–10.
[17] Apoc. 7: 4, 9.
[18] Matt. 20: 16; 22: 14.

wide is the gate and broad is the way that leadeth to destruction and many there are who go in thereat. How narrow is
the gate and strait is the way that leadeth to life, and few
there are that find it!" [19] St. Thomas remarked on several
occasions that although everything is ordered for good in
the universe as a whole, and in the different species, yet if
we consider the human race from the time of original sin,
evil is more prevalent in this sense, that those who follow
the senses and their passions are greater in number than those
who follow right reason; "in man alone does evil appear as
in the greater number." [20] The elect are an elite class.[21] St.
Thomas maintains, however, that the number of the angels
who were saved exceeds the number of devils,[22] and he wrote
the same about the angels in another of his treatises, pointing out that "evil is found as in the smaller number in the
angels, because many more remained faithful than fell, and
perhaps even more than all the devils and men to be condemned. But in man good appears as in the smaller number
. . . because of the corruption of man due to original sin,
and the very nature of human conditions . . . in which the
secondary perfections that direct human actions are not innate, but either acquired or infused." [23]

In his theological treatise we read: "The good that is
proportionate to the common state of nature is to be found
in the majority; and is wanting in the minority. The good
that exceeds the common state of nature is to be found in
the minority, and is wanting in the majority. . . . Since
eternal happiness, consisting in the vision of God, exceeds
the common state of nature, and in so far as this is deprived

19 *Ibid.*, 7: 13 f.
20 *Loc. cit.*, Ia, q.49, a.3 ad 5um; q.63, a.9 ad 1um; Ia IIae, q.71, a.2 ad
3um; *I Sent.*, d. 39, q.2, a.2 ad 4um; *C.G.*, III, 6; *De pot.*, q.3, a.6 ad 5um;
De malo, q.1, a.3 ad 17um; a.5 ad 16um.
21 *Ibid.*, Ia, q.23, a.7 ad 3um.
22 *Ibid.*, q.63, a.9.
23 *I Sent.*, d. 39, q.2, a.2 ad 4um.

of grace through the corruption of original sin, those who are saved are in the minority." [24]

Let us bear in mind that, according to the passage of the commentary on the Sentences just quoted, which this last quotation does not contradict, if we include among the elect both angels and men, then the number of the elect is perhaps greater than that of the reprobates.

It is the common opinion of the Fathers and early theologians that the majority of human beings are not saved. They mention in favor of this opinion Basil, John Chrysostom, Gregory of Nazianzus, Hilary, Ambrose, Jerome, Augustine, Leo the Great, Bernard, and Thomas Aquinas. In more recent times we have Molina, Bellarmine, Suarez, Vasquez, Lessius, and St. Alphonse. In the last century, of those who depart from this common opinion, we have Father Faber in England, Bishop Bougaud in France, and Father Castelein, S.J., in Belgium.

Especially in the case of all those who lived before the coming of our Lord, and of those who have not had the gospel preached to them, it would seem that the formula of St. Thomas is verified that "in man evil appears as in the greater number," [25] although God never commands what is impossible, and He gives to all sufficient graces to keep the commandments as made known to them by conscience.[26] On the contrary, it seems well enough established that the greater number of the baptized, both children and adults, is saved. There are many children who die in the state of grace before attaining the use of reason.

We cannot say whether the greater number of non-Catholic baptized adults are saved.[27] On the contrary, it is probable that the majority of adult Catholics attain eternal life, and

[24] *Loc. cit.,* Ia, q.23, a.7 ad 3um.
[25] *Ibid.,* Ia, q.49, a.3 ad 5um.
[26] Denz., no. 1,677.
[27] Cf. Hugon, O.P., *Dogmatica,* I, 317.

this because of the efficacy of redemption and the sacraments.[28]

Throughout this question that is so mysterious, it is well for us to recall here what Pius IX said about this subject in his encyclical to the bishops of Italy on Indifferentism, which is as follows: "It is known to us and to you that those who labor under invincible ignorance concerning our most holy religion and who, diligently observing the natural law and its precepts that are engraved in the hearts of all by God, and being ready to obey Him, lead an honest and upright life, can, through the operative power of divine light and grace, attain eternal life, since God, who clearly intues, scrutinizes, and knows the minds, impulses, thoughts, and habits of all, because of His supreme goodness and clemency, by no means will allow anyone to be punished eternally who was not guilty of any wilful offense. But very well known also is the Catholic dogma, namely, that no one outside the Catholic Church can be saved, and those contumaciously resisting the authority of this Church, pertinacious in their dissension, cannot obtain eternal salvation." [29]

[28] Cf. Father Buonpensiere, O.P., *De Deo uno,* in Ia, q.23, a.7; Tanquerey, *De Deo uno, De praed.,* no. 41.

[29] Denz., no. 1,677. This statement must be interpreted according to the tenor of the preceding. As the supreme pontiff had just said that no one will be punished eternally who is not guilty of any wilful offense, this statement can mean only that those who wilfully remain outside the Catholic Church, when they are convinced that it is the true Church, cannot be saved. (Tr.)

CHAPTER V

Conclusion

THE TRANSCENDENCE OF THE MYSTERY
OF PREDESTINATION

It remains for us to say a few words about the transcendence of this supernatural mystery and about the mode of knowledge by which in this life we are better able to reach it in the obscurity of faith. It is one of the most striking examples of what may be termed light and shade in theology.

In the study of God's mysteries, especially the reconciliation of the mystery of predestination with God's universal will to save, we are struck by the ever increasing evidence of certain principles which, however, can be intimately reconciled only in the impenetrable obscurity of the Deity. There we have one of the most striking illustrations of light and shade. The principles to be reconciled are like the two quadrants of an intensely luminous semicircle enveloping a deeper and inaccessible obscurity. The more luminous the two quadrants of the semicircle become, the more this increases in a way the obscurity of the mystery that dominates them. On the one hand, we see, indeed, the more clearly that God cannot command what is impossible, and that He wills consequently the salvation of all men; on the other hand, we realize that no one thing is better than another unless it is loved more by God, and the more, too, we see that these two principles, so certain when viewed separately, although they appear to be contrary, can be reconciled only in the eminence of the Deity that is supremely obscure for us.

This mystery is far more obscure than is the reconciliation of God's foreknowledge, decrees, and grace with our freedom of will. If God is God, it follows that He is omnipotent and must be able to move our free will suavely and strongly, especially to the performance of salutary and meritorious acts. Otherwise, how can we explain the free and meritorious acts which our Lord Jesus Christ's human will had infallibly to accomplish here below for our salvation; or again how can we account for Mary's "fiat" which she had freely and infallibly to give on the day of the Annunciation, so that the Savior might be given to us?

Certainly there is a mystery in the reconciliation of the freedom of our meritorious acts with God's infallibly efficacious decrees. Yet far more obscure is the mystery of evil permitted by God. Whereas the mysteries of grace, which for us are obscure, are as clear as can be in themselves, the mysteries of iniquity are obscure in themselves, evil being a privation of light and goodness. From this it follows that the solution of the great mystery with which we are confronted, that of the reconciliation of predestination, connected as it is with God's universal will to save, is to be found, as St. Augustine and St. Thomas viewed it, in the incomprehensible and ineffable union of infinite mercy, justice, and supreme liberty. This was often formulated by these two great doctors who said that, if God grants the grace of final perseverance to this particular person, He does so because of His mercy; if He does not grant it to a certain other, as to Judas, it is through just punishment for previous sins and for having finally resisted the last call of grace.

It is a profound mystery which is the result of the intimate union of the three infinite perfections of mercy, justice, and sovereign liberty. The obscurity is great, but we see that it is not the outcome of absurdity or incoherence. Two absolutely certain principles lead us to it, the first being that "God never commands what is impossible," and the other that "no one thing would be better than another, unless it were loved more by God."

In this case, particularly, we grasp the truth of what St. Thomas said about faith, that "it is of things not seen." The object of faith is essentially obscure; it is neither seen nor known.[1] But living faith that is united with charity is, as a rule, accompanied by the gift of understanding which in the literal sense of Holy Scripture penetrates the meaning or spirit of the mysteries. It is also accompanied by the gift of wisdom, which gives one a relish for them. Then the great believers realize that in the mysteries of faith, what is more obscure about this translucid obscurity is what is more divine, the Deity itself, in the inaccessible eminence of which are reconciled mercy, justice, and liberty. What is more obscure in the mysteries then appears as supremely good, and whereas the intellect is incapable of assenting to them as evident by the light of reason, the will, actuated by the very pure love of charity, gives its supernatural and immediate adherence to them.[2]

This explains, then, why interior souls who have to undergo the passive purifications of the spirit,[3] are generally very much tempted against hope when they think of predestination. These temptations are permitted by God so as to make these souls feel the necessity of rising above human arguments by prayer, a purer faith, and a most loving confidence and abandonment. This is then infused contemplation, the fruit of the gifts of understanding and wisdom, by means of which one begins to reach in a truly higher way, in the obscurity of faith, the culminating point of the mystery which we are discussing. Then it is that we begin to have a foretaste of the fruits of this exalted doctrine and, to quote the words of the Vatican Council, that we attain "a certain very fruitful understanding of the mystery." [4]

The spiritual fruits of this mystery which concerns us here

---

1 *Summa theol.*, IIa IIae, q.1, a.4, 5.

2 *Ibid.*, IIa IIae, q.27, a.4; q.45, a.2.

3 Cf. St. John of the Cross, "Dark night of the soul."

4 Denz., no. 1796.

could not be better expressed than by quoting in conclusion two of Bossuet's letters on this subject. In his reply to a certain person who was tormented in mind, how to reconcile the fact of God's willing the salvation of all men with the mystery of predestination, he said: "There are many called and few chosen, said Jesus Christ. All of those who are called can come if they wish to; free will is given to them for this reason, and the purpose of grace is to conquer their resistance and help them in their weakness. If they do not come, they have only themselves to blame; but if they come, that is because they received a certain divine touch urging them to make good use of their free will. They owe their fidelity, therefore, to God's special goodness, for which they must be extremely grateful, and this teaches them to humble themselves and say: 'What hast thou that thou hast not received? And if thou hast received, why dost thou glory?' [5]

"All that God does in time, He foresees and predestines from all eternity. He foresaw and predestined in detail all the means by which He had to inspire His followers with fidelity, obedience, and perseverance. That is what predestination means.

"The benefit of this doctrine is to have us place our will and liberty in God's hands, asking him to direct this will so that it may never stray from the right path, and thanking Him for all the good that it does and believing that He operates in it without weakening or destroying it, but, on the contrary, elevating, strengthening, and granting it to make good use of itself, which is the most desirable of all good things. . . . We must not, therefore, attribute the cause of salvation to him who wills or to him who runs, but to God who shows mercy. This means that neither their running nor their willing are the primary cause, and still less the only cause of their salvation; but this cause is the accompanying and preventing grace that gives them strength to continue until the end, and this grace

[5] I Cor. 4: 7.

does not act alone; for we must be faithful to it; and to accomplish this effect, it gives us the power to co-operate with it, so that we can say with St. Paul: 'Yet not I, but the grace of God with me.' [6]

"God is the author of all the good we do. It is He who brings it to completion, just as it is He who begins it. His Holy Spirit forms in our hearts the petitions He wishes to grant. He foresaw and predestined all that; for predestination is nothing else. In all this we must believe that no one perishes, no one is cast off as a reprobate, except through his own fault. If human reasoning finds a difficulty in this, and cannot reconcile all phases of this holy and inviolable doctrine, faith must continue to reconcile all things, at the same time waiting until God causes us to see everything in Him, the fountain-head.

"The whole doctrine of predestination and grace may be summed up briefly in these words of the prophet: 'Destruction is thy own, O Israel; thy help is only in Me.' [7] So it is. If we do not see the consistency in all this, it suffices for us that God knows, and we must humbly believe Him. God's secret is His own." [8]

In this the soul finds peace, not in descending by means of reasoning below faith, but, on the contrary, by aspiring to the contemplation of God's intimate life, a contemplation which, since it is above human reasoning, proceeds from faith enlightened by the gifts of the Holy Ghost.

It is fitting to recall here that the formal motive of Christian hope, like that of the other two theological virtues, must be the uncreated Being. It is, therefore, not our personal effort but God helping.[9] Moreover, the certainty of hope differs from that of faith in this, that it is a certainty in which the will participates; it is also a certainty of tendency, not exactly the certainty of salvation (for this would require a special revela-

6 *Ibid.*, 15: 10.
7 Osee, 13: 9.
8 *Œuvres*, XI, 133 f.
9 *Loc. cit.*, IIa IIae, q.17, a.5.

tion), but it is the certainty of tending toward salvation, relying upon God's promises and help, so that "thus hope tends with certainty toward its end, sharing, as it were, in the certainty of faith." [10] There is security in this.

This peace is established, if the soul trustfully abandons itself to God, not as the quietists do, but by doing its best every day to accomplish God's will as made known by the commandments, the spirit of the counsels, and daily occurrences, and in all else abandoning itself to the divine will of good pleasure; for we are certain beforehand that this Will can will and permit nothing except what is for the manifestation of divine goodness, for the glory of Christ the Redeemer, and for the spiritual and eternal welfare of those who love God and persevere in this love.[11]

To another person who wrote him, saying: "My reasonings on predestination, in spite of myself, disturbed me very much in mind," Bossuet replied again as follows: "When these thoughts come to the mind, and only useless efforts are made to dispel them, they must end in causing us to abandon ourselves completely to God, assured that it is infinitely better to leave our salvation in His hands than to rely on our own strength. Only by thus doing shall we find peace. The whole doctrine of the divine Master's secret is that we must adore Him and not claim to fathom Him. We must lose ourselves in this impenetrable height and depth of divine wisdom and plunge ourselves as if lost in His immense goodness, though expecting everything from Him, without however relaxing our efforts, which He demands from us for our salvation." [12]

It is Christian contemplation which, above the reasoning of theological arguments, penetrates beyond the literal meaning of the Gospel, so as to reach the spirit of the mysteries and

10 *Ibid.*, IIa IIae, q. 18, a. 4.

11 On this point consult St. Francis de Sales, *Love of God*, Bk. VIII, chaps. 5, 9; Bk. IX, chaps. 1–8; also *Conference* II. (Eng. tr. by Dom Mackey, O.S.B.)

12 *Loc. cit.*, p. 444.

taste their sweetness. It soars not only far above the errors that are contrary to Semipelagianism and predestinationism, but also above the conflict of theological systems. It finds its refuge in the Immutable, in the very spirit of God's word. It is this by all means that makes us understand what a doctor of the Church, St. John of the Cross, wrote to show that, if the soul makes too much of what seems clear, this alone accounts for the far distant recoil from the abyss of faith.

"The understanding must remain in darkness, and must journey in darkness, by love and in faith, and not by much reasoning. You must be careful not to misunderstand me. . . . The Holy Spirit illumines the understanding which is recollected, and illumines it according to the manner of its recollection. The understanding cannot find any other and greater recollection than in faith. For the purer and more refined the soul is in faith, the more it has of the infused charity of God; and the more charity it has, the more it is illuminated and the more gifts of the Holy Spirit are communicated to it, for charity is the cause and the means whereby they are communicated to it. And although it is true that, in this illumination of truths, the Holy Spirit communicates a certain light to the soul, this is nevertheless as different in quality from that which is in faith, wherein is no clear understanding, as is the most precious gold from the basest metal; and, with regard to its quantity, the one is as much greater than the other as the sea is greater than a drop of water. For in the one manner there is communicated to the soul wisdom concerning one or two or three truths, etc., but in the other there is communicated to it the sum total of divine wisdom, which is the Son of God, who communicates Himself to the soul in faith.

"And if you tell me that this is all good, and that the one impedes not the other, I reply that this impedes it greatly if the soul sets store by it; for to do this is to busy itself with things which are quite clear and of little importance, yet which are quite sufficient to hinder the communication of the abyss of faith, wherein God supernaturally and secretly instructs the soul, and exalts it in virtues and gifts." [13]

In other words, grace by a secret instinct sets us at peace concerning our salvation and the intimate reconciliation in God of infinite justice, mercy, and sovereign liberty. Grace, by this secret instinct, sets us thus at peace, because it is itself a real and formal participation in the divine nature, in God's intimate life in the very Deity, in which all the divine perfections are absolutely identified.

If we stress too much our analogical concepts of the divine attributes, we set up an obstacle to the contemplation of the revealed mysteries. The fact that these concepts are distinct from one another, like small squares of mosaic reproducing a human likeness, is why they harden the spiritual aspect of God for us. Wisdom, absolute liberty, mercy, and justice seem in some way to be distinct in God, and then His sovereignly free good pleasure appears in an arbitrary light, and not entirely penetrated by wisdom; mercy seems too restricted, and justice too rigid. But by faith illumined by the gifts of understanding and wisdom, we go beyond the literal meaning of the Gospel and imbibe the very spirit of God's word. We instinctively feel, without seeing it, how all the divine perfections are identified in the Deity, that is superior to being, the one, the true, the intellect, and love. The Deity is superior to all perfections that are naturally susceptible of participation, these being contained in it formally and eminently without any admixture of imperfection. The Deity is not naturally susceptible of participation, either by angel or man. It is only by grace, which is essentially supernatural, that we are permitted to participate in the Deity, in God's intimate life, inasmuch as this latter is strictly divine. Thus it is that grace is instrumental in causing us mysteriously to reach, in the ob-

[13] St. John of the Cross, *Ascent of Mount Carmel,* Bk. II, chap. 29, nos. 5-8 (Eng. tr. by Allison Peers.)

scurity of faith, the summit where the divine attributes are identified. The spiritual aspect of God for us is no longer hardened. We do not see His countenance, but we instinctively feel it, and this secret instinctive feeling, in the supernatural abandonment of ourselves, gives us peace.

PART III

GRACE AND ITS EFFICACY

In this third part we shall treat of grace, especially of actual efficacious grace by which the effects of predestination are realized in time, namely: vocation, justification, and merits. Our chief purpose will be to study the relations between efficacious grace and sufficient grace that is offered and even given to us. We shall also see that the foundation for the distinction between these two graces is, according to the teaching of St. Thomas, the consequent will of God (which concerns the infallible realization of good at the present moment), and the antecedent will (which concerns good absolutely considered and not as determined by certain circumstances).[1] By His antecedent will, God wills to save all men (for it is good that all be saved); by His consequent will, He wills efficaciously, all things taken into consideration, to save the elect.[2]

That we may proceed in an orderly manner in this third part, we shall first treat of efficacious grace and sufficient grace according to the Scripture and the declarations of the Church; then we shall discuss the divine motion in general, and premotion such as St. Thomas and the Thomists understood it.

[1] *Summa theol.*, Ia, q.19, a.6 ad 1um.
[2] See pp. 72–75, 80–84.

CHAPTER I

EFFICACIOUS GRACE AND SUFFICIENT GRACE ACCORDING TO SCRIPTURE AND THE DECLARATIONS OF THE CHURCH

THE PROBLEM

WE know it to be certain according to revelation, which is contained in Scripture and tradition, that there are many actual graces granted by God which do not produce the effect (at least the complete effect) intended, whereas others do. The former are called *sufficient* and *merely sufficient*. They give the power (proximate or remote) to perform a good act, though they do not effectively bring one to perform this very act. Man resists their appeal. The latter graces are called *efficacious*, because they cause us to act, so that we may perform the salutary act.

Hence arises the question: What is the principle in distinguishing between these two kinds of graces? In other words: The grace that is called efficacious, is it so of itself, intrinsically, because God efficaciously wills it so, or is it only extrinsically so, by reason of our consent foreseen by God?

The errors of the Reformers and the Jansenists gave rise to animated discussions on this question. It was at that time that the term *sufficient* was technically determined in meaning in opposition to the term *efficacious*.[1]

---

1 Cf. Father Chenu, O.P., "On the meaning of the word 'sufficient' according to St. Thomas," in the *Revue des Sciences Phil. et Théol.*, May, 1933. The author shows, following Nicolaï, that for St. Thomas "sufficient" is at times a synonymous term for 'efficacious' (Ia, q.46, a.1, obj. 9; I Cor. c. 15, lect. 2; *De verit.*, q.14, a.1); in certain cases, however, he has given them opposite meanings (IIIa, q.79, a.7 ad 7um; *De verit.*, q.29, a.7 ad 4um; III Sent., d. 13,

The importance of the problem is evident because of the very opposition raised against it by the contrary heresies and the teachings of the Catholic theologians. We may say that for the Pelagians actual grace (for instance, the preaching of the gospel) is made efficacious by our good consent, and inefficacious by the perversity of the human will. For the Reformers and the Jansenists, there are two kinds of actual interior graces. One kind is efficacious of itself, the other is inefficacious and even is not truly sufficient.

For the Thomists, there are two kinds of actual interior graces; one kind is intrinsically efficacious of itself; for it causes us to perform the good act; the other is inefficacious but truly sufficient; for it gives us either the proximate or remote power to perform the good act.[2] For the Molinists, actual sufficient grace is itself either extrinsically efficacious, by reason of our consent that is foreseen by God by means of the *scientia media,* or else it is inefficacious and merely sufficient.[3]

DECLARATIONS OF THE CHURCH

The Church declared against Jansenism that there are graces truly and merely sufficient. They are truly sufficient because they really give the power to perform a good act; and they are merely sufficient because, through our own fault, they do not produce their effect, or at least the complete effect intended.

---

q.2, a.2, q.2, ad 5um; d. 19, q.1, a.2; *In Hebr.,* c. 9, lect. 5; *in I ad Thess.* 2: 5).

According to the author of this article, the famous distinction that is nowadays accepted, bears on its face the mark of its modern origin (for we find traces of it in the fourteenth and fifteenth centuries), and of the preoccupation of those who imposed it, such as Lessius and Catharinus.

[2] Cf. Joannem a S. Thoma, O.P., *Curs. theol., De gratia,* disp. XXIV; Salmanticenses, *Cursus theol., De gratia,* disp. V, dub. 7; Lemos, O.P. *Panoplia gratiae,* Vol. IV, Part 2a, p. 36; Del Prado, O.P., *De gratia et libero arbitrio,* Vol. II, chaps. 1–3.

[3] Cf. Molina, *Concordia,* in the index under the title *Auxilium efficax.*

This teaching of the Church is clearly seen in the condemnation as heretical of the first proposition of Jansenius, which reads as follows: "Some of God's commandments are impossible of fulfilment for the just according to their present powers, though they desire and strive to observe them; they stand in need, too, of the grace that would make them possible of fulfilment."[4] Quesnel and the pseudo-synod of Pistoia were also condemned for having denied the existence of truly sufficient grace.[5] The second proposition of Jansenius is very much like the first. It reads: "In the state of fallen nature interior grace is never resisted."[6] This was tantamount to saying that the only actual interior grace is efficacious grace.

After the condemnation of the five propositions of Jansenius, the great Arnauld[7] admitted a little grace, which gives the power to act in general, though it does not really give this power at the moment when needed. The Catholic theologians showed that this little grace, for which the great Arnauld contended, does not safeguard the traditional teaching; for it must really be possible to keep the commandments not only in general, but in each particular case when occasion arises.[8]

Besides this, the Church teaches that there is an actual efficacious grace and that this latter does not restrain liberty. That there is such a grace follows from the condemnation of Pelagianism and Semipelagianism, which did not, strictly speaking, deny that grace gives the power to act, but they denied that it causes one to will and to act. Against these heresies the Second Council of Orange defined: "As often as we perform good acts, God works in us and with us, that

4 Denz., no. 1,092.

5 *Ibid.*, nos. 1,359 f., 1,521.

6 *Ibid.*, no. 1,093.

7 *Dissert. quadripart. de gratia efficaci;* and *Apologie pour les Saints Pères,* Bk. IV.

8 Cf. Guillermin, O.P., *Revue Thomiste,* 1901–03, five important articles on sufficient grace. Consult especially 1902, p. 47 ff.

we may act." [9] There is therefore a grace that effectively operates, although it does not exclude our co-operation, but requires and elicits it.

As for the fact that efficacious grace does not restrain our liberty, this is clearly affirmed by the Council of Trent.[10] The constant teaching of the Church affirms this, according to which the meritorious act is the result of both human freedom and efficacious grace. According to this teaching, sufficient grace leaves us with no excuse before God for having sinned, and efficacious grace does not permit us to glory in ourselves when we have performed a good act.

WHAT IS THE FOUNDATION IN SCRIPTURE FOR THE DISTINCTION BETWEEN SUFFICIENT GRACE AND EFFICACIOUS GRACE?

The Scripture often speaks of the grace that does not produce its effect, and this because of man's resistance. In the Old Testament we read: "I called and you refused. I have spread forth My hands all the day to an unbelieving people, who walk in a way that is not good after their own thoughts." [11] In the Gospel, Jesus says: "Jerusalem, Jerusalem, thou that killest the prophets and stonest them that are sent thee, how often would I have gathered together thy children, as the hen doth gather her chickens under her wings, and thou wouldest not?" [12] St. Stephen, the first martyr, said to the Jews before he died: "You stiffnecked and uncircumcised in heart and ears, you always resist the Holy Ghost." [13] St. Paul wrote: "And we helping do exhort you that you receive not the grace of God in vain." [14]

All these quotations show that there are truly sufficient

[9] Denz., no. 182.
[10] Ibid., no. 814; see also nos. 797, 1,094.
[11] Prov. 1: 24; Is. 65: 2.
[12] Matt. 23: 37.
[13] Acts 7: 51.
[14] II Cor. 6: 1.

graces, which however, are fruitless because of our resistance. This doctrine is proved also from what St. Paul says to Timothy: "God will have all men to be saved and to come to the knowledge of the truth . . . for Jesus gave Himself a redemption for all, a testimony in due times." [15] This means that God wills to make it really possible for all to keep His commandments.

On the other hand the Scripture often affirms the existence of efficacious grace that produces its effect, the salutary act. This point is made particularly clear in the texts from the Scripture quoted by the Second Council of Orange against the Semipelagians, such as: "I will give you a new heart and put a new spirit within you; and I will take away the stony heart out of your flesh and will give you a heart of flesh. And I will put My spirit in the midst of you, and I will cause you to walk in My commandments and to keep My judgments and do them." [16] St. Paul also wrote: "It is God who worketh in you both to will and to accomplish, according to His good will." [17] And Jesus said: "My sheep shall not perish for ever. And no man shall pluck them out of My hand." [18] Hence these words of the Second Council of Orange: "As often as we perform a good act, God works with us that we may act." [19] Farther on [20] we shall quote scriptural texts similar to these, such as: "As the divisions of waters, so the heart of the king is in the hand of the Lord; whithersoever He will He shall turn it." [21] "As the potter's clay is in his hand, to fashion and to order it; so man is in the hand of Him that made him, and He will render to him according to His judgment." [22]

[15] I Tim. 2: 4 f.
[16] Ezech. 36: 26 f.
[17] Phil. 2: 13.
[18] John 10: 27 f.
[19] Denz., no. 182.
[20] Chap. 7, no. 3.
[21] Prov. 21: 1; cf. Esther 13: 9; 14: 13.
[22] Eccli. 33: 13; cf. 33: 24–27.

It seems, indeed, according to the language of Scripture, that the efficacious grace of which it speaks is efficacious of itself, and not merely because God foresaw we would consent to it without offering any resistance.

Hence we see that for St. Thomas and his school, the distinction between efficacious grace and sufficient grace has its ultimate foundation in the distinction between God's consequent will (which concerns good infallibly to be realized at the present moment) and his antecedent will (which concerns good taken in the absolute sense and not as considered in certain determined circumstances), such as, for instance, the salvation of all men in so far as it is good for all to be saved.[23] From this antecedent or universal will to save come the sufficient graces that make it really possible for us to keep the commandments, without causing anyone, however, effectively to do so. God's consequent will in its relation to our salutary acts is the cause, on the contrary, of our effectively fulfilling our duty.

This doctrine appears to have the solid support of Holy Scripture. The same must be said of the Thomist teaching that actual grace, which is of itself efficacious as regards an imperfect act, such as attrition, is truly sufficient as regards a more perfect act, such as contrition.

Hence this is the question at issue: Is the grace that is said to be efficacious, truly so of itself intrinsically, or is it merely extrinsically efficacious by reason of our consent that is foreseen by God? In other words, how are we to conceive the divine motion that inclines our will and causes it to perform the salutary act? The relations between sufficient grace and efficacious grace are evidently connected with this question. Is efficacious grace included in the sufficient help that is granted to all, just as the fruit is included in the flower?

All Thomists agree in saying that, if a man did not resist

[23] *Summa theol.*, Ia, q. 19, a.6 ad 1um.

sufficient grace, he would receive the efficacious grace required to enable him to do his duty. But here again is the mystery: for to resist sufficient grace is an evil that can come only from us; whereas not to resist sufficient grace is a good that cannot be solely the result of our action, but one which must come from God who is the source of all good. How then shall we conceive the divine motion, the various modes of this, and its efficacy?

CHAPTER II

The Divine Motion in General

For a proper understanding of what the Thomists mean by the expression "physical premotion," we must recall what led them to adopt it.

They understand this to be the answer to the question clearly put by St. Thomas, when he asks whether God moves all secondary causes to act.[1] They answer first that the Scripture does not leave room for any doubt about this, since it says that "God worketh all in all. For in Him we live and move and are." [2] Even if it is a question of our free acts, the Scripture is no less positive in affirming that He is the prime Mover, for we read: "Lord . . . Thou hast wrought all our works for us. For it is God who worketh in you, both to will and to accomplish, according to His good will." [3] These scriptural texts are so clear, they state so plainly that the action of the creature depends upon God's influx or upon the divine causality, that even Suarez, although opposed to the theory of physical premotion, wrote that it would be an error against the faith to deny the dependence of the creature in its actions upon the first Cause.[4]

Equally clear stands the case from the philosophical point of view; for just as the participated and limited being of creatures depends upon the causality of the first Being, who is the self-subsisting Being, so also does their action: for there is no reality that can be excluded from His controlling

1 *Summa theol.*, Ia, q. 105, a.5.
2 I Cor. 12: 6; Acts 17: 28.
3 Is. 26: 12; Phil. 2: 13.
4 *Disp. met.*, disp. 22, sect. I, par. 7.

influence. It is not a question, therefore, in this case of the necessity or existence of the divine influx, without which no creature would act, but rather of the nature of this influx and of the way in which it operates.

In the first place we shall see, in pointing out the manifest errors to be avoided, what physical premotion is not, so as to enable us to state more precisely afterward what it is. We say then: (1) It is not a motion such as to render the action of the secondary cause superfluous. This is directed against occasionalism. (2) It is not a motion that would interiorly compel our will to choose this particular thing rather than a certain other. This is directed against determinism. (3) Neither is it, at the opposite extreme of both occasionalism and determinism, simply a simultaneous concurrence. (4) Nor is it an indifferent and indeterminate motion. (5) It is not a purely extrinsic assistance given by God.

We shall see more clearly further on that physical premotion is: (1) A motion and not an *ex nihilo* creation, without which our acts, created in us *ex nihilo,* would not be the result of the vital action of our faculties and would no longer be ours. It is a passive motion that is received in the creature and that is consequently something distinct either from the divine action which it presupposes, or from our action which follows it. It is (2) a physical and not a moral motion or one that is the result of an object proposed to it that attracts it. (3) It is, as regards our freedom of action, not necessitating but predetermining, or it is not a formal but a causal predetermination, in the sense that it guarantees the intrinsic infallibility of the divine decrees and moves our will to determine itself to a certain determinate good act (the determination to a bad act, since it is itself bad and defective, comes on these grounds from a defective cause and not from God). Finally, we shall see that the predetermination, since it is both formal and causal, is prior to the motion. It is identical, according to the teaching of St. Thomas, with the divine predetermining decrees that have reference to our salutary acts; whereas the formal and no longer causal determination is the very one of our already determined free act, which still remains free even after its determination, just as God's act is free. The careful study of these different aspects of the problem is necessary so as to avoid any confusion of thought, and it is expedient for us to begin with the negative phase of this problem, for the expression "predetermining physical premotion" is used precisely to exclude a simultaneous concurrence and an indifferent premotion.

CHAPTER III

WHAT DOES NOT CONSTITUTE PHYSICAL PREMOTION

1) THE divine motion must not be understood in the sense held by the occasionalists in that God alone would act in all things, so that it is not the fire that gives heat, but God in the fire, the latter being the occasion of this. If such were the case, remarks St. Thomas,[1] secondary causes would not be causes, and, not being able to act, their presence would be to no purpose. Moreover, their impotence would prove that God was incapable of communicating to them the dignity of causality, action, and life, being like an artist who can produce only lifeless works (and this would imply lack of power in the Creator). Moreover, occasionalism leads to pantheism. This is clear, because action follows being, and the mode of action the mode of being. If there is but one action, which is God's action, then there is but one being; creatures are absorbed in God; universal being is identical with the divine being, as ontologist realism postulates, a fond theory of Malebranche and one that is closely associated, according to his notion, with occasionalism.

St. Thomas, having thus refuted the occasionalism of his time, adds that God, who created and maintains secondary causes in being, applies them to act. He says: "God not only gives things their form, but He also preserves them in existence, and applies them to act, and is moreover the end of every action." [2]

2) The divine motion, since it does not render the action of

---

[1] *Summa theol.,* Ia, q. 105, a. 5.
[2] *Ibid.,* q. 105, a. 5 ad 3um; cf. *Contra Gentes,* III, 67; *De potentia,* q. 3, a. 7.

secondary causes superfluous but gives rise to it, cannot be necessitating, in the sense that it would suppress all contingency and liberty. But, under the divine influx, secondary causes act as befitting their nature, either necessarily, as the sun gives light and heat, or contingently, as fruits become more or less ripe in time; or else freely, as in the case of man who chooses. St. Thomas connects even this property of divine motion with the sovereign efficacy of God's causality, who does not only what He wills but as He wills it; who brings it about not only that we will but that we freely will. On this point he writes: "Since, then, the divine will is perfectly efficacious, it follows not only that things are done which God wills to be done, but also that they are done in the way that He wills. Now God wills some things to be done necessarily, some contingently, to the right ordering of things, for the building up of the universe." [3]

The divine motion does not therefore suppress freedom of action, but actualizes it. It eliminates only potential indifference, and in return gives it the actual dominating indifference of the free act, an indifference that persists after it is already determined. This is the only indifference there is in God, and it persists in the unchangeable free act by which He preserves the world in existence. It is of this actual indifference that St. Thomas speaks when he says: "And just as by moving natural causes He does not prevent their acts being natural, so by moving voluntary causes He does not deprive their actions of being voluntary: but rather is He the cause of this very thing in them; for He operates in each according to its own nature." [4]

3) In opposition to occasionalism and determinism, would the divine motion be merely a simultaneous concurrence as Molina will have it to be? Molina considers the primary and secondary causes as two partial and co-ordinated causes pro-

[3] *Ibid.*, Ia, q. 19, a.8.
[4] *Ibid.*, Ia, q.83, a.1 ad 3um; cf. Ia IIae, q.10, a.4.

ducing one and the same effect, similar, he says, to two men pulling a boat: "The total effect, indeed, comes both from God and from the secondary causes; but it comes neither from God nor from secondary causes as total but as partial causes, each at the same time requiring the concurrence and influx of the other cause, just as when two men are pulling a boat." [5] From this point of view, even if the total effect is produced by each of the two causes, in this sense that one without the other would produce no effect, in such a case the secondary cause is not premoved by the first. The concurrence of this latter is merely simultaneous, as when two men are pulling a boat, the first exerting no influence upon the second to cause it to act. "God's universal concurrence." says Molina, "does not immediately exert an influence on the secondary cause, so as to premove it to act and produce its effect, but it immediately exerts an influence on the action and the effect, along with the secondary cause." [6]

Apart from this simultaneous concurrence, which is necessary for every act, Molina admits, indeed, a particular grace for salutary acts; but this latter is not a physical motion, attracting the will by reason of the object proposed to it.

The author of the *Concordia* acknowledges, moreover, that this conception of the simultaneous concurrence, which is necessarily connected, in his opinion, with his definition of liberty and his theory of the *scientia media,* is not the view held by St. Thomas. After setting forth what the Angelic Doctor said [7] on the subject of the divine motion, he writes: "I am confronted by two difficulties: (1) I do not see what is this application in secondary causes, by which God moves and applies these causes to act. I think rather that the fire heats without any need of its being moved to act. And I candidly confess that I have difficulty in understanding this

5 *Concordia,* q. 14, a. 13, disp. 26 (end).
9 *Ibid.*
7 *Loc. cit.,* Ia, q. 105, a. 5.

motion and application which St. Thomas requires in second-ary causes. . . . (2) There is another difficulty: according to this doctrine, God does not concur immediately (*immedia-tione suppositi*) in the action and effect of secondary causes, but only through the intervention of these causes." [8]

Molina could have found the solution of these two diffi-culties in a well-known passage of St. Thomas,[9] in which it is stated that God's immediate influence is also exercised on the being of the action or effect of the secondary cause, for this latter cannot be the proper cause of its act in so far as it is being, but only in so far as it is this individual act, its own. In this effect, what is more universal, as being, depends upon the more universal cause, and the more particular depends upon the particular cause. St. Thomas remarks: "The more universal effects must be reduced to the more universal and prior causes. Now among all effects the most universal is being itself." [10] Being, in so far as the being of things is con-cerned, is an effect that belongs properly to God, by way of creation *ex nihilo* and of conservation in being, or by way of motion, which is the case of the being itself of our acts, for these were at first in our faculties as potential acts.

But what is of greatest interest for us now in Molina's ob-jection, is the way in which he avows that St. Thomas ad-mitted that the divine motion applies secondary causes to act, which means that St. Thomas admitted not merely a simul-taneous concurrence, but a premotion. This word "premo-tion" may seem to be a pleonasm, because every true motion has a priority, if not of time at least of causality over its effect, and in this particular case it has, for St. Thomas, a priority over the action of the secondary cause thus applied to act. The Thomists use the word "premotion" solely for the pur-pose of showing that the motion of which they speak is truly

[8] *Concordia*, p. 152, 1876 ed.
[9] *De potentia*, q.3, a.7 ad 7um.
[10] *Loc. cit.*, Ia, q.45, a.5.

a motion that applies the secondary cause to act, and that it is not merely a simultaneous concurrence.

Is not this latter absolutely the very opposite of occasionalism and determinism or fatalism? If, in truth, the divine concurrence is merely simultaneous, it is no longer true to say that God moves secondary causes to act, since He does not apply them to their operations. We have in this case merely two partial and co-ordinated causes, not two total causes which, in their very causality, are subordinated the one to the other, as St. Thomas had said.[11] Moreover, Molina expressly stated: "For us, the divine concurrence does not determine the will to give its consent. On the contrary, it is the particular influx of the free will that determines the divine concurrence to act, according as the will is inclined to will rather than not to will, and to will this particular thing rather than a certain other." [12] The secondary causes, far from being determined by God to act, by their action determine the very functioning of the divine causality which, of itself, is indifferent.

But, if this is so, then there is something that is beyond the scope of the universal causality of the first agent; for, in fine, the influence exerted by the secondary cause is truly something; it is a perfection for it to pass into act, even a perfection so precious that Molinism is totally concerned in safeguarding it, and it is so delicate that even God, they say, cannot contact it.

The great difficulty is this: How could the will, which was only in the state of potency, give itself this perfection which it did not possess? This means that the greater comes from the less, and this is contrary to the principles of causality and of the universal causality of the first agent. St. Thomas was of the opinion that to refute determinism, instead of attacking the principle of causality, we must insist on the tran-

11 *Ibid.*, Ia, q. 105, a. 5 ad 2um; q. 23, a. 5, corp.
12 *Concordia,* q. 23, a. 4, 5, disp. 1, m. 7 ad 6um.

scendent efficacy of the first Cause, the only one capable of causing in us and with us that our acts be performed freely, since it is more intimate to us than we are to ourselves, and since this free mode of our acts is still being and for this reason depends upon Him who is the cause of all reality and good.

Furthermore, the Thomists say that if the divine concurrence, far from inclining the will infallibly to determine itself to perform this particular act rather than a certain other, is itself determined by the particular influx of the free will to function in this particular way rather than in a certain other, then the tables are turned: God by reason of His foreknowledge and causality, instead of determining is determined. This means that by His *scientia media* He foresees what choice a certain person would make, if placed in certain circumstances. Instead of being the cause of this foreseen determination, He is determined and therefore perfected by this determination which, as such, in no way comes from Him. Now there is nothing more inadmissible than to posit a passivity or dependence in the pure Act, who is sovereignly independent and incapable of receiving any perfection whatsoever.

This stands out as the great objection against the Molinist theories of the *scientia media* and simultaneous concurrence, as we have elsewhere shown.[13]

4) May we say that the divine motion is an indifferent motion by which God would determine us only to an indeliberate act, so that the free will alone would determine itself and the divine motion, to perform this or that particular act? Some theologians thought so, especially Father Pignataro.[14]

13 Cf. *Revue Thomiste*, "The dilemma, God determining or determined," June, 1928, pp. 193–211; see also *"God, His existence and His Nature,"* II, 529–62.

14 Cf. *De Deo Creatore*. On page 519 of this work the author wrote: "This motion constitutes the will as directly and proximately ready to choose"; and

The Thomists reply,[15] that this theory and the *scientia media* mutually support each other, and that it has to contend with several of the difficulties pointed out against the preceding. Something real would still be excluded from God's universal causality. There would be a determination that is independent of the sovereign determination of pure Act, a finite good independent of the supreme Good, a second liberty that would be acting independently of the first Liberty. That which is better in the work of salvation, the determination of our salutary act, would not come from the Author of salvation. Contrary to this, St. Paul said: "It is God who worketh in you, both to will and to accomplish, according to His good will. For who distinguisheth thee? Or what hast thou that thou hast not received?" [16] St. Thomas said the same in formulating the principle of predilection: "Since God's love is the cause of goodness in things, no one thing would be better than another, if God did not will greater good for one than for another." [17]

This doctrine of indifferent premotion, like that of simultaneous concurrence, cannot solve the dilemma: "God determining or determined: there is no other alternative." Willingly or unwillingly, it leads to the positing of a passivity or dependence in Him who is pure Act, especially in His foreknowledge (*scientia media*) as regards our free determinations, even the noblest which, as free determinations, would not come from Him. Concerning these God would not be the cause of them, but merely a passive onlooker.

---

he adds: "That the divine motion is determined to move in one particular way those things which by nature are so determined, this I concede; that it is so determined in contingent things, this I deny." The *Ami du Clergé* (February 21, 1935, pp. 392–94) assures us that when this work was published (1899), even Father Billot did not hesitate to declare this opinion to be absolutely unintelligible. On this point consult the second appendix at the end of this book.

15 Cf. Father del Prado, O.P., *De gratia et libero arbitrio*, III, 162.

16 I Cor. 4: 7; Phil. 2: 13.

17 *Loc. cit.*, Ia, q.20, a.3.

For these reasons, the Thomists admit that since God is the first Cause of all existing things, with the exception of sin, even as regards our salutary free acts, the divine decrees are of themselves infallibly efficacious or predetermining, and the divine motion that gives infallible assurance of their execution is not indifferent and undetermined, but brings us infallibly to perform a certain salutary act that is efficaciously willed by God, by causing in us and with us even that this act is performed freely. Later on we shall see that this teaching is completely in agreement with what St. Thomas says.[18]

Therefore the Thomists use the expression "predetermining physical premotion" only for the purpose of excluding the theories of simultaneous concurrence and indifferent premotion. If these theories had not been proposed, as Thomas de Lemos remarked on several occasions, the Thomists would have been satisfied to speak about divine motion as St. Thomas did, for every motion as such is a premotion, and every divine motion, as divine, cannot receive a determination or perfection that is not virtually included in the divine causality. We always come back to the same inevitable dilemma: "God determining or determined."

5) Is the divine motion purely an extrinsic help given by God, or is His action identical with His essence, without which nothing created is received in the operative potency of the creature, so as to make it pass into act, for instance, so as to cause our will to perform a vital and free act?

Some theologians thought so, as cardinals Pecci and Satolli in the time of Leo XIII; as also did bishops Paquet and Janssens, O.S.B., in more recent times. These theologians teach, of course, against the Molinists and Suarezians, that the *scientia media* is inconceivable and that the divine influx necessary for the free act is an intrinsically efficacious motion.

---

18 *Ibid.*, Ia, q.14, a.5,8; q.19, a.4; a.6 ad 1um; q.19, a.8; q.83, a.1 ad 3um; Ia IIae, q.10, a.4 ad 3um; q.79, a.2; *De veritate*, q.22, a.8,9.

But they add—and in this they think that they have Cajetan's authority on their side—that the divine decree and concurrence are not predetermining and that there is no created motion received in the operative potency of the creature so as to cause it to pass into act. As far as they can see, God's help is merely extrinsic.[19]

Father del Prado shows [20] that there is no *via media* between the doctrine of the predetermining decrees and the theory of the *scientia media;* for the divine knowledge of conditionally free acts of the future presupposes indeed a divine decree or it does not. If we reject the *scientia media* and say that it does, then the decree is predetermining, for otherwise it could not infallibly make known the conditionally free act of the future or the conditionate future. Undoubtedly, this decree does not precede our acts by a priority of time but of nature and causality, and it is measured by the sole instant of motionless eternity. Does it follow, as Cardinal Satolli says,[21] that by the determination of this divine decree there is no longer any mystery? Not at all, say the Thomists, for the mystery remains in this sense, that this predetermining divine decree reaches even to what is more obscure for us, even to the free mode of our acts, and to the physical act of sin without it being at all the cause, however, of the disorder that is in this act. The same must be said for the divine motion, for it, too, has a priority not of time but of causality over our acts, and this kind of priority was admitted by Cajetan,[22] as well as by the other Thomists.

Is there no created motion that is received in the secondary cause? Some thought that by the words "physical premotion" the Thomists meant to qualify God's uncreated

19 Cf. Satolli, *De operat. div.,* disp. II, lect. 3; Paquet, *De Deo uno,* disp. VI, q. 1, a. 5.

20 *Loc. cit.,* III, 496, 501–07.

21 *Loc. cit.*

22 *Com. in Iam,* q. 19, a. 8. Cajetan here excludes priority of time, but not of nature. Cf. N. del Prado, *loc. cit.*

action, conceiving it as being in relation to ours. In that case there would be no created motion.

The doctrine of St. Thomas and his disciples is very clear on this point. They teach in common that even God's action *ad extra* is formally immanent and virtually transitive,[23] and that there is no real relation on God's part toward us; there is only a relation of dependence of the creature on God, and this is not reciprocated.[24] Thus the creative action is formally immanent and eternal, although it produces, at the time willed in advance by God, an effect in time.[25] Whereas the formally transitive action, such as the heating of water by the coal fire, is an accident that proceeds from the agent and terminates in the patient, the divine action *ad extra* cannot be an accident; it is really identical with God's very essence. It is therefore formally immanent, and, though not having the imperfections of the formally transitive action, it resembles this latter in so far as it produces either a spiritual or corporeal effect that is really distinct from it. It is in this sense that it is said to be virtually transitive, for it contains eminently within itself all the perfection of a formally transitive action, without any of the imperfections that essentially belong to this latter.

From this we see that God's uncreated motion bears only an analogical resemblance to the motion of a created agent that is incapable of interiorly and infallibly moving our will to choose this or that.[26] The greater number of the objections against the divine premotion are due to the fact that the divine action is conceived as being univocal with created action, which latter does not go so far as to cause our acts to be performed freely.[27]

---

[23] *Loc. cit.,* Ia, q.25, a.1 ad 3um; *Cont. Gent.,* II, 23, par. 4; chap. 21, par. 3.
[24] *Ibid.,* Ia, q.13, a.12.
[25] *Cont. Gent.,* II, 35.
[26] *Loc. cit.,* Ia, q.19, a.8; q.105, a.4; Ia IIae, q.9, a.4.
[27] Cf. Zigliara, O.P., *Summa phil., Theol. nat.,* Bk. III, chap. 4, a. 4, par. 5.

But from the fact that the secondary cause cannot be independent of the divine action, does it follow that there is no created motion received in the secondary cause, and one that is prior to the operation of this latter according to a priority not of time but of causality? Does it follow that actual grace, whether it is operating or co-operating, is identical either with God's uncreated action or with the salutary act of which it is said to be the cause?

St. Thomas replies in an article in which he has treated this question *ex professo* and at very great length. He writes as follows: "What God effects in the natural thing by which it actually acts, is solely of the intentional order, since it has a certain incomplete being, just as colors are in the air and artistic power in the artificer's instrument. . . . A power peculiarly its own could have been conferred on the natural thing, as a form permanently inhering in it; but power could not have been given for it to act in the production of being as the instrument of the first Cause, unless it were given the power to be the universal principle of being. Neither could it be given the natural power to move itself, or to preserve itself in being. Hence just as it is evidently unreasonable to expect that the instrument be given the power to act apart from the artificer's artistic movement, so also the natural thing could not have the power conferred upon it to act apart from the divine action." [28]

In like manner, when speaking of actual grace, St. Thomas distinguishes the divine motion received in us both from God and from our acts of knowing and loving, saying of actual grace that "it is an effect of God's gratuitous will . . . inasmuch as man's soul is moved by God to know or will or do something." [29] In another of his works he expresses himself still more clearly: "The motion of the mover precedes the

[28] *De potentia*, q.3, a.7 ad 7um.
[29] *Loc. cit.*, Ia IIae, q.110, a.2.

motion of the mobile object, both intellectually and causally." [30] And again he says: "The secondary agent receives
the complement of its power from the primary Agent." [31]

The objection has been raised [32] that this received divine
motion would limit the scope of the divine causality, which
would stand in need of this determined disposition so as to
bring about the action of the secondary cause. And, moreover, it is a contradiction to maintain that the secondary
cause is determined to act by an ultimate formality and that,
notwithstanding, it determines itself.

Father del Prado [33] replies to this by remarking that it is
not the first Cause that stands in need of this determination
received in the secondary cause, but it is this latter that needs
to be moved or applied to its act by the first Cause. The scope
of the divine causality is in no way limited by this, for God
needs only to will efficaciously so as to realize what He wills.

To the second difficulty the Thomists reply that there
would certainly be a contradiction in maintaining that the
secondary free cause is determined to act by an ultimate
formality that is peculiarly its own act, and that it determines
itself to this act. But we must not confound the motion that
causes the secondary cause to act, with the action of this
latter. Motion, for instance, efficacious grace, is given for the
purpose of action, and is not identical with it. Likewise, the
heating of water by the fire is not identical with the warmth
of this water upon surrounding objects. Moreover, as we shall
see more clearly in the following chapters, the expression
"predeterminating premotion" does not mean a formal, but
a causal, predetermination.

We have just seen what, according to classic Thomism, is
meant by divine motion. By it we see, as the Thomists say,

[30] *Cont. Gent.*, III, 150, par. 1.
[31] *Ibid.*, III, 66, par. 4.
[32] Cf. Satolli, *De operat. div.*, disp. II, lect. 3.
[33] *Loc. cit.*, III, p. 479.

how removed is the true doctrine of St. Thomas from these two extremes, in that it rises above and beyond them.

On the one hand, the divine motion does not render the activity of the secondary cause superfluous, as occasionalism concluded, nor does it suppress freedom of action but actualizes it. On the other hand, the divine motion is not merely a simultaneous concurrence, or an indifferent and undetermined premotion that would be under the necessity of receiving from us a perfection and a new determination not contained in its causality. Nor is it a purely extrinsic help given by God.

CHAPTER IV

What Physical Premotion Actually Is According to Classic Thomism

For a proper understanding of this expression, we need merely make use of the very words of St. Thomas in explaining the terms: motion, premotion, physical, and predetermining.

1) It is a motion that is passively received in the secondary cause so as to induce it to act, and, if the secondary cause is vital and free, so as to induce it to act vitally and freely, as we have seen St. Thomas said. This motion which, in the supernatural order is called actual grace, is really distinct both from God's uncreated action upon which it depends, and from the salutary act to which it is directed.[1] On this point all the Thomists are agreed. They say, as for instance John of St. Thomas does: "This motion cannot be the very action of the created cause, since this motion is prior to such action and brings it about; it is not, therefore, the action of the created cause, for it cannot move the cause as agent but as patient." [2]

We can explain this divine motion that is received in the secondary cause by comparing it with creation in the passive sense, about which St. Thomas spoke at considerable length.[3] By this we do not mean, as at times it has been said, that the motion in question here is creation, for our acts are not created in us *ex nihilo,* as is the case with the spiritual soul

---

[1] *Summa theol.,* Ia IIae, q.110, a.2; q.111, a.2.
[2] *Cursus phil., Phil. natur.,* q.25, a.2.
[3] *Loc. cit.,* Ia, q.45, a.3.

when it is united with the body. They are vital acts, produced by our faculties or operative powers, and these powers, created and preserved in being by God, need to be moved so as to receive the complement of causality of which St. Thomas speaks. Neither indeed is grace, whether habitual or actual, created *ex nihilo;* but it is drawn from the obediential potentiality of the soul, upon which it depends as an accident.[4]

But if the divine motion in question here is not creation, in the strict sense of the term, then it can come only from the creative cause, for only this latter is capable of producing the whole being of a given effect and all its modes, whether the effect be necessary or free. On this point St. Thomas, commenting on Aristotle, says: "The divine will is to be understood as existing outside the order of beings, like a cause that profoundly pervades all being and all its differentiae; and since the possible and the necessary are differentiae of being, therefore necessity and contingency in things originate from this same divine will."[5]

Furthermore, although the motion that applies us to act is not creation, yet for several reasons it is not unlike it. Active creation and active motion are analogous, as also are passively considered creation and passive motion by which the secondary cause, as St. Thomas says, is applied to its act. Let us see in what this twofold analogy consists.

If creation in the active sense is a divine and eternal action, which is formally immanent and virtually transitive, creation in the passive sense is the real relation of dependence upon God on the part of the creature that comes into existence; for "creation imports a relation of the creature to the Creator, with a certain newness or beginning."[6] In like manner, preservation in the active sense is continued creative

4 *Ibid.,* Ia IIae, q.113, a.9; *De virtutibus in commune,* a.10 ad 2um et 3um.
5 *Perihermenias,* I, lect. 14; cf. *Com. in Met.,* VI, lect. 3; Ia, q.19, a.8.
6 *Loc. cit.,* Ia, q.45, a.3 ad 3um.

action and, in the passive sense, it is the real relation of constant dependence of the being of the creature upon God.

Now just as the being of the creature is really dependent
upon the divine creative and conservative action, so also is
the action of the creature really dependent upon the divine
action that is called motion. We do not say that God creates
our acts of knowing and willing; He does not produce them
ex nihilo; for, in such event, these acts would no longer be
either vital or free. Nor do we say that God merely sustains
these acts which begin at a precise moment, though before
they did not exist. We say that God moves us to perform
them ourselves vitally and freely.

To avoid all equivocation, just as we distinguish between
active and passive creation, so we must distinguish here [7]
between two similar acceptations of the word "motion." We
have: (1) the active motion that in God, as we have said, is
a formally immanent and virtually transitive action; (2) the
passive motion by which the creature, though it had only
the power to act, is passively moved by God to become actually in act; then there is: (3) the action itself of the creature, which in us is the vital and free act of the will.

This distinction is commonly made to explain the influence
of one created agent over another, of fire, for instance, over
water. In this case we have: (1) the action of the fire: actual
heating of water; (2) the effect of this action upon the water:
it is heated; (3) the action of the heated water upon surrounding objects.

In like manner, external objects and light exert an influence on the eye that is aroused to action, then the eye receives an impression, a likeness of the object, and finally it
reacts by the vital act of vision. Again, in like manner, our
immaterial will, by an immaterial action that is formally
immanent and virtually transitive, exerts an influence upon
our sensitive faculties and bodily organs so as to cause them

[7] Zigliara, *Summa phil., Theol. nat.,* Bk. III, chap. 4, a. 4, nos. 3-5.

to act. This is what St. Thomas calls the active use of the will,[8] which is followed by the passive use of the faculties moved to act, and finally we have the act of these faculties, an act that is immediately produced, elicited by them, and commanded by the will.

We must not, therefore, confuse the divine motion that is passively received in the secondary cause, either with the divine active motion which is God Himself, or with the action produced by the secondary cause. Now this confusion is made by those who say, as Satolli does,[9] that the will cannot be determined by God to act and yet determine itself to this act. It would be a contradiction, if the will received from God its voluntary act complete in itself, as if it had been created *ex nihilo;* then it would no longer be possible for the will to produce this act. But what the will receives is merely a passive motion by which it is applied to act according to its nature, which means that it acts vitally and freely. This motion, however, cannot be given to it by any created or creatable spirit, however powerful it may be, but only by God, the Author of its nature and inclination to universal good, by God who preserves it in existence, and who is more intimate to it than it is to itself. As Zigliara points out,[10] when persons object to physical premotion, they generally take in an active sense what Thomists take in a passive sense; they confound physical premotion either with the divine un-created action, which we are incapable of receiving, or else with our own action that supposes premotion instead of being identical with it.

The Thomists commonly define the motion received by our will as "a divine motion by which our will is reduced from the potency of willing to the act of willing." [11] These last words do not mean that God produces in us and *without*

---

[8] *Loc. cit.,* Ia IIae, q.16, a.1.
[9] *De operat. div., op. cit.*
[10] Zigliara, *loc. cit.*
[11] *Ibid.*

us the act of willing, but that our will is moved by Him to perform itself, and vitally, this act which is called volition. And therefore, as Zigliara remarks,[12] the act which the will is passively brought to perform is not its own vital and free operation, as the opponents of this doctrine suppose. It is a supernatural movement or impulse, an actual efficacious grace by which it performs its act, whether this be its first vital though indeliberate act, or successive acts that terminate a discursive deliberation. Thus it is that the actual efficacious grace, which inclines our will to perform the salutary act, is called "the first proximate act," and the salutary act itself is called "the second act," even if it be a question of the first salutary act.

Just as water does not heat unless it is heated, so every secondary cause, our will, for instance, acts only if it is pre-moved by God, the very first cause. If it were otherwise, then this something of reality in the transition to act, which is required for the performance of vital and free actions, would be withdrawn from God's universal causality that includes everything of reality and goodness external to Himself.

Only by confusing physical premotion with our voluntary act can anyone conclude that our will under the influence of this motion, which is said to be in conformity with its nature, is no longer mistress of its act.

2) In what sense is the divine motion called premotion? To move and to be moved are correlative and synchronous terms. There is no priority of time of active over passive motion; they are coincident, for it is the same thing that is produced by the mover and that is received in the movable object, namely, the movement that proceeds from the mover into the movable object.[13]

We must get away, therefore, from imaginations which picture physical premotion as an entity which, like a small

12 *Ibid.*
13 Cf. S. Thomam, in *Phys. Arist.* III, lect. 4, no. 10.

winch placed by God in our will, would precede in time our voluntary act: "The motion of the mover precedes the movement of the movable object both intellectually and causally." [14] We have here only a priority of causality, as in the case of the eternal decree, which transcends time, and the divine motion of this decree assures its execution. But with regard to this decree, we must say that it is measured by the unique instant of immobile eternity, which corresponds unchangeably to every successive instant of time, as the apex of a pyramid corresponds to all the points of its base and to each of its sides. With regard to the motion received in the created will, it is received at the very moment of time in which the voluntary act is produced. In the case of the angels, it is discrete time that is measured by its successive acts, and this has nothing to do with the sun's movement. In the case of human beings, it is the continuous time of day and hours, because of the sensible movement of our imagination and organism, and this is inseparable from our intellectual and volitional acts.

From this we see that physical premotion and the free act following it instantaneously, do not depend infallibly upon what precedes them in time—that is, in the past—but only upon what precedes them in the ever unchangeable present (*nunc stans*) of eternity, which is the measure of the divine decrees.

The Thomists, too, cannot admit without a distinction the Molinist definition of liberty, that it is a faculty which, if we presuppose all that is required for the will to act, it can still act or not act. If, by the words "presupposed all that is required for it to act" is meant only what is required as a prerequisite by a priority of time, then this definition is absolutely true; but if, by these words, is meant what is required as a prerequisite by a simple priority of causality— namely, the divine motion and the final practical judgment

[14] *Contra Gentes,* III, 150, par. 1.

that precedes the voluntary election—then the definition is no longer true except by the aid of a distinction. Under the influence of the divine efficacious motion that extends even to the free mode of our acts, our will, in performing the act efficaciously willed by God, by reason of its unlimited scope, in that it is specified by universal good, retains the real power not to perform the act and to perform even the contrary act (*remanet potentia ad oppositum*); but it is impossible for the will, under the influence of the divine efficacious motion, actually to omit the performance of the act efficaciously willed by God, or actually to perform the contrary act. St. Thomas is explicit on this point. Of various texts it suffices to quote the following: "If God moves the will to anything, it is incompossible with this supposition, that the will be not moved thereto. But it is not impossible simply. Consequently it does not follow that the will is moved by God necessarily." [15] Bannez did not say anything more forcible than this.

The potential indifference which the faculty had before performing its act has been replaced by the actual indifference of the act itself that is already determined, and it tends with a dominating indifference toward a particular good that is absolutely out of all proportion to the universal scope of the will that is specified by universal good. The act does not cease to be free because it is determined; otherwise no act of the divine will would be free, since these acts are determined from all eternity and are unchangeable. Potential indifference is not essential to liberty, and is not to be found in divine liberty, in which there is no actual indifference of pure Act with regard to any finite good; it is not to be found in the freest of our acts that still remain free after their determination.

The word "premotion" indicates therefore a priority not of time but merely of reason and causality, and, if this

[15] *Loc. cit.,* Ia IIae, q. 10, a. 4 ad 3um.

priority did not exist, there would no longer be motion but merely simultaneous concurrence, such, says Molina, as of two men drawing a boat, the first exerting no influence over the second, but each acting independently on the boat. That is not the way God concurs in the action of the secondary cause; for He applies this latter to perform its act without which this reality, which is the transition from the state of inactive potency to the performance of the act, would be excluded from the divine universal causality.

3) The premotion is called physical not by reason of its opposition to the metaphysical or spiritual, but to distinguish it from moral motion, which moves the will by way of an objective attraction, by proposing a good to it.

St. Thomas often distinguished between these two motions: the movement of the will as to the specification of its act being called thus since it is derived from the object or end, and the other as to the exercise of its act which is derived from the agent.[16] He pointed this out particularly in another passage [17] where it is stated that God moves every secondary cause: (1) as final end, for every operation is for the sake of some good, real or apparent, which participates in a likeness to the supreme Good; (2) as first Agent from whom every subordinated agent receives its power to act. Applying this to the will, he had just said: "Wherefore in both ways it belongs to God to move the will; but especially in the second way by an interior inclination of the will." [18]

In this preceding article St. Thomas explains these two kinds of motion with reference to the intellect and the will, saying that these two faculties are moved both by the object proposed to them and, as to the exercise of their act, by God. St. Thomas adds that God alone seen face to face can irresistibly attract our will, because it is only He who can adequately

16 *Ibid.*, Ia IIae, q. 10, a. 2.
17 *Ibid.*, q. 105, a. 5.
18 *Ibid.*, a. 4; cf. ad 3um.

satisfy our capacity for loving.[19] As for the motion that concerns the exercise of the act, this can be received only from
the will itself, and this by a prior act from God, who alone
is capable of creating from nothing the spiritual soul and
directing it to universal good. The order of agents must correspond to the order of ends.[20]

This explains, then, how God, in thus moving our will, by
interiorly inclining it, does not force it; for He moves it in
accordance with its inclination to universal good; He actualizes this general inclination and causes it powerfully and
suavely to confine itself with a dominating indifference to a
certain particular good, thus freely willed with a view to
happiness, since man naturally wills to be happy and seeks
happiness in everything he wills.

St. Thomas observes that our acts would be neither free
nor meritorious, if the will were moved by God in such
manner that it nowise would move itself; but it is not so.
He says: "But since its being moved by another does not
prevent its being moved from within itself, as we have stated
(ad 2um), it does not therefore forfeit the motive for merit
or demerit." [21]

This last point is explained in another article,[22] in which
it is stated that the will, in so far as it wills the end, moves
itself to will the means. St. Thomas remarks that, if the will
could not move itself, if it were only moved by God, then it
would never will what is sinful. The complete reply, which
has been so much discussed, is as follows: "God moves man's
will, as the universal Mover to the universal object of the
will which is good. And without this universal motion man
cannot will anything. But man determines himself by his
reason to will this or that, which is true or apparent good.

19 *Ibid.*, Ia IIae, q. 10, a. 2.
20 *Ibid.*, Ia IIae, q. 9, a. 6.
21 *Ibid.*, Ia, q. 105, a. 4 ad 3um.
22 *Ibid.*, Ia IIae, q. 9, a. 3.

Nevertheless, sometimes God moves some specially to the willing of something determinate, which is good; as in the case of those whom He moves by grace, as we shall see later on (q. 109, a. 2)." [23]

Some Molinists claimed, according to this text, that for St. Thomas the divine motion is not predetermining, and that by the same motion which incites a person to will happiness, one would perform a good act (at least naturally good), whereas another would commit sin.

This interpretation contradicts many texts of St. Thomas, and in the first place it is against the principle of predilection on several occasions formulated by him, according to which, "since God's love is the cause of goodness in things, no one thing would be better than another, if God did not will greater good for one than for another." [24] Now in the Molinist interpretation of the text with which we are concerned,[25] it would happen that of two men equally helped and loved by God, one would become better than the other by this naturally good act, for instance, which consists in paying one's debts. He would become better without having received more from God. It would not depend on the free Cause of all good that there is more of good in this man rather than in that other.

Moreover, this Molinist interpretation is contrary to what St. Thomas explicitly states in many texts,[26] and to the concluding words of the text we are discussing, which are: "Nevertheless, sometimes God moves some specially to the act of willing something determinate, which is good; as in the case of those whom He moves by grace, as we shall see later on." [27]

23 *Ibid.*, Ia IIae, q.9, a.6 ad 3um.
24 *Ibid.*, Ia, q.20, a.3.
25 *Ibid.*, Ia IIae, q.9, a.6 ad 3um.
26 *Ibid.*, Ia IIae, q.10, a.4 ad 3um.
27 *Ibid.*, Ia IIae, q.9, a.6 ad 3um.

The commentators [28] of St. Thomas generally admit that it is a question of operating grace, which St. Thomas discusses later on.[29] We shall see that it is so when we come to explain the three propositions of this text just quoted. In doing so we shall appeal to the three principal modes by which God moves us: (1) before we deliberate: to will happiness in general; (2) after we deliberate: to will a certain particular good about which we deliberated; if the act is supernatural it is in this case performed under the influence of co-operating grace; (3) above and independent of our deliberation: by the special inspiration of the Holy Spirit, which is an operating grace; of such a nature are the acts which are performed by means of the gifts of the Holy Ghost.

Several Molinists recognize that, according to St. Thomas, in this last case there is a predetermining premotion, but they add: then the act is neither free nor meritorious.[30] Contrary to this, St. Thomas holds that the acts performed by means of the gifts of the Holy Ghost, by the gift of piety, for instance, are free and meritorious.[31] The purpose of the gifts is precisely to dispose us to receive in a docile manner the special inspiration of the Holy Ghost, that it may be a means of merit for us. Thus the Blessed Virgin was moved powerfully and suavely to utter infallibly and freely her "fiat" on the day of the annunciation in view of the redemptive purpose of the incarnation, which was destined most certainly to come to pass.[32]

---

[28] Cf. Billuart, *De actibus humanis*, diss. III, a. 3; N. del Prado, O.P., *De gratia et lib. arb.*, I, 236; II, 228, 256; Garrigou-Lagrange, *God*, II, 80, no. 35, p. 158.

[29] *Loc. cit.*, Ia IIae, q.3, a.2.

[30] Cf. Father de Guibert, S.J., *Etudes de théologie mystique*, p. 170.

[31] *Loc. cit.*, Ia IIae, q.68, a.3, c et ad 2um.

[32] The teaching of St. Thomas on operating grace (Ia IIae, q.3, a.2) and on the special inspiration of the Holy Ghost received by the gifts gives special trouble to the Molinists. That is why they are led to modify it considerably, and to say that this special inspiration inclines one to an act that is not free and not meritorious, which, in its turn, prompts one (like actual grace) to

4) In what sense is premotion said to be predetermining, although not necessitating, that is, although in conformity with the nature of our free will which must remain mistress of its act? It is a question here not of a formal but of a causal predetermination.[33] The Molinists generally say that if God by His motion determines the will to will this rather than that, then it can no more determine itself. This confounds causal predetermination, which inclines us strongly and suavely to determine ourselves, with formal determination, which is that of the voluntary act already determined, and which follows the other according to a posteriority not of time but of causality.

Some authors [34] admit physical premotion, but by no means predetermination. And yet, as Cardinal Zigliara said,[35] pre-

---

perform an act that is subsequently meritorious and that is produced by means of the virtues.

Hence in that the gifts of the Holy Ghost do not immediately tend toward the performance of meritorious acts, it follows that the mystic life or infused contemplation (which is the result of faith illumined by the gifts of understanding and wisdom) is not the formal way of sanctity, but is a gift in itself of an extraordinary kind like visions and revelations; for sanctity cannot consist of acts that are not meritorious.

As besides, the seven gifts are in all the just, these theologians are led to admit two modes of operation for the acts performed by means of the gifts; there is the *ordinary* mode dependent upon graces called medicinal, by which the non-meritorious acts that precede justification are performed; the other mode is *extraordinary*, and it is such that the first has no connection with the second. Hence we cannot see how acts so different and heterogeneous, between which there is no subordination of inferior to superior, can proceed from the same habit. Several of these theologians go so far as to deny the principle of the specification of the habits by their formal objects and the specific difference between the gifts of the Holy Ghost and the infused virtues. This completely changes the teaching of St. Thomas about the gifts, and they strive to show that in the *Theological Summa* he even modified what he had said on this point in his *Commentary on the Sentences*.

In other words, the Molinists are hard put to it by the teaching of St. Thomas on operating grace (Ia IIae, q.3, a.2), whether this refers to the acts performed by means of the gifts or to the justification of the adult or to the first voluntary act of the angel or to the liberty of the blessed or to the liberty of Christ's impeccability.

[33] Cf. Zigliara, *Theol. nat.*, Bk. III, c. 4, a. 4, par. 6.
[34] Cf. Pignataro, S.J., *De Deo Creatore*, p. 519.
[35] *Loc. cit.*

motion and predetermination mean the same thing; but premotion refers to omnipotence, and predetermination to the predetermining decree of the divine will. The divine will predetermines that a certain salutary act, for instance, Mary's fiat, St. Paul's conversion, Magdalene's or the good thief's, shall be accomplished in time, on a certain day, at a certain hour, and that it shall be accomplished freely; then Omnipotence interiorly moves the human will without in the least forcing it, so as to assure the execution of the decree.

St. Augustine wrote on this as follows: "Certainly we observe His commandments, if we will. . . . Certainly we will, when we will; but He causes us to will what is good, of this it being said that it is God who worketh in you, both to will and to accomplish (Phil. 2: 13). Certainly it is we who act when we act; but He causes us to act by enabling the will to act efficaciously, who says 'I will cause you to walk in My commandments and to keep My judgments, and do them' (Ezech. 36: 27). . . . For it is He who operates first that we may will, and who co-operates with us when we will, bringing what we will to completion." [36]

The divine motion received in the secondary cause is predetermining in so far as it gives infallible assurance of the execution of a divine decree. It is not a formal but a causal predetermination; whereas that of the decree is both formal and causal. Finally, the determination of our voluntary act already performed is formal and not causal; but, as we said, far from excluding the actual dominating indifference, it implies this; for the free act already determined remains free; even the immutable act of divine liberty remains free in spite of its immutability. This is what St. Thomas says: "God alone can move the will, as an agent, without violence. Hence it is said: 'The heart of the king is in the hand of the Lord: whithersoever He will He shall turn it' (Prov. 21: 1). And: 'It is God who worketh in you both to will and

[36] *De Gratia et lib. arb.*, chaps. 16 f.

to accomplish, according to His good will' (Phil. 2: 13).

"Some, nevertheless, unable to understand how God can cause in us the movement of the will without prejudice to liberty, have endeavoured to give a false exposition to the authorities quoted. They say, in fact, that God causes in us the power to will, and not by causing us to will this or that. This is the exposition of Origen (3 Peri Archon) who defended free will in a sense contrary to the aforesaid authorities. . . . But the authority of Scripture is in manifest opposition to all this; for it is said: 'O Lord, Thou hast wrought all our works in us' (Is. 26: 12). Hence we receive from God not only the power to will, but also our very operations. Further, the very words of Solomon: 'Whithersoever He will He shall turn it' (Prov. 21: 1) show that the divine causality extends not only to the will, but also to its act. . . . Therefore in spiritual things every movement of the will must be caused by the first will.

"The saying of Damascene in the Second Book (*De orthod. fide*, c. 30), that God foreknows but does not predetermine the things which are in our power, is to be understood as meaning that the things which are in our power are not subject to the divine predetermination in such a way as to be necessitated thereby." [37]

In this interpretation given by St. Thomas of this text of St. John Damascene we have non-necessitating predetermination declared to be the very teaching of St. Thomas; otherwise he would have purely and simply admitted the words of Damascene: "He does not predetermine." In the construction of the phrase by St. Thomas, "non" refers directly to "quasi," which means that our elections or free acts are submitted to the determination of Providence, but not as though imposing necessity on them. In other words, this predetermination is non-necessitating, for it extends even to the free mode of our acts which, pertaining to being, comes under

[37] *Contra Gentes,* III, 88 (end), 89 (end), 90 (end).

the adequate object of Omnipotence; and what is not so included is only evil, since it comes from the deficient cause.[38]

On this subject St. Thomas writes: "Acts of choice and will are under the immediate governance of God (that is, not through angelic intermediaries). . . . God alone is the cause of our willing and choosing." [39] "Although God's action alone has a direct bearing on man's choice, nevertheless the angel's action has a certain bearing on man's choice by way of persuasion." [40] "The operation of an angel and of a heavenly body disposes a man to choose; whereas the operation of God gives completion to his choice. . . . Man does not always choose what his guardian angel intends, nor that to which the heavenly body inclines him: whereas he always chooses in accord with God's operation in his will. Hence the guardianship of the angels is sometimes frustrated . . . whereas divine providence never fails." [41] "Man can be directed to all things by the one divine disposition (that is what happens in the case of the predestined)." [42]

"Among the parts of the whole universe the first distinction to be observed is between the contingent and the necessary. . . . Therefore it belongs to the order of divine providence not only that such and such an effect be produced, but that it be caused necessarily, and that some other effect be produced contingently." [43] "The divine providence is the *per se* cause that this particular effect will happen contingently. And this cannot fail." [44] "God foresaw that it would happen contingently. It follows then infallibly that it will be, contingently and not of necessity." [45] "For all things are

[38] *De veritate,* q.5, a.5 ad 1um.
[39] *Contra Gentes,* III, 91, par. 1.
[40] *Ibid.,* chap. 92, par. 1.
[41] *Ibid.,* par. 3.
[42] *Ibid.,* par. 10 (end).
[43] *Ibid.,* chap. 94, par. 9.
[44] *Ibid.,* par. 10.
[45] *Ibid.,* par. 11.

foreseen by God so as to be freely done by us. . . . It belongs to His providence sometimes to allow defectible causes
to fail, and sometimes to preserve them from failing." [46]
"Accordingly, by knowing His essence, God knows all the
things to which His causality extends. Now this extends to
the works of the intellect and will. . . . Therefore God
knows both the thoughts and the affections of the mind." [47]

All these quotations from the *Contra Gentes* show that for
St. Thomas the divine motion, which directs us to perform
salutary acts, is a motion that concerns the exercise of the
act or a physical motion which, of itself and infallibly, inclines us, without compulsion, to perform this particular act
rather than a certain other, and this because the divine
causality extends even to the free mode of our acts; for this
latter still pertains to being. This means that for St. Thomas
the divine motion is predetermining although not necessitating.

We find the same doctrine expounded in the following
passage: "God can change the will from the fact that He
Himself operates in the will as He does in nature; hence, as
every natural action of the will, inasmuch as it is an action,
not only is from the will as immediate agent, but is also
from God as first Agent who operates more vigorously; hence,
as the will can change its act for another, much more so can
God." [48] The text is clear. The human will as secondary
cause determines itself to perform a certain free act; therefore much more so can God as the first Cause, who operates
more vigorously, incline the will infallibly to determine itself to perform this particular act rather than a certain other.
Thus He is the cause of St. Paul's conversion, of Magdalene's
or of the good thief's. [49]

46 *Ibid.,* par. 13.
47 *Ibid.,* I, 68. Also *Quodl.,* q.12, a.6.
48 *De veritate,* q.22, a.8.
49 *Ibid.,* q.22, a.9; *De malo,* q.6, a.1 ad 3um; also *Com. in I Periher.,* lect. 14.

In all these texts we see that for St. Thomas the divine causality extends even to the free mode of our determinations, so that everything real and good in them depends upon God as the first Cause, and upon us as secondary cause. In this sense the divine motion is predetermining and not necessitating.

The peculiar nature of predetermination is especially affirmed by St. Thomas, when commenting on our Lord's words: "My hour has not yet come." [50] "By this is meant," says St. Thomas, "the hour of His passion, which is determined for Him not of necessity, but according to divine providence." It is evidently here a question of a determining and infallible but not necessitating decree of the divine will. In like manner, commenting on the verse, "They sought therefore to apprehend Him: and no man laid hands on Him, because His hour was not yet come," [51] he says: "By this is meant His hour predetermined not from fatal necessity but by the three divine Persons." Again, commenting on St. John's words, "Jesus knowing that His hour had come, that He should pass out of this world to the Father," [52] he says: "Neither are we to understand by this that fatal hour, as if subjected to the course and disposition of the stars, but the hour determined by the disposition of divine providence." And concerning the words of our Lord, "Father, the hour is come; glorify Thy Son," [53] he remarks: "Neither is it the hour of fatal necessity, but of His Father's ordination and good pleasure."

All these texts evidently point to a predetermining and infallible divine decree that refers to the hour Jesus speaks of as His own, and hence even to the free act which He had infallibly to perform in willing to die for our salvation. These texts also refer to the permissive decree as regards

50 John 2: 4.
51 *Ibid.*, 7: 30.
52 *Ibid.*, 13: 1.
53 *Ibid.*, 17: 1.

the sin of Judas, who before this hour could do no harm to our Lord.

It has been claimed that the expression, "God does not determine from necessity," is not found in the writings of St. Thomas.[54] His commentary on the passages of St. John, which we have just quoted, show, on the contrary, that the hour of Jesus in which He freely offered Himself in the garden of Gethsemane and in which Judas betrayed Him, was not from necessity determined and fixed by God.

Finally, we find the same teaching in the *Theological Summa* of St. Thomas, where he gave it its definite shape. We shall quote only the principal texts. St. Thomas begins by saying: "Determined effects proceed from His own infinite perfection according to the determination of His will and intellect."[55] There we have the eternal predetermining decree. How does it safeguard our liberty? St. Thomas explains this in the fundamental text to which he always has recourse: "Since, then, the divine will is perfectly efficacious, it follows not only that things are done which God wills to be done, but also that they are done in the way that He wills. Now God wills some things to be done necessarily, some contingently."[56] St. Thomas states this objection: "Every cause that cannot be hindered, produces its effect necessarily. But the will of God cannot be hindered. For the Apostle says: 'Who resisteth His will?' (Rom. 9: 19.) Therefore the will of God imposes necessity on the things willed."[57] Instead of replying to this by stating, as the defenders of the *scientia media* do, that God foresees what we shall freely decide upon doing, he says: "From the very fact that nothing resists the divine will, it follows that not only those things happen that God wills to happen, but that they happen necessarily or

[54] Cf. A. d'Alès, *Dict. apol.*, art. "Providence," append. "Prédetermination physique."
[55] *Loc. cit.*, Ia, q.19, a.4.
[56] *Ibid.*, a.8.
[57] *Ibid.*, obj. 2a.

contingently according to His will." [58] We have already seen the reply to this objection.[59] This text also expresses with all possible clarity, that the intrinsic and infallible efficacy of the decrees and the divine motion, far from destroying the liberty of our acts, causes it; for this efficacy extends even to the free mode of these acts, and this still pertains to being.

St. Thomas said the same in the following passage: "God, therefore, is the first cause, who moves causes both natural and voluntary. And just as by moving natural causes He does not deprive their actions of being voluntary: but rather is He the cause of this very thing in them; for He operates in each thing according to its own nature." [60]

Elsewhere St. Thomas explains, as he did when commenting on Damascene's statement that "God foreknows our intentions, but does not predetermine them." [61] Briefly St. Thomas replies as follows: "Damascene calls predestination an imposition of necessity, after the manner of natural things which are predetermined towards one end. This is clear from his adding: He does not will malice, nor does He compel virtue. Whence predestination is not excluded by Him." [62] This text shows that St. Thomas, in excluding necessitating admits non-necessitating predetermination that implies, in his opinion, predestination. On this point he says: "Predestination most certainly and infallibly takes effect, yet it does not impose any necessity." [63]

All these texts enable us to see clearly the meaning of passages occurring further on in the *Theological Summa* of St. Thomas on this subject. Thus we read: "Since, therefore, the will is an active principle, not determinate to one thing, but having an indifferent relation to many things, God so moves

---

[58] *Ibid.*, ad 2um.
[59] Cf. *Contra Gentes*, III, 94, par. 11.
[60] *Loc. cit.*, Ia, q.83, a.1.
[61] *Contra Gentes*, III, 90 (end).
[62] *Loc. cit.*, Ia, q.23, a.1 ad 1um.
[63] *Ibid.*, a.6.

it that He does not determine it of necessity to one thing." [64]
Throughout this question St. Thomas used the expression
"not to move of necessity" as meaning, to move without necessitating. It is in this same sense that he says here "He does
not determine of necessity to one thing," as he said in the
passages just quoted from his commentary on St. John's Gospel that have reference to the "hour" of Jesus appointed by
Providence. In all cases it is a question of a non-necessitating
predetermination, which extends even to the free mode of
our acts.

St. Thomas repeats even here that "the divine will extends
not only to the doing of something by the thing which He
moves, but also to its being done in a way which is fitting to
the nature of that thing. And therefore it would be more
repugnant to the divine motion, for the will to be moved
of necessity, which is not fitting to its nature, than for it to
be moved freely, which is becoming to its nature." [65] This
means that God cannot by His motion necessitate the will
to will a particular good that is presented to it as good under
one aspect, and that is not good under another. [66] Such an
object, which is absolutely inadequate to the universal scope
of the will, specifies the free act, in virtue of the principle
that acts are specified by their object; therefore the act of
the will that concerns a particular good thus proposed by
the intellect under the form of an indifferent judgment,
cannot be other than free. This constitutes, for St. Thomas,
the very definition of a free act; [67] whereas the Molinist definition of liberty abstracts from the specifying object, saying:
"Liberty is the faculty which, granted all that is required
as a prerequisite for the will to act, it can either act or
not act." The Thomists, considering that the free act, like
every act, is specified by its object, say with the Council of

[64] *Ibid.*, Ia IIae, q. 10, a.4, c.
[65] *Ibid.*, a.4 ad 1um.
[66] *Ibid.*, q. 10, a.2.
[67] *Ibid.*, q. 10, a.2.

Trent that, "under the influence of the divine efficacious motion, the will still has the power to resist. It can resist if it so wills, but under the influence of efficacious grace it never so wills, just as Socrates when seated can rise, but he is never at the same time both seated and standing. "It is even commonly accepted doctrine among them that "it implies a contradiction for the will, when the judgment is indifferent, to be necessitated by the divine motion, which is itself efficacious." [68] Just as the will cannot will an unknown good, one that is not proposed to it by the intellect, so also it cannot will any other good than that which is proposed to it; it cannot necessarily will what is proposed to it as not necessarily desirable. The act specified by this object cannot but be free, and the divine efficacious motion cannot change its nature; therefore it is not necessitating.

However, when it is efficacious, it causes the will infallibly to will freely this particular good rather than that other; it is in this sense that it is predeterminating. Such is, indeed, the mind of St. Thomas. There can be no doubt about this if we read the reply to the third objection of this article from which we have just quoted. [69]

The objection which St. Thomas states is the one that will always be brought up by the Molinists. It is as follows: "A thing is possible, if nothing impossible follows from its being supposed. But something impossible follows from the supposition that the will does not will that to which God moves it; because in that case God's operation would be ineffectual. Therefore it is not possible for the will not to will that to which God moves it." Therefore it wills of necessity. St. Thomas far from saying that God foresees our consent, replies as follows: "If God moves the will to anything, it is incompossible with this supposition that the will be not moved thereto. But it is not impossible simply. Consequently

[68] Cf. Billuart, *Cursus theol., De actibus humanis,* diss. II, a.5.
[69] *Loc. cit.,* Ia IIae, q.10, a.4.

it does not follow that the will is moved by God necessarily." [70] The will truly has the power to perform the contrary act, but this act, which is really possible, is never really present under the influence of efficacious grace, for this latter would no longer be efficacious. That is why actual resistance is said to be incompatible with efficacious grace. So Socrates when sitting has it in his power to stand, but he cannot at the same time stand and sit; he must sit, while he is seated.[71]

This is one of the clearest texts on this point. It evidently affirms an infallible, but not necessitating predetermination. It is another way of expressing what, as we have just seen, St. Thomas said: "From the very fact that nothing resists the divine will, it follows that not only those things happen that God wills to happen, but that they happen necessarily or contingently, according to His will." [72] In another of his works he wrote: "God foresaw that it would happen contingently. It follows then infallibly that it will be, contingently and not of necessity." [73]

The distinction between the possible and the compossible is tantamount to the distinction between the divided and composite senses, as St. Thomas points out when he says: "The fact that God wills any created thing is necessary on the supposition that He so wills, on account of the immutability of the divine will, but is not necessary absolutely." In other words, there is necessity of consequence or a conditional necessity, but not of consequent, as in the case of a strict syllogism, the minor of which is contingent. Then he goes on to say: "So the same must be said of predestination. Wherefore one ought not to say that God is able not to predestinate one whom He has predestined, taking it in a

---

[70] *Ibid.*, ad 3um.
[71] For a criticism of this illustration as applied to efficacious grace, see Pohle-Preuss, *Grace*, p. 243. (Tr.)
[72] *Ibid.*, Ia, q.19, a.8 ad 2um.
[73] *Contra Gentes*, III, 94, par. 11.

composite sense, though absolutely speaking, God can pre-destinate or not. But in this way the certainty of predestination is not destroyed." [74]

St. Thomas speaks just as clearly in his treatise on grace, saying: "God's intention cannot fail. . . . Hence if God intends, while moving, that the one whose heart He moves should attain to grace, he will infallibly attain to it, according to John 6: 45: 'Everyone that hath heard of the Father and hath learned cometh to Me.' " [75] Similarly he says: "The Holy Spirit infallibly effects whatsoever He wills. Hence it is impossible for these two things to be at the same time true: that the Holy Spirit will to move anyone to perform an act of charity, and that this person lose the virtue of charity by committing sin. For the gift of perseverance is included among God's benefits, whereby most certainly are liberated whoever are liberated, as Augustine says (*De dono persever.*, chap. 14)." [76]

So we see that for St. Thomas the foreseeing of a free determination that would depend solely upon ourselves, is not the foundation for this divine certainty. It has its foundation in a decree of the divine will, the execution of which is assured by the divine motion. [77]

All these texts presuppose a divine predetermining but not necessitating decree, which extends even to the free mode of our acts; and they affirm the presence of a divine motion that assures the infallible execution of this decree. In this sense, too, it is justly said to be predeterminating and non-

[74] *Loc. cit.*, Ia, q.23, a.6 ad 3um; cf. Ia, q.14, a.13 ad 3um.

[75] *Ibid.*, Ia IIae, q.112, a.3, c.

[76] *Ibid.*, IIa IIae, q.24, a.11.

[77] *Ibid.*, Ia, q.14, a.8; q.19, a.3,4, c. et ad 4um; a.8; *De veritate*, q.6, a.3; Quodl. XII, a.3,4; All things are predetermined and ordained is declared to be but a Scotist infiltration into the school of Thomism. Cf. H. Schwamm, *Das gottliche Voherwissen bei Duns Scotus und seinen ersten Anhangern*, Innsbruch, 1934. See also on this subject M. Congar, *Praedeterminare et Praedeterminatio*, according to St. Thomas, *Rev. Sci. Phil. et Théol.*, August, 1934, pp. 363–71. Likewise, P. V. Doucet, O.F.M., in *Archiv. Franc. Hist.*, 1931, pp. 391–92, who is against Schwamm.

necessitating. It causes the will infallibly to determine it-self, to perform this particular act rather than a certain other, and it causes in us and with us all that there is of reality and goodness in this act.[78] Only evil, which is a disorder, is not included within the scope of its causality; it is excluded from the adequate object of Omnipotence, and far more so than sound is from the object of sight.[79]

Of late years people have written: "For God to have in-fallible knowledge of our free acts He does not need to in-ject the element of a free determination into the drama of our liberty, and that such a process of knowledge would be truly anthropomorphism; it would be the knowledge of ef-fects in their proximate cause, which is not a divine process."

The Thomists never claimed for God the necessity of a created motion, so that He may have infallible and eternal knowledge of our acts; for this motion, as such, since it is received in the created will, exists only in time. They always said God knows our free acts in His eternal decree, and that His motion assures its execution in time. As a matter of fact, without this eternal decree, such a future free act would not be present in eternity as the object of divine intuition rather than its contrary act. God foresaw from all eternity that Paul would freely be converted on his way to Damascus on a cer-tain day and at a certain hour, because He had decided to convert him efficaciously in this manner. Without this decree, Paul's conversion would pertain only to the order of possible things and not to that of contingent futures.

The Molinists never proved that God cannot infallibly move our will to determine itself freely to perform a certain act; for it cannot be proved that God's universal and sover-eignly efficacious causality cannot extend even to the free mode of our acts. This mode is still being, and is therefore possible of realization; it is included consequently in the

78 *Ibid.*, Ia, q.23, a.5.
79 *Ibid.*, Ia IIae, q.79, a.1.

adequate object of Omnipotence, and beyond this there is only evil, which is a privation and a disorder.

This sublime doctrine makes all the more its demand upon us when we consider what influence God has upon the most heroic acts of the saints, upon the "fiat" of Mary on the day of the annunciation, and upon the meritorious acts of Jesus, whose human will here on earth, an image of the divine will, was both most free and impeccable.[80]

How does the divine motion adapt itself to the very nature of the secondary cause? We must take this to mean, say the Thomists, that the divine motion is actively modified by our will which receives it, for the will, in so far as it receives, is passive. But God adapts Himself in His motion to the nature of secondary causes, which means that He moves them according to their nature. Thus a great artist adapts his motion to the various instruments which he uses.[81] Thus St. Thomas, commenting on St. Paul's words on this point: "May He fit you in all goodness that you may do His will, doing in you that which is well pleasing in His sight through Jesus Christ," [82] writes: "When God incites a person to be of good will, He applies him, that is He makes him apt. . . . Interiorly . . . only God makes the will apt, who alone can change the will: 'The heart of the king is in the hand of the Lord; whithersoever He will He shall turn it' (Prov. 21: 1). Hence it is said: Doing in you: 'For it is God who worketh in you, both to will and to accomplish' (Phil. 2: 13). But what will He do? What is pleasing in His sight, that is, He will cause you to will what is pleasing to Him." [83]

Finally, the Thomists admit that physical premotion is entitled to be called simultaneous concurrence, when the created will is already in act; but it is a simultaneous con-

---

80 Cf. St. Thomas, IIIa, q.18, a.4 ad 3um, and the commentators apropos of the agreement between Christ's liberty and His impeccability.

81 Cf. Zigliara, *Theol. nat.*, Bk. III, chap. 4, a. 4, par. 5.

82 Heb. 13: 21.

83 *Com. in Ep. ad Heb.*, 13: 21.

currence that differs from Molina's in this, that it is primarily a premotion to apply the secondary cause to act.[84] Under the influence of this concurrence, the secondary cause becomes the instrumental cause of what is more universal in the effect produced, namely, of its very being in so far as it is being; whereas it is the proper cause of this effect in so far as it is this individual effect. Thus my will is the proper cause of my voluntary act and the instrumental cause of the very being of this act, in virtue of the principle: "The more universal effects must be reduced to the more universal and prior causes." [85] St. Thomas also says: "Furthermore, we find that according to the order of causes is the order of effects, which must be so because of the similarity between effect and cause. Neither can the secondary cause exert its effect on the primary cause by its own power, although it is the instrument of the primary cause as regards the effect of this latter. . . . And for this reason nothing acts to produce being except by God's power. For being itself is the most common and first of effects, and therefore it belongs to God alone to produce such an effect by His own power." [86] The created will is therefore the proper cause of its act in so far as it is this individual act; but it is the instrumental cause of being as regards the being of its act, vital and instrumental being, of course, as St. Thomas remarks.[87] In like manner this apple tree is the proper cause of this particular fruit, although God is the proper cause of the being of this same fruit.

To sum up what we have just said as to what physical premotion is, and to dispel the false notions that have often been entertained about it, let us say:

1) It is a motion received in the created operative potency

84 Cf. Goudin, O.P., *Phil. Met.*, q.3, *de praemotione*, a.2; also Zigliara, *loc. cit.*, chap. 5 (end).

85 *Loc. cit.*, Ia, q.45, a.5.

86 *De potentia*, q.3, a.7 (end).

87 *De veritate*, q.24, a.1 ad 5um.

in order to apply it to act. It is therefore a motion distinct both from the uncreated action that it presupposes, and from our action that follows it at the same moment. Efficacious grace is neither God nor the salutary act to which it is ordained. Thus our action remains truly our own; it is not created in us from nothing, but proceeds vitally from our faculty that is applied to its act by the divine premotion.

2) It is a physical motion, *as regards the exercise of the act,* and not a moral motion, or as regards the specification of the act, a motion that results from the attraction of a proposed object. Of all the agents that are distinct from our will, God is the only one, moreover, who can so move it interiorly according to its natural inclination to seek universal good, which He alone was able to give it. Under the influence of this motion, it moves itself.

3) It is a premotion according to a priority not of time, but of reason and causality.

4) It is predetermining, according to a causal predetermination distinct from the formal determination of the act that follows it. This means that it moves our will by an intrinsic and infallible efficacy to determine itself to perform this determinate good act rather than a certain other. The determination to perform a bad act, since it is itself bad and deficient, for this reason does not come from God, but from a defectible and deficient liberty. The divine predetermining motion is therefore not necessitating, for, like the divine predetermining decrees, the execution of which it assures, it extends even to the production in us and with us of the free mode of our acts, which is still being, and thus it is included in the adequate object of Omnipotence, and besides this there is only evil.

CHAPTER V

CONFORMITY OF THIS DOCTRINE WITH THE MIND OF ST. THOMAS

ALL the holy Doctor's texts just quoted in explanation of what this motion is and what it is not, sufficiently prove that this doctrine which we have just set forth is truly his own. By way of synthesis, and to save the reader the trouble of summarizing these texts, we shall draw attention here to the leading ones and certain others that are of importance. The necessity of giving a precise answer to certain objections obliges us to repeat ourselves to some extent.

"Determined effects proceed from God's own infinite perfection according to the determination of His will and intellect." [1] There we have the eternal predetermining decree, which is an elective act of the divine will, and this is followed up by the command of the divine intellect. Now the divine motion assures the execution of this decree in time. It is in this sense that it is said to be predetermining.

A little further on St. Thomas states this objection: "But the will of God cannot be hindered. Therefore the will of God imposes necessity on the things willed." [2] This is the ever recurring objection against the divine predetermining decrees. St. Thomas replies: "From the very fact that nothing resists the divine will it follows that not only those things happen that God wills to happen, but that they happen necessarily or contingently according to His will." The divine predetermining decree, far from destroying the liberty of our

[1] *Summa theol.*, Ia, q.19, a.4.
[2] *Ibid.*, a.8, obj. 2a.

choice because of its ineffable efficacy, causes it in us by reason of this transcendent efficacy which belongs only to God
and which extends even to the free mode of our choice; for
this mode, which is the dominating indifference of willing
as regards a good with an admixture of non-good, is still
being, and it is thus included in the adequate object of divine
power; whereas the disorder of sin cannot be included. As
St. Thomas remarks: "And just as by moving natural causes
God does not prevent their acts being natural, so by moving
voluntary causes He does not deprive their actions of being voluntary, but rather is He the cause of this very thing
in them." [3]

On the infallible efficacy of the predetermining decrees
and of the divine motion St. Thomas writes as follows: "The
operation of an angel merely disposes a man to choose;
whereas the operation of God gives completion to his choice.
. . . Man does not always choose what his guardian angel
intends. . . . Hence the guardianship of the angels is sometimes frustrated . . . whereas divine providence never
fails." [4] And again he writes: "Accordingly, by knowing His
essence God knows all things to which His causality extends.
Now this extends to the works of the intellect and will. . . .
Therefore God knows both the thoughts and affections of
the mind." [5] He does not know our affections independently
of His causality, but in His causality that extends even to
our most intimate affections. Does this include even our free
choices? Undoubtedly. Concerning this St. Thomas writes:
"Therefore all movements of will and choice must be traced
to the divine will: and not to any other cause, because God
alone is the cause of our willing and choosing." [6] It is a question of our elections or free choices as elections and not
merely as actions; for it concerns their free determination

[3] *Ibid.*, Ia, q.83, a.1 ad 3um.
[4] *Contra Gentes*, III, 92.
[5] *Ibid.*, I, 68.
[6] *Ibid.*, III, 91.

which God knows in so far as He causes it in and with us, as was said in the preceding text.[7]

Let us again refer to the objection St. Thomas states about Damascene, who wrote: "God foreknows all that is in us, but does not predetermine it all." [8] He replies: "Damascene calls predestination an imposition of necessity, after the manner of natural things which are predetermined towards one end. This is clear from his adding: He does not will malice, nor does He compel virtue. Whence predestination is not excluded by him." [9] St. Thomas says the same in another of his works: "The saying of Damascene (second book of *De orthod. fide,* c. 30), that God foreknows but does not predetermine the things which are in our power, is to be understood as meaning that the things which are in our power are not subject to the divine predetermination in such a way as to be necessitated thereby." [10]

Sylvester of Ferrara had pointed out, long before Bannez, that "Gregory of Nyssa in his book (*De homine*) and Damascene (second book of *De orthod. fide*) seem to say that what is within us is not subject to divine providence. But St. Thomas replies that this means nothing else than that the divine determination does not impose necessity upon what is within us." [11]

Father Synave, O.P., wrote not long ago: "What St. Thomas thought, indeed, about this question is beyond doubt, for he said that 'what is within us is not subject to divine providence as if necessitated by it.' St. Thomas admits, therefore, a divine non-necessitating determination: the wills and choices of man are submitted to the determination of divine providence, though this determination does not impose necessity on them. It is not right to say that, according

7 Cf. *Quodl.,* XII, a.6.
8 *De orthod. fide,* Bk. II, chap. 30.
9 *Loc. cit.,* Ia, q.23, a.1 ad 1um.
10 *Contra Gentes,* III, 90 (end).
11 *Com. in Contra Gentes,* III, 90 (end).

to the constant usage of St. Thomas, the idea of necessity is necessarily implied in the verb 'to determine.' It is not correct to say that the expression 'not of necessity determining' is equivalent to 'not determining.' . . . May we at least assert that 'to determine of necessity to one thing' is but a clearer and more forcible way of saying 'to determine to one thing'? No more so. Another text, as precise as the preceding, will show us that this equation of the two expressions is as false as the preceding, it being but a variant of the former by the addition, in the two terms compared, of the expression 'to one thing.' Replying to St. John Damascene who affirms that 'what is within us is not predetermined by God but comes from our free will,' St. Thomas says: 'Damascene's statement is not to be understood as meaning that all which is within us, that what is subject to our choice, is excluded from the scope of divine providence; but it means that all these things are not so determined to one thing, as in the case of those beings that are not endowed with free will.' [12]

"Human acts, in that they depend upon our choice, are therefore truly determined to one thing. If these acts were not so determined, St. Thomas would have said that they are not determined by divine providence to one thing, as those beings that are not endowed with free will. But one will have noticed that the phrase contains the word 'so' to which the negative particle at the beginning of the sentence belongs, so that it reads: 'they are not so determined to one thing by divine providence, as those beings are that are not endowed with free will.' The determination to one thing of free acts is not accomplished in the same way as the determination to one thing of acts that are not free. Now we know the nature of the determination to one thing of acts that do not depend upon free will. Everyone agrees that it is a necessitating determination. It is therefore a case of recognizing a twofold determination to one thing: a non-necessitating

[12] *De veritate,* q.5, a.5 ad 1um.

and a necessitating determination. The former pertains to free acts, and the latter to those that are not free." [13]

In another article Father Synave confirmed this interpretation with an argument that is quite conclusive. "If the word 'determine' implies necessity," he says, "why does not St. Thomas accept St. John Damascene's formula? . . . The result of that would be to make St. Thomas speak to no purpose. Lest it make no sense, the negative phrase of St. Thomas: 'What is within us is not submitted to the determination of divine providence as if it received from it a necessitating trait,' is to be taken as meaning that what is within us is submitted to the determination of divine providence, although this determination does not impose necessity upon it. There is no need of copious gloss, or even of any gloss, so as to reach this obvious meaning. . . . Words are words. It seems to me, in accordance with the most elementary laws of criticism, that we must accept this expression, 'determination of divine providence' as clearly established; if it conflicts with a system or a preconceived view of determination, we should either reform the one or abandon the other." [14]

We have proved this at length elsewhere,[15] and we must likewise take note of the following famous text of St. Thomas: "Since, therefore, the will is an active principle, not determinate to one thing, but having an indifferent relation to many things, God so moves it that He does not determine it of necessity to one thing, but its movement remains contingent and not necessary, except in those things to which it is moved naturally." [16]

Non ex necessitate must be translated here by *not of necessity*, as it must throughout this tenth question.[17] The *non*

13 *Revue Thomiste,* January, 1927, p. 74.
14 *Ibid.,* p. 241.
15 *Revue de phil.,* 1926, pp. 379, 423, 659; 1927, p. 303.
16 *Summa theol.,* Ia IIae, q. 10, a. 4.
17 *Ibid.,* Ia IIae, q. 10, a. 2, 3.

does not belong to *determinat,* but to *ex necessitate.* To understand it otherwise would result in a faulty translation throughout this question. Thus, in another place we read: "Therefore the will is not moved of necessity to either of the opposites." [18] And again: "It will not of necessity tend to this particular good." [19] Also the following replies to objections: "If it (the object) is lacking in any respect, it will not move of necessity. . . . But other things without which the end can be gained, are not necessarily willed by one who wills the end." [20]

All these texts prove that there is no doubt about the mind of St. Thomas. For him there is no necessitating predetermination; he admits, as regards our free acts, a non-necessitating divine predetermination. This is made still clearer from the state of the question in the famous article just quoted, in which it is determined with marvelous precision in two of the opening objections, these being the same as those always brought forward by the opponents of Thomism. They are as follows: "Every agent that cannot be resisted moves of necessity. But God cannot be resisted, because His power is infinite. But something impossible follows from the supposition that the will does not will that to which God moves it; because in that case God's operation would be ineffectual." [21]

St. Thomas replies to these objections, without referring in the least to the divine foreknowledge of our consent by means of a knowledge that would make us think it approaches either proximately or remotely to the *scientia media* of Molina. On the contrary, he insists upon the transcendent efficacy of the divine causality, for he writes: "In reply to the first objection we must say that the divine will extends not only to the doing of something by the thing which He

18 *Ibid.,* a.2, sed contra.
19 *Ibid.,* c.
20 *Ibid.,* ad 1um et ad 3um; cf. *ibid.,* a.3, sed contra, et c.
21 *Ibid.,* a.4, obj. 1a et 3a.

moves (and here we have election as a voluntary act), but also to its being done in a way which is fitting to the nature of that thing (and here we have the free mode of this election, which is produced by God in and with us, when He moves us to a particular salutary act in preference to a certain other, and this in virtue of the intrinsic efficacy of His motion, which man positively does not resist). And therefore it would be more repugnant to the divine motion, for the will to be moved of necessity, which is not fitting to its nature, than for it to be moved freely, which is becoming to its nature." [22]

In like manner, St. Thomas again affirms the intrinsic efficacy of the divine motion against which the objection was raised; but he replies that under the influence of this motion which man positively does not resist, he retains the power to resist. He could resist if he so wills; but under the influence of this most powerful and gentle motion he never wills to resist. In reply to this objection, he says: "We must say that if God moves the will to anything, it is incompossible with this supposition that the will be not moved thereto, because in that case God's operation would be ineffectual (as stated in the objection). But it is not impossible simply. Consequently it does not follow that the will is moved by God necessarily." [23] In order to grasp the exact meaning of St. Thomas' replies, we must not separate them, as is so often done in this case, from the objections he is seeking to solve.

There is no possibility of doubt. It is a case here of non-necessitating predetermination. Under the influence of this most powerful and gentle motion the Virgin Mary infallibly and freely uttered her "fiat" for the fulfilment of the mystery of the incarnation, which had infallibly to be fulfilled. Under the influence of this motion St. Paul was freely converted when on his way to Damascus, and the martyrs remained

[22] *Ibid.*, ad 1um.
[23] *Ibid.*, ad 3um.

firm in the faith and in their love for God in the midst of their torments. At least this is the way St. Thomas understood it. To put a different construction upon these texts would be to drain them of their metaphysical contents. The terms would cease to have any meaning.

The expression "non-necessitating predetermination" is found even several times in his works, as we have pointed out, especially in his commentary on St. John's Gospel, apropos of the hour of the passion, which is pre-eminently Christ's hour. All these expressions signify a decree of the divine will that is non-necessitating but predetermining premotion assuring the infallible execution of this decree, and this in a different way both for good and bad acts, for God is the cause of only the reality and goodness of our acts. As for moral disorder, whenever it occurs, He permits it, though in no way causing it, either directly or indirectly. This disorder comes solely from the deficient cause and is not included in the adequate object of indefectible Omnipotence, just as sound is not included in the object of sight. The expression, predetermining and non-necessitating "physical premotion," is therefore quite in conformity with the mind and even the terminology of St. Thomas.

It has been alleged at times that certain texts of the holy Doctor can be interpreted in the opposite sense. Goudin, O.P., pointed out: (1) that when St. Thomas denies predetermination, the context shows that he then has in mind necessitating predetermination as Damascene understands it.[24] (2) When St. Thomas says that the will determines itself, he is speaking of secondary causes; and it is clear that the deliberation is ordained to the determination of choice, which is a free act of the will. This is affirmed by St. Thomas in the famous text which we shall examine in the next chapter, it reads as follows: "God moves man's will, as the

[24] *Phil. Met.*, disp. II, q.3, a.7.

universal Mover to the universal object of the will, which is good. And, without this universal motion, man cannot will anything. But man determines himself by his reason to will this or that which is true or apparent good. (Certainly it is so in the order of secondary causes. That is why man deliberates, and thus sin is possible, which answers the objection put by St. Thomas.) Nevertheless, sometimes God moves some specially to the willing of something determinate, which is good; as in the case of those whom He moves by grace, as we shall state later on." [25] In the following question it is stated that this divine motion to will something determinate is not necessitating, because this infallibly efficacious influx extends even to the free mode of our choice: "It is incompossible with this supposition, that the will be not moved thereto. But it is not impossible simply." [26]

3) When St. Thomas says that God at times moves the will without implanting anything in it, he means, without producing in it an infused habit. [27]

4) Finally, St. Thomas has drawn a distinction between a general motion to universal good and a particular motion for this particular act, an act, for instance, of contrition. It remains true as he said: "that no matter how perfect a corporeal or spiritual nature is supposed to be, it cannot proceed to its act unless it be moved by God." [28] The notion of physical, predetermining, and non-necessitating premotion is therefore quite in agreement with the teaching of St. Thomas. We can assure ourselves of this by reading his earliest commentators, those who wrote long before Bannez. A

[25] *Contra Gentes,* III, 90 (end), a text previously quoted. See also *De veritate,* q.22, a.6, in which he spoke of a determination to one thing by a natural inclination or by way of nature, which is most certainly necessitating, and is therefore quite different from that which concerns us here; cf. *loc. cit.,* Ia IIae, q.9, a.6 ad 3um; cf. Ia IIae, q.109, a.6; q.111, a.2, q.112, a.3.

[26] *Ibid.,* q.10, a.4, c. et ad 3um.

[27] *De potentia,* q.3, a.7; *De veritate,* q.22, a.8.

[28] *Loc. cit.,* Ia IIae, q.109, a.1.

compilation of their texts was made by Father Dummermuth, O.P.[29]

[29] Cf. *S. Thomas et doctrina praemotionis physicae*, 1886 ("De mente S. Thomae," pp. 23–181; "De vetere schola S. Thomae," pp. 427–557, especially Capreolus, pp. 454–82; Ferrariensis, pp. 482–95; Cajetanus, pp. 495–506). How the earlier Jesuit theologians interpreted the mind of St. Thomas, such as Toletus, Molina, and Suarez, may be read pp. 685–754.

See also Dummermuth, *Defensio doctrinae S. Thomae de praemotione physica, Responsio ad R.P.V. Frins, S.J.*, Louvain and Paris, 1895. An examination of the texts of St. Thomas, objects of the controversy and the doctrine of the first Thomists, pp. 317–401; cf. Father Guillermin, O.P., "Sufficient grace," in the *Revue Thomiste*, 1902, pp. 75 f. (five articles). Cf. Dr. J. Ude, *Doctrina Capreoli de influxu Dei in actus voluntatis humanae*, p. 158. There are various reasons given in proof that Capreolus taught physical predetermination. Dr. J. Ude relates that he had undertaken to write this work because he thought Capreolus was rather opposed to physical predetermination; but an examination of the texts of this great commentator of St. Thomas, made him see that the opposite was the case. Cf. Father N. del Prado, O.P., *De gratia et libero arbitrio*, 1907, II, 141–253: "De natura physicae praemotionis juxta doctrinam sancti Thomae, et de diversis perfectionis gradibus in physica praemotione."

Cf. Garrigou-Lagrange, O.P., articles on non-necessitating predetermination in the *Revue Thomiste*, 1924, pp. 494–518; in the *Revue de philosophie*, 1926, pp. 379–98; 423–33; 659–70; and in 1927, pp. 303–24; by the same author, "Le dilemme: Dieu déterminant ou déterminé," in the *Revue Thomiste*, 1928, pp. 193–210; also "*God, His existence and His nature*," II, 529–62. Father Synave, O.P., "Prédétermination non-necessitante et prédestination nécessitante," in the *Revue Thomiste*, 1927, pp. 72–79; 240–49, a reply to Father d'Alès; by the same author, in the *Bulletin Thomiste*, 1928, pp. 358–68, a criticism of the work by Father d'Alès: *Providence et libre arbitre*, 1927, in which are re-assembled the articles which we answered in the *Revue de philosophie*, 1926–27. Cf. Garrigou-Lagrange, "La grace infailliblement efficace et les actes salutaires faciles," in the *Revue Thomiste*, November, 1925, March, 1926.

See also R. Martin, O.P., "Pour Saint Thomas et les thomistes contre le P. Stuffler, S.J.," in the *Revue Thomiste*, 1924–26, a series of articles. Cf. Ven. Carro, O.P., "El Maestro Pedro de Soto y las controversias theologicas en el siglo XVI" (Salamanca, Vol. X, 1931). By the same author, "De Soto a Banez," in the *Ciencia tomista*, 1928, pp. 145–78, and in the *Angelicum*, 1932, fasc. 4, pp. 477–81. Cf. M. J. Congar: "Praedeterminare et praedeterminatio chez S. Thomas," in the *Revue des Sc. phil. et théol.*, August, 1934, p. 363.

CHAPTER VI

THE DIFFERENT WAYS IN WHICH PHYSICAL PREMOTION OPERATES

FATHER del Prado has discussed this question at length.[1] He shows it to be the opinion of St. Thomas, by numerous texts taken from his works, that God moves our intellect and will in three ways: (1) before the act of deliberation; (2) after this act; (3) by a movement of a higher order. St. Thomas noted these three ways in which the divine motion operates both in the order of nature and of grace.

In the natural order God moves our will: (1) to will happiness in general (or to wish to be happy); (2) to determine itself to choose this particular good by an act of discursive deliberation; (3) He moves it by a special inspiration that excels any deliberation, such as happens with the man of genius and with heroes, as Aristotle [2] remarked and also one of his disciples [3] who argued as Plato would have done.

Likewise, in a proportionate manner, in the order of grace, God moves our will: (1) to direct itself to its supernatural end; (2) to determine itself to the use or practice of the infused virtues by means of a discursive deliberation; (3) He moves it in a manner that excels any deliberation by a special inspiration, and the gifts of the Holy Ghost render us docile to this movement.

Whether it be in the natural or in the supernatural order, the first manner of movement precedes the deliberation of

---

[1] *De gratia et libero arbitrio*, Vol. II, 1907, chapter 7, pp. 201–25; 245–58.
[2] *Nicomachean Ethics*, Bk. VII, chap. 1.
[3] *Eudemian Ethics*, Bk. VII, chap. 14; cf. St. Thomas, Ia IIae, q.68, a.1.

the will as regards the means; [4] the second follows or accompanies it; the third mode excels it. St. Thomas has enumerated these three ways.[5] It suffices here to give in English the first of these texts which, though several seem to be ignorant of this, is explained by the following texts, especially by those that treat of grace, to which St. Thomas refers them.

"God moves man's will as the universal Mover to the universal object of the will, which is good. (Thus man wills to be happy.) And without this universal motion, man cannot will anything. But man determines himself by his reason, to will this or that, which is true or apparent good. Nevertheless, sometimes God moves some specially to the willing of something determinate which is good; as in the case of those whom He moves by grace, as we shall see later on." [6]

Having seen in what physical premotion does and does not consist, and what are its different modes, we must speak of the reasons why the Thomists affirm the necessity of its being admitted.

[4] *Summa theol.,* Ia IIae, q.13, a.3; q.24, a.1 ad 3um.

[5] *Ibid.,* Ia IIae, q.9, a.6 ad 3um; q.68, a.2,3; q.109, a.1,2,6,9; q.111, a.2; *De veritate,* q.24, a.15.

[6] *Ibid.,* Ia IIae, q.9, a.6 ad 3um; cf. q.109, a.2,6; q.111, a.2. Space does not permit us here to give all these texts. On the text just quoted and its relation to the others, see Father N. del Prado, *op. cit.,* I, 236; II, 228, 256. Consult also the author's "Perfection chrétienne et contemplation," Vol. I, pp. 355–70; cf. *supra,* p. 266 note 32.

CHAPTER VII

REASONS FOR AFFIRMING PHYSICAL PREMOTION

WE shall here consider these reasons in the following order: (1) in general; (2) with reference to the divine decrees concerning our salutary acts; (3) so as to explain the efficacy of grace.

GENERAL REASONS FOR ADMITTING PHYSICAL PREMOTION

1) The Thomists ultimately give two general reasons for affirming physical premotion; one of these is to be sought in God, the other in the secondary cause. Fundamentally the reason is the same, though viewed under two aspects.

First reason. God is the first Mover and first cause to whom are subordinated, even in their action, all secondary causes. Now, without physical premotion we cannot safeguard in God the primacy of causality or the subordination of secondary causes in their very action. Therefore physical premotion is the reason why all secondary causes are subordinated to God as first Mover and first Cause.

The major is certain both in philosophy and in theology. It would be rash to deny it. As, indeed, it is certain that God is the supreme Being, upon whom all beings as such immediately depend, it is equally certain that God is the supreme efficient cause to whom all secondary causes are subordinated even in their action. Subordination in action follows subordination in being, just as action follows being. To deny this major would be to deny the first two classical proofs for the existence of God as set forth by St. Thomas.[1]

[1] Summa theol., Ia, q.2, a.3.

The minor becomes evident to us, if we take note of the fact that subordination of causes in their action consists in this, that the first cause moves or applies secondary causes to act, and that secondary causes act only because they are moved by the primary cause. St. Thomas states this clearly as follows: "Where there are several agents in order, the second always acts in virtue of the first: for the first agent moves the second to act. And thus all agents act in virtue of God Himself." [2] Now this is the very definition of physical premotion, which has a priority not of time but of causality over the action of the created agent. The Thomists confirm this argument by pointing out that neither simultaneous concurrence nor moral motion suffices to safeguard the subordination of causes.

2) Second reason. It finds its explanation in the indigence of the secondary cause. Every cause that is not of itself actually in act, but only in potentiality to act, needs to be physically premoved to act. Now such is the case with every created cause, even the free cause. Therefore every created cause needs to be physically premoved to act.

The major is certain. The classical proofs for God's existence, such as St. Thomas understands them, have their foundation in this principle, and to refuse to admit this major is to say that the greater comes from the less, the more perfect from the less perfect; for actually to act is a greater perfection than being able to act. If, therefore, the faculty to act were not moved, it would always remain in a state of potency and would never act. St. Thomas, too, said: "Everything that is at one time an agent actually and at another time an agent in potentiality, needs to be moved by a mover." [3]

The minor is no less evident. If a created cause were of itself actually in act, it would always be in act and never in potentiality. Our intellect would always actually know all the

[2] *Ibid.,* Ia, q.105, a.5.
[3] *Ibid.,* Ia IIae, q.9, a.4.

intelligible things it can know, and our will would always actually will all the good things that will be willed by it. Moreover, this created cause, instead of being moved to act would be its own action; but, for that, it would have to be its very being, to exist of itself; for action follows being, and the mode of action the mode of being, as St. Thomas often says.[4] Therefore every created cause, that it may act, needs to be physically premoved by God.

The free cause is no exception; for its action, as being, depends upon the first Being; its action as action, upon the first Agent; and as a free action, upon the first Free.[5] Furthermore, the free cause is particularly indifferent of itself or undetermined whether to act or not to act, to will this or that, and for this reason it stands particularly in need of a divine motion to cause it to determine itself.[6] The stars obey God without knowing Him and they are powerless to disobey; that the human will may freely obey Him it needs a special divine motion or a grace that, without forcing it, will cause it actually and freely to make its choice.

The special laws that govern human liberty cannot be contrary to the universal laws of the real that govern the relations between created being and God. They cannot be an exception to these most universal laws, but are subordinate to them.

Such are the two reasons why Thomists generally affirm physical premotion. We say that they are two aspects of one and the same fundamental reason: on God's part, the primacy of His causality, and as regards the created cause, the indigence of this latter.

3) Insufficiency of the other explanations. These two reasons are confirmed by the insufficiency of the other explanations. The primacy of the divine causality and the

4 *Ibid.*, Ia, q.54, a.1.
5 *Ibid.*, Ia IIae, q.79, a.2.
6 *Ibid.*, Ia, q.19, a.3 ad 5um.

subordination of causes are not indeed safeguarded, so the Thomists say, either by simultaneous concurrence or by the fact that God gave secondary causes the faculty to act.

a) Simultaneous concurrence does not move the secondary cause to act; and exerts no direct influence upon it, causing it to act; but this concurrence has only a simultaneous influence with it upon its effect, just as two men pulling a boat or two horses drawing a carriage. If it were otherwise, then this concurrence would not be merely a simultaneous but also a previous motion. It would have a priority of causality over the action of the secondary cause. By simultaneous concurrence God would be only the co-principle of our acts, but not the first Cause. There would be two partial and co-ordinated causes (at least of causality, if not of effect) and not two total and subordinated causes. Whereas for the Thomists the whole of the created action comes from God as the primary cause and from the created agent as the secondary cause.[7]

b) Moral motion also fails to explain it. This can, of course, constitute the subordination of causes in the order of final causality, for the end morally or objectively moves by way of attraction; but it does not do so in the physical order of efficient causality, and it is with this that we are concerned. God, indeed, is first Mover and first Cause in this physical order of efficient causality, and not merely in the order of moral causality by way of attraction or end. If it were not so, then He would be the first Mover only as regards agents endowed with intellect, since only these are capable of being moved morally by having an object proposed to them which attracts them.

c) Finally, it is not enough to say with Durandus of St. Pourçain [8] that God gave to secondary causes and preserves in them the faculty of action. St. Thomas excludes this opin-

[7] *Ibid., Ia*, q. 105, a. 5 ad 2um.
[8] In *IIum Sent.*, d. 1, q. 5.

ion as erroneous.[9] It was admitted by Pelagius and was not enough to declare him orthodox. Finally, it does not establish the subordination of causes in action but merely in being. Now action follows being, and the mode of action the mode of being. Dependence in action follows therefore dependence in being.

Furthermore, it is only God who can interiorly move our will to the exercise of its act, for He alone created and preserves it, and can move it according to the natural inclination He gave it for universal good. The order of agents corresponds to the order of ends, and therefore the most universal efficient cause can move to universal good which, as such, is realized in God alone.[10] Every other cause would necessitate, which means that it could not cause in us and with us that our acts should be performed freely.[11]

Suarez objected to this, saying that our will is *of itself,* if not formally at least virtually, in act, and that thus it can pass into act without a divine motion.[12] It is easy to reply to this objection by saying that the virtual act is distinct from the action resulting from it. Is there, or is there not, a becoming in this? Is its action eternal, or, on the contrary, did it appear in time? This appearance is something new, and this becoming presupposes an active power which was not its own activity, which did not even act but was only able to act. And then, how does the virtual act reduce itself to the second act which it did not have? To say that it did so by itself, is to posit an absolute beginning, which is repugnant to reason; for the greater does not come from the less, being from nothing. The virtual act was therefore reduced to its second act by an eternal mover which, in the last analysis, must be its own activity and which cannot be the subject of becoming.

The reply to Suarez has often been that before the created

9 *Contra Gentes,* III, 88.
10 *Loc. cit.,* Ia, q.105, a.4; Ia IIae, q.9, a.6.
11 *Ibid.,* Ia IIae, q.10, a.4.
12 Cf. *Disp. met.,* disp. 29, sect. 1, no. 7.

will acts, its act is contained in it not *virtually* and *eminently,* as God contains creatures and as the divine intuition contains human reasoning; but it is contained virtually and potentially, which means that it can produce its act as a secondary cause acting under the influence of the primary Cause.

Moreover, it is not enough to say that God moves man to will to be happy, or to will good in general; for when our will afterwards wills some particular good, there is then a new actuality, which must depend as being upon the first Being, as free act upon the first Free, as ultimate actuality upon the supreme Actuality who is pure Act, and, if this free act is good and salutary, it must depend as such, not only by reason of its object, but also as to the exercise of its act, upon the source of all good and the Author of salvation. St. Thomas, too, said: "No matter how perfect a corporeal or spiritual nature is supposed to be, it cannot proceed to its act unless it be moved by God." [13]

Such are the general reasons for affirming physical premotion. They become clear if we consider them with reference to what revelation teaches us concerning the divine decrees and efficacious grace.

PHYSICAL PREMOTION AND THE DIVINE DECREES AS THEY RELATE TO OUR SALUTARY ACTS

Physical premotion presupposes these decrees and the infallible execution of them. These decrees are admitted by almost all the theologians who do not accept the Molinist theory of the *scientia media.* This means that they are admitted by the Thomists, the Augustinians, and the Scotists, who in a general way grant the case of the dilemma: God determining or determined, no other alternative. In other words, if God has not from all eternity determined our sal-

[13] *Loc. cit.,* Ia IIae, q. 109, a. 1.

utary free acts, then He is passive or dependent upon His knowledge as regards the free determination made by a certain man if placed in certain circumstances (and it is only for God to place him or not in these circumstances). As regards this free determination which, as a free determination, does not come from God, He is not the author but merely the spectator of it. Now we can admit no passivity or dependence in the pure Act, who is sovereignly independent as regards everything created, as to contingent things, whether absolute or conditional.

In the opinion of the theologians just referred to, the existence of these divine predetermining decrees concerning our salutary free acts has its foundation not only in the notion which the philosopher perforce must have of God and His independence, but also in divine revelation as contained in Scripture and tradition.

1) Scriptural texts. We have the following prayer of Mardochai: "O Lord, Lord, almighty King, for all things are in Thy power, and there is none that can resist Thy will. . . . Thou art the Lord of all and there is none that can resist Thy majesty. . . . Hear my supplication and turn our mourning into joy." [14] In the same book Queen Esther prays as follows: "Give me a well ordered speech in my mouth, in the presence of the lion (the king), and turn his heart to the hatred of our enemy; that both he himself may perish and the rest that consent to him." [15] Further on we read: "And God changed the king's heart into mildness," [16] and he issued an edict in favor of the Jews. From these words we see that the infallibility and efficacy of the decree of God's will have their foundation evidently in His omnipotence and not in the foreseen consent of King Assuerus. This makes St. Augustine say, when explaining these words: "By a most secret and most

14 Esther 13: 9, 11, 17.
15 Ibid., 14: 13.
16 Ibid., 15: 11.

efficacious power He converts and transforms the king's heart from indignation to lenity." [17]

In the Book of Psalms we read: "He hath done all things whatsoever He would." [18] Everything He wills not conditionally, but absolutely, He does, even man's free conversion, as in the case of King Assuerus. Hence the "heart of the king is in the hand of the Lord; whithersoever He will He shall turn it." [19] The same thought is expressed somewhat differently as follows: "As the potter's clay is in his hand, to fashion and order it . . . so man is in the hand of Him that made him." [20] Isaias announces various events that will happen against the pagan nations by means of human intervention, especially the ruin of Babylon, and he concludes as follows: "The Lord of hosts hath sworn, saying: Surely as I have thought, so shall it be. And as I have purposed, so shall it fall out. . . . For the Lord of hosts hath decreed, and who can disannul it? And His hand is stretched out, and who shall turn it away." [21] The hand of God signifies His omnipotence; here again the infallibility and efficacy of the divine decree do not at all have their foundation in the foreseeing of human consent.

It is even declared that God gives the good consent: "And I will give you a new heart and put a new spirit within you; and I will take away the stony heart out of your flesh and will give you a heart of flesh . . . and I will cause you to walk in My commandments and to keep My judgments and do them . . . and you shall be My people and I will be your God." [22]

Jesus also said: "Without Me you can do nothing," [23] in

[17] *I ad Bonifatium,* chap. 20.
[18] Ps. 113: 3.
[19] Prov. 21: 1.
[20] Eccli. 33: 13 f.
[21] Is. 14: 24–27.
[22] Ezech. 36: 26–28.
[23] John 15: 5.

the order of salvation. Speaking of deceivers, He said: "There shall arise false Christs . . . and shall show great signs and wonders." [24] Of His followers He said: "My sheep hear My voice. And I know them, and they follow Me. And I give them life everlasting, and they shall not perish for ever. And no one shall pluck them out of My hand. That which My Father hath given Me is greater than all; and no one shall snatch them out of the hand of My Father." [25]

Again, in like manner, every time Jesus speaks of the "hour" of His passion, He says that it has from all eternity been determined by a divine decree, and that before this hour no one will be able to lay hands on Him. God is therefore the master of the human will to such an extent that it cannot sin except at the time permitted by God from all eternity; also the kind of sin has been permitted without God being directly or indirectly the cause of it. Thus we read in the Gospel: "They sought therefore to apprehend Him; and no man laid hands on Him, because His hour had not yet come." [26] Of this hour the Evangelist writes: "Jesus knowing that His hour was come . . . having loved His own . . . He loved them unto the end." [27] "Father the hour is come." [28] We have observed that the hour appointed by Providence is not of necessity determined. Now this is the hour of Christ's greatest free act. The act is one that had therefore been from all eternity the object of a divine positive predetermining decree. It is also the hour of the greatest sin, that of deicide. This act had been from all eternity the object of a divine decree that was not positive but permissive, so that this sin was not due to happen before this hour, or in any other way except that permitted by God.[29]

24 Matt. 24: 24.
25 John 10: 27–30.
26 *Ibid.*, 7: 30.
27 *Ibid.*, 13: 1.
28 *Ibid.*, 17: 1; cf. Com. of St. Thomas on these texts of St. John.
29 *Summa theol.*, IIIa, q.46, a.2; q.47, a.3,6.

Likewise, St. Peter on the day of Pentecost said to the Jews: "This same being delivered up, by the determinate counsel and foreknowledge of God, you by the hands of wicked men have crucified and slain. Whom God hath raised up." [30] It is also to be noticed that in this text "the determinate counsel, τῇ ὡρισμένῃ Βουλῇ," precedes foreknowledge: προγνώσει τοῦ Θεοῦ. As St. Thomas says: "God by His eternal will preordained Christ's passion for the deliverance of the human race." [31]

In like manner, St. Paul says of the resurrection: "Him God raised up the third day; and gave Him to be made manifest, not to all the people, but to witnesses preordained by God." [32] He points out the effect of this upon the Gentiles as follows: "And the Gentiles hearing of it were glad . . . and as many as were ordained to life everlasting believed." [33] He refers to the divine predetermination in these words: "God hath determined for all mankind the appointed time and the limits of their habitation." [34] St. Paul relates that after his conversion, Ananias said to him: "Brother Saul, look up. And I the same hour looked upon him. But he said: The God of our fathers hath preordained thee that thou shouldst know His will and see the Just One and shouldst hear the voice from His mouth. For thou shalt be His witness." [35] And freely but infallibly St. Paul testified concerning our Lord.

Finally, it was St. Paul himself who said: "To them that love God all things work together unto good: to such as according to His purpose are called. For whom He foreknew, He also predestinated. . . . But when Rebecca had conceived . . . when the children were not yet born . . . that the purpose of God according to election might stand, not of works of Him

30 Acts 2: 23.
31 Loc. cit., IIIa, q.47, a.3.
32 Acts 10: 40 f.
33 Ibid., 13: 48.
34 Ibid., 17: 26.
35 Ibid., 22: 13–15.

that calleth, it was said to her: the elder shall serve the younger.
. . . What shall we say then? Is there injustice with God? God
forbid! For He saith to Moses: I will have mercy on whom I
will have mercy. And I will show mercy to whom I will show
mercy. So then it is not of him that willeth, nor of him that
runneth, but of God that showeth mercy." [36] In this text it is
clear that the election, the eternal decree of the divine will,
does not depend upon the foreseen consent of the human will.
God's sovereign independence cannot be more clearly affirmed.

Other passages are equally to the point: "If God, willing
. . . to show the riches of His glory on the vessels of mercy
which He hath prepared unto glory," [37] where is the injustice?
"But in all these things we overcome, because of Him that hath
loved us." [38] "Hath God cast away His people? God forbid!
. . . Of old He said to Elias: I have left Me seven thousand
men that have not bowed their knee to Baal. Even so then,
at the present time also, there is a remnant saved according
to the election of grace. And if by grace, it is not now by works:
otherwise grace is no more grace. What then? That which
Israel sought, he hath not obtained; but the election hath
obtained it. And the rest have been blinded." [39]

Similarly, St. Paul said: "For who distinguisheth thee? Or
what hast thou that thou hast not received?" [40] According to
St. Paul what distinguishes the just person from the impious
one, what even begins to distinguish him, when the just person
begins to be converted, that also he received. Long afterward
St. Thomas said: "Since God's love is the cause of goodness in
things, no one thing would be better than another, if God did
not will greater good for one than for another." [41] It is the

[36] Rom. 8: 28; 9: 11–18.
[37] *Ibid.*, 9: 23.
[38] *Ibid.*, 8: 37.
[39] *Ibid.*, 11: 1–7.
[40] I Cor. 4: 7.
[41] *Loc. cit.*, Ia, q.20, a.3.

principle of predilection, which applies both in the natural and supernatural orders, and this for salutary acts either difficult or easy to perform. This principle is of absolute universality, and it supposes that God's love for us is efficacious of itself and not because of our foreseen good consent, since God, the source of all good, is the primary cause of this good consent. This principle of predilection, so clearly formulated by St. Paul and so boldly affirming God's sovereign independence, is balanced by this other principle, that "God never commands what is impossible, and makes it really possible for all adults to obey the commandments when these are binding on them," as explained by St. Paul who says: "God will have all men to be saved." [42]

How is this second principle reconciled with the principle of predilection? That is an inscrutable mystery. For this we should have to see the Deity and thus realize how infinite mercy, justice, and sovereign liberty, or God's independence, are there reconciled.

We read the same in St. Paul's epistles: "As He chose us in Him [Jesus Christ] before the foundation of the world, that we should be holy and unspotted in His sight . . . [and not because He foresaw our holiness]. Who hath predestinated us unto the adoption of children through Jesus Christ unto Himself, according to the purpose of His will, unto the praise of the glory of His grace [and not that of man's free will], in which He hath graced us in His beloved Son. . . . In whom we are also called by lot, being predestinated according to the purpose of Him who worketh all things according to the counsel of His will. That we may be unto the praise of His glory, we who before hoped in Christ." [43] It is not a question here merely of the general election of Christians, for it is stated that one particular Christian is better than a certain other: "For who distinguisheth thee? Or what hast thou that thou

---

[42] I Tim. 2: 4; see above, pp. 72–75, 80–84.
[43] Eph. 1: 4–7, 11 f.

hast not received?" [44] If God's love is the source of all good, no one thing would be better than another, unless it were loved more by God. Again St. Paul says: "For it is God who worketh in you, both to will and to accomplish, according to His good will." [45] Therefore, so the Thomists think, the free determination of the salutary act comes, as from its primary source, from God, who is the first Free and the first Goodness, from God, who is the Author of salvation.

2) Theological argument. The same doctrine is set forth by St. Thomas when he speaks of the divine consequent or nonconditional will: "The will is directed to things as they are in themselves, and in themselves they exist under particular qualifications. Hence we will a thing simply inasmuch as we will it when all particular circumstances are considered; and this is what is meant by willing consequently. Thus it may be said that a just judge wills simply the hanging of a murderer, but in a qualified manner or antecedently he would will him to live, to wit, inasmuch as he is a man. Thus it is clear that whatever God simply wills takes place; although what He wills antecedently may not take place." [46]

In this passage St. Thomas gives us the principle of the distinction between intrinsically efficacious grace (which infallibly assures the execution of the divine consequent will for salutary acts, whether these be easy or difficult), and sufficient grace (which corresponds to the divine antecedent will by which God wills to make it possible for all to keep the commandments and obtain salvation).

Why does St. Thomas think that everything which God wills by His consequent or unconditional will is infallibly fulfilled? The reason given by St. Thomas is not because God foresees our consent, but because "nothing may fall outside the order of the universal cause; under which all particular causes are

[44] I Cor. 4: 7.
[45] Phil. 2: 13.
[46] *Loc. cit.,* Ia, q. 19, a.6 ad 1um.

included." [47] Only the good which God willed or the evil which He permitted can happen; for no secondary cause can act without His concurring in the act.

The Council of Orange had said: "Let no one glory in what he may seem to have, as if he did not receive it from God." [48] The Council of Trent also said: "For God, unless men be themselves wanting to His grace, as He began the good work, so will He perfect it [working in them to will and to accomplish]." [49]

In the opinion of the Thomists, not to admit predetermining decrees in God with regard to our salutary acts, is to make it impossible for one to solve the dilemma: God determining or determined, no other alternative. Thus we must admit a certain passivity or dependence in God as regards the free decision that a certain man would make if placed in certain circumstances, and that he will make if actually placed in such circumstances. Is not God's dependence upon man's decision admitted by Molina in the following passage? "The *scientia media* on no account is to be called free, both because it precedes every free act of the divine will, and also because it was not in God's power to know by this knowledge anything else than He actually knew. Furthermore, not even is it natural in this sense, as if it were to such a degree innate to God that He could not know the opposite of that which He knows by this knowledge. For if the created will were to do the opposite, as it truly can, He would have known even this by the same knowledge, but not that He actually knows it." [50] This means that it is not in God's power to foresee by the *scientia media* something else than what He knows by it; but He would have known something else by it if the created will, on the supposition that it were placed in certain circumstances, had made a different choice. Now, then, can we avoid saying that God's

[47] *Ibid.*, Ia, q.19, a.6.
[48] Denz., no. 189; cf. can. 20, 22.
[49] *Ibid.*, no. 806; Phil. 2: 13.
[50] *Concordia*, q.14, a.13, disp. 52, Paris ed., 1876, p. 318.

foreknowledge depends upon the choice which the created free will would make if it were placed in certain circumstances, and which it will make if actually placed in such circumstances? Evidently it follows as a logical conclusion for Molina that actual grace, which results in the salutary act, is not intrinsically efficacious,[51] and that with an equal or even a less grace a particular sinner is converted, whereas a certain other with greater help is not converted.[52] In the opinion of the Thomists, this cannot be reconciled with what St. Paul says: "For who distinguisheth thee? Or what hast thou that thou hast not received?" [53]

On the contrary, if we admit the divine predetermining decrees with regard to our salutary acts, namely, intrinsically and infallibly efficacious decrees, which cause even our acts to be performed freely, actuating our liberty, then it follows that actual grace, which is followed by the salutary act, must also be intrinsically efficacious, so as to assure the infallible execution of the decree which it presupposes. In the opinion of the Thomists,[54] actual grace can be intrinsically efficacious only on condition that it is a predetermining physical but non-necessitating premotion, in the sense explained at the beginning of this third part. It remains for us to prove this.

PREDETERMINING PHYSICAL PREMOTION AND THE EFFICACY OF GRACE

It is of faith that God grants us efficacious graces which are not only followed by the good consent of free will, but which in a certain manner produce it: for efficacious or effective grace makes us act. The Pelagians and Semipelagians denied this. They did not refuse to admit that grace gives us the *power* to perform a good act, but they denied that it causes us to will and

51 *Ibid.*, pp. 230, 459.
52 *Ibid.*, pp. 51, 565.
53 I Cor. 4: 7.
54 Cf. Billuart, O.P., *De gratia,* diss. 5, a.7.

do the act. The second Council of Orange explaining the words of St. Paul, "It is God who worketh in you, both to will and to accomplish," [55] declares against the Semipelagians: "If anyone, that we may be cleansed from sin, contends that God awaits the consent of our will, and does not confess, however, that even our wish to be cleansed is effected in us by the infusion and operation of the Holy Ghost, such a one resists this same Holy Spirit . . . and the Apostle proclaiming for our benefit that it is God who worketh in you both to will and to accomplish, according to His good will." [56]

Now grace, which causes us to perform a good act, which works in us both to will and to accomplish, makes us do the good deed, is not merely virtually efficacious (in actu primo) in the sense that it gives us really the power to act in a salutary manner, for this power is already given by sufficient grace even when the salutary effect does not follow; but it is actually efficacious or effective, for, as the Council of Orange says: "As often as we do any good act, God works in us and with us that we may act." [57] In these words we have the expression of Christian faith, and it is also of faith that under the influence of efficacious grace so conceived, man retains his liberty of action.[58]

In addition to this the Thomists and many other theologians interpreting these texts of the Scripture and the councils as implying divine independence, which they consider is compromised by the scientia media, see in this the affirmation that grace is efficacious of itself, and not because of our foreseen consent.

It is of importance to note here that the doctrine of intrinsically efficacious grace, which is admitted by almost all theo-

[55] Phil. 2: 13.

[56] Denz., no. 177; cf. no. 182: "For as often as we do any good act, God works in us and with us that we may act"; also consult Denz., nos. 176, 179, 183, 185, 193, 195, see also Indiculus de gratia Dei, nos. 131–35, 139, 141 f.

[57] Ibid., no. 182.

[58] Ibid., no. 814.

logians who reject the theory of the *scientia media*, means far more for the Thomists than their explanation of predetermining physical premotion. Likewise, provided it is within the power of our will to move our hand as it pleases, it is of little consequence for us to know by means of what nerve centers it does so. Among the Thomists, Billuart pointed this out. He said in substance that the theologians explain in various ways the efficacy of grace; some by means of delectation and moral influence, others by physical predetermination, though they do not apply this to natural acts, or to the material element in sin. But, strictly speaking, these are philosophical questions, whereas grace efficacious of itself in virtue of God's omnipotent will, independently of the creature's consent and the *scientia media*, this we defend as a theological conclusion that is connected with the principles of the faith and proximate to the faith (proximately definable). If we exclude the Molinists, this opinion is held by almost all the schools.[59] The Thomists perceive, indeed, that this statement of intrinsically efficacious grace is implied in the scriptural texts previously quoted concerning the intrinsic efficacy of the divine decrees.[60] Similarly, they connect this doctrine with the principle of predilection, namely: "No one thing would be better than another, if God did not will greater good for one than for another." [61]

Now if we admit the fact of intrinsically and infallibly efficacious grace, how can we account for it except by saying that it is so by reason of the predetermining physical premotion in the sense just explained? It has been proposed, of course, to explain this efficacy by means of a moral causality in that the object attracts the will, and so some have spoken, such as Berti and Bellelius, of a victorious delectation, others of a multiplicity of graces that attract the will, or of a series of indeliberate and inefficacious good movements that incline the

59 *De Deo*, diss. 8, a.5 (end).

60 Billuart, *loc. cit.*, diss. 5, a.6; in more recent times, cf. N. del Prado, *op. cit.*, III, 150 ff.; E. Hugon, *De gratia*, p. 202.

61 *Loc. cit.*, Ia, q.20, a.3.

will to make the salutary choice, and it has even been proposed to assign to this moral motion, in one or the other of the above mentioned modes, a physical but non-predetermining pre-motion.

It is the common teaching of the Thomists in the tractate on grace, that the explanations are insufficient. The funda-mental reason they give is that God cannot infallibly move the will by means of a moral or objective motion. Now in-trinsically efficacious grace is that by which God infallibly moves the will to make the salutary choice. Therefore intrinsi-cally efficacious grace cannot be explained by simply a moral or objective motion.

The major of this premise rests upon the principle that by a moral or objective motion the will is reached only through the medium of the intellect by way of objective attraction, and is not infallibly drawn by this motion. Undoubtedly, God seen face to face would infallibly attract our will because He ad-equately satisfies its capacity for love. But every attraction, however exalted it may be, is unable fully to satisfy this ca-pacity and is fallible; it leaves the will undetermined whether to consent or not, especially so with a weak will, with one that is hard and indocile to the divine call, so long as it is not in-trinsically changed.

It does not solve the difficulty to say that this moral motion is accompanied by a celestial and victorious delectation. This latter, which is admitted by several Augustinians, such as Berti, cannot make the grace intrinsically and infallibly effi-cacious; for, often enough, it does not even accompany the motion, and when present does not infallibly produce its effect. Often enough it is ineffective, for some are converted who were not disposed precisely because they were drawn by a celestial delectation that is superior to earthly things; for they were drawn by reason of an inclination to good that is not always a victorious delectation, but is inspired by the fear of divine chastisements and other motives. Even saints perform many good works without experiencing this victorious delectation; and they are, at times, in a state of very great aridity, as for instance, is the case with those who are undergoing the dark night or passive purification of the soul. When this celestial delectation is present, it solicits undoubtedly our free will to act, but it does not infallibly attract the will; for it does not fully satisfy the capacity of the will for love, as would be the case of God seen face to face; for the will can incline us to think of something else.[62] As a matter of fact, in his choice man is not always influenced by the greatest delectation that suddenly presents itself; he chooses what appears to him to be the best right at the moment, even for the sole motive that it is of obligation, without any previous delectation, and the superior delectation then follows the choice, just as joy follows the fulfilment of one's duty.

The multiplicity of the graces of attraction would not give the salutary acts an infallible efficacy; for the will still remains undecided whether to consent or not, although it is ardently solicited or inclined to give its salutary consent. Thus the persecutors promised all the goods of this world to the holy martyrs, at the same time attempting to frighten them by the threat of all the torments; but neither these promises nor threats of torments could infallibly influence their liberty of action. In like manner, inefficacious good movements incline the will to make the salutary choice, but they cannot infallibly cause this act; for they, too, leave our free will *undecided.* They do not effect the free choice, to say nothing of the fact that they often have to contend with great temptations and the fickleness of our free will in the performance of good.

Finally, an indifferent physical premotion that moves man to will to be happy, without inclining him infallibly to will this particular good, it, too, leaves our free will undecided. It does not effect the free choice of a certain good.

The Thomists, too, conclude that moral motion is certainly

[62] *Loc. cit.*, Ia IIae, q. 10, a. 2.

required to dispose our will to make the choice, by proposing to it an object, a good that solicits or attracts it. But intrinsically efficacious grace that infallibly moves the will to make the free choice, must be the application of the will to the exercise of this act. Now this is not a moral motion, or one by way of objective attraction, but it is a physical motion. It must exert its effect immediately *from within;* on the will itself, and not through the intervention of the intellect. It must have a priority not of time but of nature or causality over the free act. It must, finally, bring the will infallibly to perform this particular free act rather than a certain other, and cause even this act to be performed freely. This means that it must be a predetermining physical and non-necessitating premotion, which can come from God alone, and from no created agent however superior; for only God can interiorly move the free will which He has ordained to universal good and which He maintains in existence. He alone by His unsullied contact can so move the will as not to destroy its liberty, and can reconcile His infallible motion with the free mode of our acts.

Theologians always granted the Thomists that it is because of this divine motion of itself efficacious, that the Virgin Mary freely and infallibly uttered her "fiat" on the day of the annunciation, that St. Paul was freely and infallibly converted on his way to Damascus, that the martyrs remained freely and infallibly faithful in the midst of most dreadful torments. But that is to concede the metaphysical principles of the doctrine, and, if they are metaphysical, they are applicable without exception to all salutary acts, whether these be easy or difficult to perform. The foregoing principles that have been formulated do not take into consideration the greater or less degree of difficulty.

On the other hand, the infallibility of the divine motion which is affirmed by the Jansenists and Quesnel [63] in terms practically the same as those of St. Thomas, is the denial of

[63] Denz., nos. 1,360–63.

liberty, as well as of sufficient grace and responsibility on the sinner's part. The Jansenists consider grace of itself efficacious to be necessary by reason of the weakness of human nature and not because of the creature's dependence upon God. They hold that in the state of innocence intrinsically efficacious grace was not necessary for the performance of a good act. It is necessary only since the fall because of the consequences of original sin, in that only freedom from coercion remains to us and not free will (freedom from necessity).

To sum up, intrinsically and infallibly efficacious grace, which in more precise language means predetermining and non-necessitating premotion, is required not only for salutary acts difficult to perform, but also for those that are easy; and this holds good either for the commencement or continuance in the performance of good works. "Since, indeed, God's love is the cause of goodness in things, no one thing would be better than another [by reason of an initial or final salutary act, by one that is easy or difficult to perform, in the beginning or for its continuance], if God did not will greater good for one than for another." [64]

[64] *Loc. cit.,* Ia, q.20, a.3.

CHAPTER VIII

The Divine Motion and the Freedom of our Salutary Acts

THE question has been raised against the Thomist thesis that it destroys liberty, as Calvinism does, in that it makes us maintain that the free will cannot resist. This is the thesis of the Reformers that was condemned by the Council of Trent defining: "If anyone shall say that man's free will, moved and aroused by God, by assenting to God arousing and calling, cannot refuse to consent, if it would, but that, as something inanimate, it does nothing whatever and is merely passive; let him be anathema." [1] This and other similar objections were made to St. Augustine by the Pelagians and Semipelagians. St. Thomas often referred to them and solved them. [2]

The Thomists reply that the Council of Trent did not wish to condemn either the doctrine of intrinsically efficacious grace or that of physical premotion, as clearly expressed by Benedict XIV and Clement XII. At the end of the sessions Paul V also had declared: "The opinion of the Friars Preachers differs very much from that of Calvin. For the Dominicans say that grace does not destroy but perfects free will, and such is its power that it leaves man to act as befits his nature, which is freely. The Jesuits, however, differ from the Pelagians who declared the beginning of salvation to be from ourselves, whereas the former teach quite the contrary." [3]

[1] Denz., no. 814.

[2] *Summa theol.*, Ia, q.19, a.8; q.115, a.4; Ia IIae, q.10, a.4.

[3] *Congregatio de Auxiliis*, August 28, 1607; cf. Schneeman, S.J., *Controv. de gratia*, p. 291. This decision of Paul V was afterwards confirmed by a decree of Benedict XIV, July 13, 1748.

Evidently the Thomist doctrine differs entirely from that condemned by the Council of Trent. According to this condemned doctrine, the free will does not co-operate with the divine action. Furthermore, there were many Thomists among the fathers of the council. One of them, Dominic Soto, was even engaged in the drawing up of these canons. It is even very probable that the fathers of the Council in the above-mentioned canon speak of an intrinsically efficacious divine motion; for it is this motion that Luther had in mind when he said it could not be reconciled with free will. Therefore the mind of the fathers is rather that the intrinsically and infallibly efficacious divine motion does not destroy free will; for, although man does not actually resist it, yet he retains the power to do so; *remanet potentia ad oppositum,* as the Thomists commonly say.

Moreover, the council had said previous to this: "For God, unless men be themselves wanting to His grace, as He has begun the good work so will He perfect it, working in them to will and accomplish." [4] These last words were generally understood by the pre-Tridentine theologians as meaning that grace is of itself efficacious, and not because God foresaw our consent.[5]

Finally, the Thomists retort by saying that it is the *scientia media* which destroys liberty; for it supposes that God previous to any divine decree sees infallibly what a particular man freely would choose if placed in certain circumstances. How, indeed, can one then avoid determinism of circumstances? In what medium can God see infallibly the determination that would arrest the appetite of the created free will, if not in the scrutiny of the circumstances that thence become infallibly determining? And not having decided in favor of a divine and non-necessitating predetermination that makes its influ-

<hr>

4 Denz., no. 806.

5 Cf. A. Reginald, O.P., *De mente Conc. Trid.;* also A. Massoulié, O.P., *Divus Thomas sui interpres,* Vol. I, diss. 2, q.9.

ence felt *strongly* and *suavely* in the very depths of the free will, is not one led to admit a very inferior sort of determinism that results from the influence exerted by external things on our spiritual will?

The canon of the Council of Trent just quoted was but the occasion of reviving an old objection. We saw that St. Thomas had already formulated it as clearly as possible, when he said: "It seems that the will is moved of necessity by God. For every agent that cannot be resisted moves of necessity. But God cannot be resisted, because His power is infinite; wherefore it is written: Who resisteth His will? (Rom. 9: 19.) Therefore God moves the will of necessity." We know that St. Thomas replied to this by saying: "The divine will extends not only to the doing of something by the thing which He moves, but also to its being done in a way which is fitting to the nature of that thing. And therefore it would be more repugnant to the divine motion, for the will to be moved of necessity, which is not fitting to its nature, than for it to be moved freely, which is becoming to its nature." [6] From this reply, what remains of the major of this objection: Every agent that cannot be resisted, moves of necessity? St. Thomas distinguishes as follows: If this agent causes the movement, without causing the being to move freely, I deny the major; if it causes the being to move and to move freely, then I concede the major. Thus man under the influence of efficacious grace remains free, although he never resists it; for it causes in him and with him even that he act freely; it actualizes his liberty in the order of good, and if he no longer is in a state of potential or passive indifference, he still has an actual and active indifference, a dominating indifference with regard to the particular good which he chooses. This good is incapable of invincibly attracting him like the vision of God face to face. He is inclined freely toward this good, God actualizing this free movement; and since its free mode still is being, it is

[6] *Ibid.*, Ia IIae, q.10, a.4 ad 1um.

included in the adequate object of divine omnipotence. Such is manifestly the doctrine of St. Thomas. The texts just quoted [7] clearly prove this to be the case.

Such is also the traditional teaching of classic Thomism. Molina concedes this at the same time that he declares his departure not only from the teaching of the Thomists, but even from that of St. Thomas.[8] Several Molinists made the same admission.[9]

This same doctrine of St. Thomas was later on expounded by Bossuet, who wrote: "Is there anything more absurd than to say that the will is not free in its act because God wills it to be free." [10] In other words: Is there anything more absurd than to say that the actualization of the free will destroys it?

This freedom in our acts is not only safeguarded, but is also produced by God in and with us. The divine motion does not force the will, because it operates according to the natural inclination of this latter. It inclines the will first toward its adequate object, which is universal good, and only after this toward an inadequate object, which is some particular good. In the first case the divine motion causes the act to be free. It operates interiorly, as was just said, in the very depths of the will, as to the universality of the same, and in a sense inclines the will toward every degree of good, before giving it the inclination to tend toward some particular good.[11]

Thus God moves us *suavely* and *powerfully* to act freely. If the divine motion were to lose its power, it would also lose its suavity. Incapable of reaching what is more delicate and intimate to us, it would remain external to us, affixed, as it were, to our created activity, something unworthy of the

[7] Cf. chap. 5.

[8] *Concordia*, pp. 152, 547.

[9] Cf. P. Mandonnet, "Notes de l'histoire thomiste," in the *Revue Thomiste*, 1914, pp. 665–79; Dummermuth, S. *Thomas et doctrina praemotionis physicae*, pp. 685–754.

[10] *Traité du libre arbitre*, chap. 7.

[11] Cf. John of St. Thomas, *Cursus theol.*, in 1am, q. 19, disp. 5, a. 5 f., nos. 37–55.

creative, conservative, and motive activity, which is more intimate to us than we are to ourselves. Our free act therefore proceeds *entirely* from us as secondary cause, and *entirely* from God as primary cause.[12] When, after deliberation, we perform the act, in virtue of the universal scope of our will and our independence of judgment that is not necessitated by the object, we retain the power not to perform the act.[13] If our free will were able of itself alone to determine itself, then it would have the dignity of the first Will and would be like to it not only analogically but also univocally. It would be purely and simply an image of the divine liberty, instead of there being a similarity of proportion between it and this latter.[14] Between the two there is similarity and dissimilarity. If we consider the similarity, we must say that it is just as easy to reconcile created liberty with the intrinsically efficacious divine motion, as it is to reconcile God's free act with His immutability. In God freedom of action is not the dominating potential indifference of a faculty that is capable of acting or of not acting. With Him it is the dominating indifference of pure Act with regard to everything created.[15] Likewise, in due proportion, under the influence of the efficacious divine motion, our liberty is no longer the potential but actual indifference of the faculty, and its actualization does not destroy this liberty.

If Molinism rejects this doctrine, the reason is because it seeks to define human liberty without any reference to the object that specifies the free act. Human liberty is a faculty that, presupposed all that is requisite for it to act, it still can either act or not act, and among these *prerequisites* it places the divine motion, which is compatible, according to this theory, not only with the power of resisting but also with the actual fact of resisting.

12 *Loc. cit.*, Ia, q.23, a.5.
13 *Ibid.*, Ia IIae, q.10, a.4 ad 1um.
14 *Ibid.*, Ia, q.19, a.3 ad 5um.
15 *Ibid.*, Ia, q.19, a.3 ad 4um; *Contra Gentes*, I, 82.

In virtue of the fundamental principle that the faculties, habits, and acts are specified by their object, in the definition of free will we must consider its specifying object, and say with the Thomists that liberty is the dominating indifference of the will with regard to good proposed to it by the reason as not in every respect good. The essence of liberty consists in the dominating indifference of the will with regard to every object proposed by the reason as at the moment good in one aspect, and not good in another, according to the formula of St. Thomas: "If the will is offered an object that is not good from every point of view, it will not tend to this of necessity." [16] There is then indifference in willing or not willing this object, a potential indifference in the faculty and an actual indifference in the free act which is not necessarily inclined toward it. Even when, in fact, the will actually wills this object, when it is already determined to will this, it is still inclined freely toward this with a dominating indifference that is no longer potential but actual. In like manner, the divine liberty that is already determined maintains us in existence. Liberty therefore arises from the infinite disproportion prevailing between the will that is specified by universal good, and a particular good which is good in one aspect, not good or insufficient in another. The Thomists also say in opposition to Suarez, that not even by His absolute power can God move our will of necessity to will a certain object, the indifference of judgment remaining as it is, so long as we judge the object to be good in one aspect and not so in another. The reason is that it implies a contradiction for the will to will of necessity the object proposed to it by the intellect as indifferent or as absolutely out of proportion to its scope.[17]

That we may better grasp how the divine motion is the cause of our free act, we must point out that this latter depends upon three different finite causalities that are mutually

---

[16] *Ibid.,* Ia IIae, q. 10, a. 2.
[17] *De veritate,* q. 22, a. 5.

related: (1) the objective attraction of particular good; (2) the direction of the intellect in forming a practical judgment; (3) the efficiency or production of the free choice by the will. The divine motion transcends these three causalities and actualizes them, without violating free will. The attraction of the end thus remains the first of the causes, and it implies a contradiction that our will be *necessitated* by the divine motion, when the judgment is indifferent or non-necessitating; for it implies a contradiction that our will should wish an object different from that which is proposed to it.

To sum up, as Bossuet said: "Is there anything more absurd than to say that the will is not free in its act, because God efficaciously wills it to be free?" [18] Is there anything more inconsistent than to say that the actualization of free will destroys it?

The great mystery, too, according to St. Augustine and St. Thomas, is not how to reconcile God's foreknowledge and His decrees with created liberty; for, if God is God, His efficacious will must extend even to the free mode of our acts. From the fact of His willing efficaciously that Paul be freely converted on a certain day at a certain time, on his way to Damascus, it must follow that Paul is freely converted; and, if in this case the effect of the divine motion on the human will does not destroy its liberty, why would it do so in other cases?

We must seek elsewhere for the reason of this great mystery. It is to be found in God's permission of moral evil or sin in this particular man or angel rather than in a certain other. St. Augustine [19] and St. Thomas [20] say that if the grace of final perseverance is granted, as it was to the good thief, that is because of God's mercy; if it is not granted, that is in just punishment as a rule for repeated sins, and for having resisted the

---

[18] *Loc. cit.*
[19] *De correptione et gratia*, chaps. 5 f.
[20] *Loc. cit.*, IIa IIae, q.2, a.5 ad 1um.

final appeal, a final resistance that God permits in this one rather than in a certain other. This makes St. Augustine say: "Why God draws this one and not that one, judge not, if thou wilt not err." [21] St. Thomas says in like manner: "No one thing would be better than another, if God did not will greater good for one than for the other." [22]

On the other hand, God never commands what is impossible. Even when Judas fell from grace, though so near to Christ His redeemer, it was still truly possible for him to comply with the divine law.

There is still one difficulty to be discussed, and this concerns the act of sin.

[21] *In Joan.*, tr. 26.
[22] *Loc. cit.*, Ia, q.20, a.3; cf. q.23, a.5 ad 3um.

CHAPTER IX

THE DIVINE MOTION AND THE PHYSICAL ACT OF SIN
PRINCIPLE

IT is certain that God is in no way the cause of sin, either directly or indirectly. He cannot be the direct cause of sin by inclining His will or a created will to it, for sin is the result of the rational creature turning away from God, its ordained end. Neither can He be the indirect cause of sin by neglecting to keep us from it, as the captain of a ship who, by his negligence, is the cause of the shipwreck, when he is not at his post watching, as he can and should be doing. Undoubtedly it happens that God does not grant certain persons the help that would keep them from sin; but that is in accordance with the established order of His wisdom and justice. He is not bound to do so. He does not owe it to Himself to keep creatures that are by nature defectible from ever failing to do their duty, and He can permit them to fail in view of a higher good. Thus He permits the sin of persecutors that the constancy of the martyrs may be made manifest.[1]

This divine permission of sin is in no way its cause, either directly or indirectly; it allows this to happen. It is but the indispensable condition. If God did not permit it, did not allow it to happen, there would be no sin. This divine permission of sin, especially in the case of the first movement by which the first sin is committed and by which the just person separates from God, is not a punishment, as the withdrawal of divine grace is the result of a transgression. Every punishment presupposes a transgression, and this latter would not

[1] *Summa theol.*, Ia, q.22, a.2 ad 2um.

be unless it were permitted by God. This divine permission of sin, which implies the non-conservation of a certain created liberty in good, is not a good; but it is not an evil, for it is not the privation of a good due to us; it is only the *negation* of a good not due to us. Philosophy teaches that privation means more than negation. God did not owe it to Himself to preserve Lucifer or Adam in a state of innocence from every transgression. He permitted Lucifer rather than a certain other angel to consent to a movement of pride in the will, and in punishment for this transgression He withdrew His grace. It is important to note here against Calvin that the withdrawal of God's grace means more than His simple permission of sin; for this withdrawal is a punishment, as St. Thomas points out.[2] Now every punishment presupposes a transgression, and every transgression presupposes a divine permission as the indispensable condition for its existence. However, the permission of a second sin is a punishment for the first.

THE DIVINE CAUSALITY AND THE PHYSICAL ACT OF SIN

This granted, it is not so difficult to understand the relation of the divine causality or physical premotion to the physical act of sin. St. Thomas writes clearly on this subject as follows: "The act of sin is both a being and an act; and in both respects it is from God. Because every being, whatever the mode of its being, must be derived from the first Being, as Dionysius declares (*De div. nom.*, c. V). Again every action is caused by something existing in act, since nothing produces an action save in so far as it is in act: and every being in act is reduced to the first Act, God, as to its cause, who is Act by His essence. Therefore, God is the cause of every action, in so far as it is an action. But sin denotes a being and an action with a defect: and this defect is from a created cause, the free will, as

[2] *Ibid.*, Ia IIae, q.79, a.3.

falling away from the order of the first Agent, God. Consequently this defect is not reduced to God as its cause, but to the free will: even as the defect of limping is reduced to a crooked leg as its cause, but not to the motive power, which nevertheless causes whatever movement there is in the limping. Accordingly, God is the cause of the act of sin: and yet He is not the cause of sin, because He does not cause the act to have a defect." [3]

The divine concurrence in the physical act of sin of which St. Thomas speaks here is not merely a simultaneous concurrence, as later on Molina contended, like that of two men drawing a boat. It is a case, indeed, of two partial causes (the partialness being of cause and not of effect, as Molina says), which means that the two causes are co-ordinated rather than subordinated in their causality. For St. Thomas, the secondary cause acts only when premoved by the first; whereas neither of the two men drawing the boat moves the other. If it were merely a simultaneous concurrence, God would not be the cause of the physical act of sin as an action; for the cause does not merely accompany the effect, but precedes it at least by a priority of nature and causality. If therefore this divine concurrence is not merely simultaneous, it is a premotion, so say the Thomists, and even, since we must be precise in meaning on this point, it is a *predetermining* though not necessitating premotion. But the predetermination is not to be applied here in the same way as in a case of a good and salutary act.

For a proper understanding of this, we must remark that this divine motion presupposes in God an eternal decree, which is positive and effective as regards the physical entity of sin, and permissive as regards the deficiency. This deficiency, as we have seen, is the result of a defectible and deficient cause. Independently of this twofold eternal decree on God's part, sin was merely possible, but it was not either a

[3] *Ibid.*, Ia IIae, q.79, a.2.

conditional or absolute future. For instance, if from all eternity God had not permitted it, the sin of Judas would not have happened; it would have been merely possible. But God having permitted it from all eternity to happen in this particular manner, place, and time, it had to happen freely and infallibly at this particular time and not before, with its particular kind of malice and not any other.[4] Therefore the sin of Judas presupposed an eternal decree, positive as regards the physical entity of the act, permissive as regards its deficiency. It is the same with every sin that happens in time.

To this eternal decree there corresponds a divine motion by which God is the first Cause of the physical act of sin as a being and an action. This divine motion can be predetermining but in a different manner from that which concerns the good and salutary act; for it depends upon an eternal decree that is not only positive and effective, but also permissive.

This can be better explained by pointing out that the divine motion as regards the exercise of the act presupposes the objective motion or the object as proposed. If this latter is defective, in so far as it does not come from God, but is the result of an evil instigation or of concupiscence, then God cannot even counsel the physical act of sin, for this objective advice could not exclude the malice of the act. In the case of a good act, on the contrary, the objective motion prerequired is good and always comes from God, at least as first Cause.

The objectivity of the defective motion having been established, there intervenes a certain lack of consideration of his obligation on the part of the one who is about to sin, a lack of consideration permitted by God but by no means caused by Him; and the lack of consideration is at least virtually voluntary, for it is the deed of one who could and ought to consider the divine law, if not always, at least before acting. It is only after this, according to a priority of nature if not of time, that the divine influence intervenes to incline the will

4 See p. 303.

to the physical act of sin, an influence which, as in the case of a good act, causes the will to choose freely and in no way compels it.

It is the common teaching, too, of the Thomists that God does not determine anyone to the material or physical act of sin before the created will, by reason of its weakness, has determined itself in a certain way to the formal element in sin. The objective motion precedes by a priority of nature the efficient motion. We cannot will a nothingness, but only a proposed object; and as regards the act of sin, the defective objective motion, which is accompanied by the lack of consideration of one's duty, precedes the divine motion that inclines the will to the physical act of sin. In other words, God moves the will to the physical act of sin only when it is already badly disposed by reason of its weakness. Thus Jesus said to Judas, who was disposed to commit sin and took pleasure in it: "That which thou dost, do quickly." [5] The Lord neither ordains nor counsels, but permits the accomplishment of the premeditated crime.[6] Unless he permitted this evil, though disapproving of it, it would not happen.

The lack of consideration of one's duty just mentioned by us, to which St. Thomas especially refers apropos of the sin in the angels,[7] is it truly voluntary and culpable? It certainly is; for, as St. Thomas again explains,[8] the fault arises from the fact that we begin to will and to act without taking the law into consideration, which we could and ought then to consider. Moreover, as the will is by nature inclined to what is truly good, it could not be inclined toward apparent good which is an evil, without being previously turned away, at least virtually, from true good, causing us not to consider this latter when the need of doing so presents itself. There is in this a resistance to sufficient grace which virtually con-

---

[5] John 13: 27.
[6] Cf. St. Thomas, *In Joan.* chap. 13, lect. 5.
[7] *Loc. cit.,* Ia, q.62, a.1 ad 4um.
[8] *De malo,* q.1, a.3 (end).

tained the offer of efficacious grace, as the fruit is contained in the flower. On account of this resistance, God can freely deprive us of efficacious grace, a privation that is a punishment and that follows by a priority of nature the lack of voluntary consideration which is the commencement of sin, whereas the simple divine permission preceded it.[9] We discussed this point of doctrine at length elsewhere.[10]

Such is the common teaching of the Thomists, as can be gathered from their commentaries on St. Thomas.[11]

Finally, we must note that predetermination to the physical act of sin as explained, is not something of primary importance in the Thomist doctrine relative to the divine decrees and motion; it is merely of secondary importance and a philosophical conclusion. What is of primary importance in this doctrine is that the divine decrees relative to our salutary acts are efficacious of themselves and not because of our consent foreseen by God. Of primary importance is the principle of predilection, which may be stated thus: "Since God's love is the cause of goodness in things, no one thing would be better than another, if God did not will greater good for one than for another." [12] Everything else is of secondary importance. Besides, this truth is related closely to the interior life. Along with the dogma of creation *from nothing*, it is the foundation of Christian humility. If we but reflect upon this truth and its scope in the interior life, then it becomes the means of dispelling all pride.

OBJECTIONS

Let us examine merely the principal objections raised against premotion with regard to the physical act of sin.

[9] *De veritate*, q.24, a.14 ad 2um.
[10] Cf. *God, His Existence*, II, 374–76, 380 ff. *Le sens du mystère*, pp. 306–09.
[11] Cf. *In Summam theol.*, Ia, q.19, a.8; Ia IIae, q.79, a.2. See especially John of St. Thomas, *In Iam*, q.19, disp. 5, a.5 f.
[12] *Ibid.*, Ia, q.20, a.3.

1) It has been said that he who moves efficaciously and determinately to the act of sin, is the cause of sin. Now, according to the Thomists, God moves in this manner. Therefore He is the cause of sin.

The major would be true if this efficacious motion could not account for the being of the action without at the same time accounting for its malice. In fact, as the Thomists say, the divine motion excludes all malice. This is what St. Thomas himself says.[18]

2) But it is insisted that God moves one to the act, as it proceeds from the will. Now the act of sin, as it proceeds from the will, is bad, for malice is not excluded. Therefore, according to this teaching, God moves one to the bad act as such.

The Thomists reply: God moves one to the act as it proceeds effectively from the will, but not as it proceeds defectively from it; for the deficiency depends solely upon a defectible and deficient cause.

Little does it matter that the physical reality of the sinful act and its moral disorder or its malice be inseparable; for this malice cannot be included in the adequate object of divine omnipotence. There is nothing more precise and more precisive, if we may so say, than the adequate and formal object of a faculty. It is that which puts within the reach of the faculty solely what concerns this latter to the exclusion of the rest. Thus, in a fruit, only color is the object of sight, and not the smell or sweetness of the fruit; and as the smell of a fruit is not included in the object of sight, so moral disorder or malice is not included in the adequate object of the divine indefectible power. Even if by an impossibility God were to will it, He could not be either the direct or the indirect cause of sin, which means the moral disorder to be found in the act. Again, in like manner, in all that is true and good, the intellect attains truth and not good, although these are not really distinct; far more so then, the divine causality is able

<hr/>

[18] *Ibid.*, Ia IIae, q.79, a.2; see *supra*, pp. 325 f.

to attain the physical entity of sin without extending to its malice, which is of another order.

3) Again, it is objected that in Thomism the sinner is not responsible for his defection; for the sufficient grace which he receives gives him only the power to keep the commandments but not actually to do so, as God demands. Certainly, sufficient grace of itself does not enable us to keep the commandments, but it is sufficient in its own way, just as one says: bread is sufficient for one's sustenance, yet it must be digested. The natural power of the intellect is sufficient for acquiring a knowledge of certain truths, yet it must institute a methodical inquiry into them so as to acquire this knowledge. Christ's passion was sufficient for our salvation, yet its merits had to be applied by the sacraments or in some other way.[14]

Moreover, sufficient grace virtually contains the efficient grace that is offered to us in it, as the flower contains the fruit. Even the most rigid Thomists, such as Lemos and Alvarez, say that God in giving sufficient help offers us in it that which is efficacious. The fruit is offered in the flower, yet it must not be destroyed by the hail, if the fruit is to develop. Likewise, efficient grace is offered to us in the sufficient; but we must be careful not to resist this latter, a resistance that would come solely from us, not from God, and that could deprive us of the proffered efficacious grace. It is also the common teaching of the Thomists that every actual grace which is efficacious as regards an imperfect salutary act, such as attrition, is sufficient as regards a more perfect act, such as contrition. If it is not followed by culpable resistance on our part, the efficacious grace of contrition will be given to us.

This efficacious grace is thus within our power, though certainly not as something that can be produced by us, but as a gift that would be granted to us if our will did not resist sufficient grace. Thus the Council of Trent teaches that "God,

14 *Ibid.,* IIIa, q.61, a.1 ad 3um.

unless men be themselves wanting to His grace, as He began the good work, so will He perfect it, working in them to will and to accomplish." [15] Sufficient grace that solicits our conversion may well go further than this. We have good reason for saying so, if we think of what our Lord did to prevent Judas from being lost. This was evidently Judas' own fault. The greatest outrage that can be committed against God is to think that He is not good enough to forgive. God never commands what is impossible, and He tells us to do what we can, and to ask of Him the grace to accomplish what of ourselves we are unable to effect.

4) There is just one more objection. It is contended that for man not to resist sufficient grace, but consent to it, efficacious grace is required, according to the Thomists' teaching. Therefore, if man resists, it is because he did not receive the efficacious grace necessary for consent. If, in fact, the bestowal of efficacious grace is the cause of one's not resisting, which is a good, then its non-bestowal is the cause of one's resisting, which is an evil. This is an application of the axiom: if affirmation is the cause of affirmation, negation is the cause of negation. Sunrise is the cause of day, and sunset is the cause of night.

The Thomists say that the reply to this must be that this axiom holds good in the case of a unique cause, such as the sun, which is either present or absent, but it does not hold good in the case of two causes, one of which is absolutely indefectible and the other defectible. Thus the bestowal of efficacious grace is the cause of the salutary act, even of the non-resistance to grace which, since it is a good, must come from the Author of all good; whereas the fact that grace is not bestowed is not the cause of the omission of the salutary act. This omission is a defect that proceeds solely from our defectibility and by no means from God. It would proceed from Him only if He were bound, if He owed it to Himself, to

[15] Denz., no. 806.

keep us always in the performance of good, and not permit a defectible creature sometimes to fail. Now He can permit this for a greater good, such as the manifestation of His mercy and justice. Thus it is true to say that man is deprived of efficacious grace because he resisted sufficient grace, whereas it is not true to say that man resists or sins because he is deprived of efficacious grace. He resists by reason of his own defectibility, which God is not bound to remedy. God is not bound to cause a defectible creature never to fail. "Destruction is thy own, O Israel: thy help is only in Me." [16] Man who is powerless of himself alone to perform the salutary act, finds his sufficiency in himself for failure. [17]

5) Some still insisted asking how we can claim that at the moment the first sin is committed, by which a just person separates from God, efficacious grace is refused because of a previous defection or an accompanying resistance? This resistance, far from preceding the divine refusal of efficacious help, follows it. Hence the sinner is not to blame.

According to the teaching of St. Thomas, it is not necessary that the first human defection precede the divine refusal of efficacious grace by a priority of time; a priority of nature suffices. In this we have an application of the principle of the mutual relation between causes, which is verified in all cases where there is the intervention of the four causes; for causes mutually interact, though in a different order. St. Thomas invokes this general principle to prove that in the justification of the sinner, which takes place in an indivisible instant, the remission of sin follows the infusion of grace in the formal and efficient order, whereas liberation from sin precedes the reception of sanctifying grace in the order of material causality. As St. Thomas says: "The sun by its light acts for the removal of darkness, and hence on the part of the sun, illumination is prior to the removal of darkness; but on the part of

16 Osee 13: 7.
17 Denz., nos. 193, 195.

the atmosphere to be illuminated, to be freed from darkness is, in the order of nature, prior to being illuminated, although both are simultaneous in time. And since the infusion of grace and the remission of sin regard God who justifies, hence in the order of nature the infusion of grace is prior to the freeing from sin. But if we look at what is on the part of man justified, it is the other way about, since in the order of nature the being freed from sin is prior to the obtaining of justifying grace." [18]

Now if justification is thus explained by the mutual relation between causes, then it must be the same for the loss of grace, which is the reverse process; for *the rule is the same for contraries*. As John of St. Thomas shows,[19] the moment man sins mortally and loses habitual grace, his deficiency, in the order of material causality, precedes the refusal of God's actual efficacious grace and is the reason for this. From another point of view, however, even the first deficiency presupposes God's permission of sin, and would not result without it. But, in opposition to justification, sin as such is the work of the deficient creature and not of God. Therefore it is true to say that purely and simply (*simpliciter* in the Scholastic sense is the opposite of *secundum quid*), sin precedes God's refusal of efficacious grace. In other words, "God forsakes not those who have been justified, unless He be first forsaken by them." [20] He withdraws habitual grace only because of mortal sin, and actual efficacious grace only because of a resistance, at least initial, to sufficient grace.

It concerns us here to note carefully against Calvin, as we did at the beginning of this chapter, that the withdrawal of divine grace spoken of by St. Thomas,[21] means far more than merely God's permission of sin; for this divine withdrawal is

---

[18] *Loc. cit.*, Ia IIae, q.113, a.8 ad 1um.
[19] *Cursus theol.*, in Iam, q.19, disp. V, a.6, no. 61.
[20] Denz., no. 804.
[21] *Loc. cit.*, Ia IIae, q.79, a.3.

a penalty.[22] Every penalty presupposes at least a first defection. This defection could not happen without God's permission, which is not at all its cause, but only its indispensable condition. The Thomists say that we thus avoid the contradiction and, instead of doing away with the mystery, we thus safeguard it.

CONCLUSION

The chiaroscuro effects of this sublime doctrine are incomparably greater than those we admire in the works of the greatest artists. On the other hand, it is absolutely clear that God cannot will evil, that He cannot be in any way either directly or indirectly the cause of sin. We are even far more certain of the absolute rectitude of the divine intentions than we are of the rectitude of our own best intentions. Consequently it is equally certain that God never commands the impossible, for that would be contrary to His justice and goodness. He wills, therefore, to make it really possible for all to keep His commandments and be saved.

On the other hand, it is absolutely beyond doubt that God is the author of all good, that His love is the cause of all created good, even of our good and salutary consent, for otherwise, what is of preference in created things would fall outside the scope of the divine causality. It follows, as St. Thomas says, in accordance with St. Augustine, that "no one thing would be better than another, if God did not will greater good for one than for another." [23] This law applies equally to the state of innocence as to the present state, and to every act, either natural or supernatural, easy or difficult, merely begun or continued. This principle of predilection that dominates all these problems, virtually contains the

22 *Ibid.*
23 *Ibid.,* Ia, q.20, a.3.

whole doctrine of predestination and the efficacy of grace to which our Lord refers when He says: "No one can snatch them out of the hand of My Father." [24]

How are these two great principles intimately to be reconciled, which taken separately are so certain: namely, the principle of the possibility of salvation for all mankind, and that of divine predilection? The answer is to be found in St. Paul's words: "O the depth of the riches of the wisdom and of the knowledge of God." [25] We must always come back to this answer, for there is no created intellect, either human or angelic, that can perceive the intimate reconciliation of these two principles before being admitted to the beatific vision. To perceive this intimate reconciliation, in fact, would be to perceive how infinite justice, mercy, and sovereign liberty are identified, without being destructive of one another in the eminence of the Deity, in God's intimate life, in that which is absolutely inaccessible and ineffable in Him.

Likewise, the more these two principles to be reconciled become evident to us, the more, by way of contrast, they appear to be obscure, with a light-transcending obscurity, the eminence of the Deity in which they are united. In this chiaroscuro of a higher order, it is of importance for us not to deny the clarity because of the obscurity, for that would be to disturb the arrangement of light and shade, for thus they are displayed to admirable effect. Let us leave the mystery where it truly belongs, and we shall increasingly realize that it must be, above all reasoning, above all speculative theology, the object of supernatural contemplation, of this contemplation that proceeds from faith enlightened by the gifts of wisdom and understanding. Thus it will begin to dawn upon us that what is more sublime in God is precisely what remains more obscure for us, or inaccessible on account of the feebleness of our sight. In this contemplation, grace, by

[24] John 10: 29.
[25] Rom. 11: 33.

a secret instinct, tranquilizes us concerning the intimate reconciliation of infinite mercy, justice, and sovereign liberty, and it does so precisely because it is itself a participation of God's intimate life. What speculative theology has to say about the divine motion must lead us to this contemplation, the purpose of which otherwise in great measure will be lost. Then all becomes clear and we understand that the resulting obscurity is not that of incoherence or absurdity, but the obscurity that is the result of too great a light for our feeble vision.[26]

Coming back to predestination, let us recall in conclusion that the gratuity of predestination in the order of intention in which the end is willed before the means, is no hindrance, in the order of execution, to the means being realized before the attainment of the end. In this case merits are necessary in the adult as preceding eternal life by which they are crowned. In this order of execution, too, the Lord says to docile and generous souls: "Refuse me nothing, and thus My graces will be able freely to pursue their course. I will that thou refusest Me nothing, so that I may have nothing to refuse thee. Thou art mine forever."

As we began this work by setting forth the stand taken by St. Augustine and his interpretation of Holy Scripture, so let us conclude with this beautiful and sublime passage that is found at the end of one of his works:

"But he that glorieth, let him glory in the Lord. . . . Let us not therefore be eager in our disputes and sluggish in our prayers. Let us pray, my beloved, let us pray that God give the grace even to our enemies and especially to our brethren and loved ones, to understand and confess that after the vast and ineffable ruin in which through one man we were all in-

---

[26] A complete bibliography of the questions in this work would be of vast size. We have pointed out the principal .works in the various chapters, and especially on p. 292. We have made special mention of the works of Fathers Dummermuth, N. del Prado, J. Ude, and Guillermin, as also the more recent controversies that occurred between the years 1924 and 1927.

cluded, no one is freed from this except by God's grace: and this is not rendered to those who receive it as being due to them on account of any merits on their part, but it is freely given to them as a pure grace regardless of preceding merits. There is no more illustrious example of predestination than Jesus Himself. . . . He who made Him of the seed of David a just man, who never would be unjust without a previous consent of His will, makes just those who are unjust, without any previous merit on their part, so that He may be the head and these His members. . . . He who made Him such that He never had nor will have His will turned to evil, makes in His members their good from being evil. And therefore He predestined Him and us, because, both for Him to be our head and for us to be His members, He foreknew not our previous merits but our future works. Those who read these things, if they understand the same, let them give thanks to God. But those who do not understand, let them pray that He may be their interior teacher from whose countenance shine forth knowledge and understanding." [27]

Jesus was predestined to be the natural Son of God before the foreseeing of His merits; for these presuppose His divine person and therefore His divine filiation. Now He is the eminent exemplar of our predestination. Let us thank Him for belonging to His Church, for having received life from Him. In Him, with Him, and by Him, the elect will thank God eternally for the gratuitous gift of their predestination, which is the source of all their divine benefits, which will have been the means of leading them to eternal life. They will understand that when the Lord rewards their merits, He crowns His own gifts. They will fully understand what St. Paul meant when he said: "Blessed be the God and Father of our Lord Jesus Christ, who hath blessed us with spiritual blessings in heavenly places, in Christ. As He chose us in Him before the foundation of the world, that we should be holy

[27] *De dono persever.*, PL, XLV, 1033-34.

and unspotted in His sight, in charity. Who hath predestinated us unto the adoption of children through Jesus Christ unto Himself, according to the purpose of His will. Unto the praise of the glory of His grace, in which He hath graced us in His beloved Son." [28] This is practically the same as what our Lord said: "My sheep hear My voice. . . . And I give them life everlasting, and they shall not perish for ever. . . . And no one can snatch them out of the hand of My Father. I and the Father are one." [29] "Father I will that where I am, they also whom Thou hast given Me may be with Me. . . . And I have made known Thy name to them and will make it known, that the love wherewith Thou hast loved Me may be in them, and I in them." [30] "And not for them only do I pray, but for them also who through their word shall believe in Me. That they all may be one, as Thou, Father, in Me, and I in Thee. . . . And the glory which Thou hast given Me, I have given to them, that they may be one, as we also are one . . . and that the world may know that Thou hast also loved Me." [31]

In conclusion let us repeat again what we said in the preface to this book. Cardinal Newman remarked that in the Middle Ages the mysteries of the faith were considered in the liturgy primarily from the point of view of infused contemplation and were given a poetic setting; later on they were viewed in the light of theological wisdom, and afterwards, from the sixteenth century, there has been at times a little too much of a tendency to view them in the inferior light of a prudence that forgets the sublimity of the divine plan and the depth of God's love, for it is only He who can thoroughly actuate our will and move it *suavely* and *firmly*.

The final effect of predestination is expressed by the liturgy in the hymn of vespers for the feast of the dedication of a

28 Eph. 1: 3–6.
29 John 10: 27–30.
30 *Ibid.*, 17: 24, 26.
31 *Ibid.*, 17: 20–23.

church in verses of unsurpassed splendor of diction. In this hymn the heavenly Jerusalem is described as being constructed of living stones, chiseled into shape by the Author of salvation, polished by bruises and blows, and fittingly arranged by the hands of Christ to remain for ever in the sacred edifice.

> Jerusalem, blessed city,
> Called the vision of peace,
> That art built up in heaven,
> Of living stones,
> And with angel cohorts circled,
> As a bride with thy attendants.
>
> Many a blow and biting sculpture
> Polished well those stones elect,
> In their places now compacted
> By the heavenly Architect,
> Who therewith hath willed forever
> That His palace should be decked.
>
> Everywhere be glory and honor
> To God most high,
> Equally to Father and Son
> And the glorious Paraclete,
> To whom praise and power
> Through everlasting ages.

APPENDIX I

Infallibly Efficacious Grace and Salutary Acts Easy to Perform

We reproduce here in substance a series of articles that appeared in the *Revue Thomiste* from November, 1925 to March, 1926, relative to a new opinion which was then proposed as being in agreement with that of the Thomists, Gonzalez and Massoulié. For a more detailed knowledge of this new opinion one may consult the two articles in the *Revue Thomiste,* only the substance of these being given here.

A NEW OPINION

We are asked to give our opinion of an interpretation that has recently been proposed of the Thomist doctrine on grace. This theory proposes to be a development of the opinion held by Gonzalez, Bancel, Massoulié, and Reginald concerning sufficient grace. Whereas the majority of the Thomists say that sufficient grace gives merely the power to perform the good act, the proximate power, the above-mentioned theologians maintain that it also gives an *impulse* to perform the good act. In their opinion, it is even a physical predetermining premotion, but a fallible one; for it does not infallibly overcome, like efficacious grace, the obstacles that may arise from temptation or free will itself. It is said that this opinion differs from that commonly held by the Thomists only for the purpose of explaining better the sinner's responsibility and real power to do good and avoid evil.

Perhaps it will complete the Thomist theory as far as culpability is concerned, but if we wish to extend its application to the order of good, to salutary acts easy to perform, it seems to us that it has serious difficulties to contend with. We should like merely to remind our readers here that this opinion of Gonzalez has already been explained at length and defended by the lamented Father Guillermin, O.P., who weighs its advantages and disadvantages, and who understood it in a far different sense from that proposed to us at the present day.[1] We should like to insist on this difference, in that it perhaps will enable us the better to discern between what truth there may be in this new interpretation and what is still very debatable.

They readily admit that a slight modification of the doctrine commonly admitted by the Thomists on the distinction between efficacious grace and sufficient grace will necessitate modifications in other points of doctrine, such as foreknowledge, providence, predestination, and reprobation. They seek, however, to persuade us that the proposed modifications cannot change, indeed, the substance of the Thomist doctrine, but are merely concerned with some unimportant details that would seem to be the result of a too rigid interpretation of the doctrine, and this seems particularly to have been verified in the case of Lemos and Alvarez. The tree would be the same, but the leaves different.

It is suggested that we return to the opinion held by Gonzalez, Bancel, Massoulié, and Reginald, according to which sufficient grace gives not only the proximate power to perform a good act, but also an impulse that actually inclines one to the performance of the good act. We said that this sufficient grace, according to these authors, is a fallibly physical predetermining motion that inclines one to the performance of the good act, but it differs from the infallibly efficacious grace in that it does not overcome the obstacles that may present themselves.

[1] Cf. *Revue Thomiste,* 1902, p. 654 ff.; 1903, p. 20.

There would seem to be a tendency to go so far with this theory as to say it often happens that this sufficient grace (impulsive) is actually the cause of salutary acts easy to perform, such as attrition or a prayer that is still imperfect. Consequently, infallibly efficacious grace would not be necessary for these salutary acts easy to perform, but only for the difficult ones such as contrition, which is entirely distinct from attrition.

These salutary acts easy to perform necessarily presuppose, so they say, only a fallibly divine motion, and anterior to this a fallibly divine decree, too. As soon as the majority of the Thomists read this objection, there arises in their minds this thought: But how can God know infallibly from all eternity in a fallible decree the free act of attrition that will be performed in time by a certain sinner in certain determined circumstances? Let us observe that the question concerns not only the predestined, but also those not predestined, who in the course of their lives will make acts of attrition.

Shall we say that God infallibly knows this free act of attrition in so far as it is present in His eternity that embraces all time? But this free act is present in His eternity rather than its contrary only because of a divine decree; otherwise it would be there on the same grounds as necessary truths and thus we fall into the error of fatalism. The foreknowledge of the act either does or does not precede the decree; there is no other alternative. Hence if the divine decree concerning the future act of attrition is fallible, God cannot have infallible knowledge of this free act except by having recourse to the Molinist theory of the *scientia media*. Now the new opinion absolutely sets aside the *scientia media* because of the implied contradictions. The divine knowledge, since it is the cause of things, cannot be *passive* with regard to conditionally free acts of the future.

It truly seems, according to this proposed new interpretation, that it may happen that with the same sufficient (im-

pulsive) grace, that this particular sinner may perform an act
of attrition and that a certain other may not, so that he who
does so would not receive more help than the other. How can
this conclusion be reconciled with the teaching of St. Thomas,
who says: "He who makes a greater effort does so because of
a greater grace; but to do so, he needs to be moved by a higher
cause"? [2] Likewise St. Paul says: For who distinguisheth thee?
What has thou that thou hast not received? [3] St. Thomas also
says: "The first cause of this diversity is to be sought on the
part of God, who dispenses His gifts of grace variously." [4] If
two sinners are placed in the same circumstances, and one of
them without being helped more than the other refrains
from placing an obstacle to grace, which the other places,
and performs the act of attrition, which the other fails to
perform, does not the former by this act distinguish himself
from the latter? And if he performs the act of attrition without the infallibly efficacious grace, why would he not, without this grace, perform the more difficult act of contrition?
Greater and less do not diversify the species. Who can say
when the more difficult act arises that would demand the
efficacious grace? [5] Are we not thus led to the acceptance of a
teaching which would have to contend with the principal
difficulties of Molinism for salutary acts easy to perform, and
with all the obscurities of Thomism for the difficult ones? [6]

To one reading this new theory the following objection

[2] *In Matt.* 25: 15; cf. *in ep. ad Eph.* 4: 7.

[3] I Cor. 4: 7.

[4] *Summa theol.,* Ia IIae, q.112, a.4.

[5] The similarity they seek to establish between the general motion and
sufficient grace, and between the special motion and efficacious grace, seems
to us contrary not only to the generally accepted interpretation among the
Thomists, but also to the text of St. Thomas in his *De veritate,* q.24, a.14,
to which these Thomists appeal in proof of their theory. Cf. Billuart, *De
gratia,* diss. 3, a.2, no. 8.

[6] Cf. del Prado, *De gratia et libero arbitrio,* III, 423. Also Schiffini, quoted
on the same page. As for the opinion held by St. Alphonse, it is conceived
from the moral and not from the metaphysical and ontological point of view,
from which St. Thomas argues in the development of his doctrine on grace.
They are on different planes.

immediately presents itself: For the acceptance of this theory it suffices, so they say, to admit that infallibly efficacious grace is not necessary so that one avoid for some time putting any obstacles in the way of that grace sufficient for salutary acts easy of performance. But the fact of not putting any obstacle in the way at the moment when the act of attrition is of obligation, would mean that this act is performed without efficacious grace.

Besides, the objection raised against foreknowledge would always be applicable. How can God in a fallible decree foresee infallibly that a particular person will not put an obstacle in the way of grace, without receiving greater help than a certain other who will do so? At least we must admit that in the latter case there is a permissive decree permitting the resistance or failure. And then in the former case in which there is no resistance, is not the divine decree infallibly efficacious, if God decides to grant a physically predetermining motion that inclines the will to act, and this without a concomitant permission of any actual failure? This would bring us back to the common teaching of the Thomists.

It will serve a useful purpose to recall how differently Father Guillermin understood this theory of Gonzalez, which he also defended, though disclosing its weak points.[7]

THE TRUE THEORY OF GONZALEZ, THE THOMIST

The proposition that infallibly efficacious grace is not necessary for salutary free acts easy to perform, far from being upheld by Father Guillermin in his exposition and defense of the theory of Gonzalez, was attacked by him, and, in his opinion, by Gonzalez and his successors.

Assuming by way of objection the teaching in support of this new theory nowadays proposed, Father Guillermin wrote:

[7] On these weak points, see Hugon, *De gratia*, p. 356. We can scarcely conceive of a physical predetermining motion that is defectible.

"There is another objection: The created free will in this life is always defectible. But they say that it does not always have to fail, not always place an obstacle to the motion of sufficient grace that inclines the will actively to good. Why, then, at least sometimes would not the will perform the good act with the help only of sufficient grace that supplies all that is necessary for a good action? Thus it will happen, if not always, at least sometimes, that sufficient grace, according to the teaching of the Molinists, becomes efficacious without having undergone any intrinsic modification, and this for the sole reason that the free will has determined of itself to give its consent or at least not to put any obstacle in the way of the sufficient motion." [8]

Father Guillermin's reply is as follows: "Evidently from the fact that the free will always has the power to fail, we cannot conclude, therefore, it will always fail, always put an obstacle to the motion of grace. But in this case the following conclusion can be legitimately drawn. Since the defectible free will can always and in all things fail, if it so wishes, and put an obstacle, it will never, in any given circumstance, be absolutely and infallibly certain that it will not actually put an obstacle in the way of good, unless a preservative power certainly prevents this obstacle from being placed. Without this preservative or victorious grace over obstacles, it will be quite possible, even probable, that in a certain case no obstacle to the motion of sufficient grace will freely be placed; it will even be morally certain that, in a long series of acts, it will once or so happen that the free will puts no obstacle in the way. But in any particular case, for it to be infallibly certain that the free will, notwithstanding its defectibility, will perform a good act, again I say that it is indispensable for the will to receive a help from God that prevents or efficaciously removes every obstacle and every defection. Now God's plans cannot be the subject of uncertainty, and His knowledge is such that He knows eternally all things, even free acts of the future, and knowing them, as the Thomists say, in His divine causality, this knowledge cannot be purely conjectural. Sufficient grace which, in moving the will to good, does not eliminate all danger of hindrance or resistance, will not then be such as to afford a certain foundation for God's infallible foreknowledge. Only efficacious grace that causes the will to perform the free act *without hindrance* assures this foundation.[9]

"But it is not only to safeguard the infallible certainty of the divine knowledge that we conclude the intervention of grace efficacious of itself is of necessity for the effective performance of every good act; there is still another more direct and more immediate reason.[10]

"It seems to us of necessity to grant that God's action reaches all beings including all their modes, and according to all the conditions of their existence. St. Augustine pays this homage to God's grace: 'It is owing to Thy grace, and to Thy mercy that Thou hast dissolved like ice the sins which I committed. I impute it also to Thy grace, whatever other sins I have not committed; for what evil was there which I was not capable of doing. I confess that all have been forgiven me as well the evils I committed by my own will, as those which by Thy providence I committed not.' [11]

"Likewise we can say," continues Father Guillermin, "that with sufficient grace, and without efficacious grace which removes indeed possible resistance, it is not necessary for the free will to resist, and it is not impossible for the same effectively to perform the good act; but, when the resistance,

[9] In this way Father Guillermin and the Thomists, whose theory he defends, avoid the *scientia media*. But how can one do so by conceding that infallibly efficacious grace is not necessary for the actual performance or even mere continuance in the performance of salutary and easy free acts, such as an act of attrition or of imperfect prayer?

[10] It must be observed that this reason applies not only to difficult but also to easy salutary acts.

[11] *Confessions*, II, 7.

which is always possible for a defective will, does not oppose the motion of grace, this does not happen without a special intervention of divine mercy whose action directs and penetrates everything that takes place in the order of good. . . .

"God's decrees do not presuppose our choice. They precede it, and when there is question of performing a good act conducive to salvation these divine decrees are positively and actively the cause of the same. Moreover, an intervention, a divine protection that is entirely external, one that removes the occasions or diminishes the intensity of the temptations would not suffice; for, even with a more powerful sufficient grace and a weaker temptation, it can still happen that the will, since it remains free and liable to fail, resists grace and yields to the temptation. Only an interior action, efficaciously determining the free will, will infallibly remove the resistance and the choice of the contrary act. . . . Only efficacious grace has the power to overcome the obstacles." [12]

This is how Father Guillermin, in explaining and defending this theory of Gonzalez, proves that he escapes incurring the contradictions implied by the *scientia media* of Molina.[13]

Not only Father Guillermin is of this opinion, but even Gonzalez.[14] He replies to the same difficulty by saying: "Efficacious grace is necessary to make sure of the actual consent of our will, but it is not necessary so as to make sure that our will have the power to be free and unimpeded from eliciting the act if it so wishes. . . . That is said to be necessary for our consent without which in fact our consent is never given, although without it this can freely and without hindrance be

---

[12] *Revue Thomiste,* 1903, pp. 23 ff.

[13] Father Guillermin also avoids (*ibid.,* p. 27) the same for the foreknowledge of sin, by means of the classical distinction between the *permissive* decree as to the disorder inherent in the act of sin, and the *positive* decree as regards the physical entity of the act of sin. We see no advantage in distinguishing between the *decree as such* and the *decree as eternal,* as a substitute for this distinction.

[14] Disp. LVIII, sect. 3.

given, if we so willed." [15] Now the free consent in this case is verified not only in acts said to be difficult, such as an act of contrition, but also in free salutary acts that are said to be easy, such as an act of attrition or of imperfect prayer, and this applies to the continuation of these acts.

Bancel, too, maintains that efficacious grace is necessary for every free salutary act, although this latter is not repugnant to sufficient grace. Bancel writes: "Although, of course, if the grace is merely sufficient, it is absolutely certain that with this grace man will not act, yet that he act is not repugnant to the nature of this grace." [16] Massoulié says the same when, defending the theory of Gonzalez de Albeda, he shows that it manages to avoid the inconveniences of the *scientia media*.[17] Gonzalez, too, explicitly says: "Fourthly, I say that of two persons equally tempted, in the case of one who consents to the promptings of the Holy Spirit, his will is always prepared for this by a greater intrinsic prevenient grace than the one who consents to the devil's suggestions." [18] It is the principle of predilection, that no one thing would be better than another unless it were loved more by God.[19] "What hast thou that thou hast not received? For who discerneth thee?" [20]

They appeal to certain texts of Gonet, which would contradict, so they say, what Lemos and Alvarez affirm about the necessity of infallibly efficacious grace for every salutary act easy of performance. But when we read the whole of these

15 Quoted by Father Guillermin, *Revue Thomiste*, 1903, p. 26, no. 1.

16 *Brevis univ. theol. cursus*, Vol. II, tr. 4, q.4, p. 381; quoted by Father Guillermin, *Revue Thomiste*, 1902, p. 662.

17 *Divus Thomas sui interpres*, Vol. II, diss. 3, q.6, a.2, p. 213, Roman ed., 1709.

18 *Com. in Iam*, q.19, a.8, disp. LVII (1637), Vol. II, p. 97; cf. *ibid.*, pp. 42, 54, 55, 60–67, 83, 86, 87. He always upholds the universality of the principle of predilection. Since God's love is the cause of goodness in things, no one thing would be better than another (even because of an act easily performed), unless it were loved more and helped more by God.

19 *Loc. cit.*, Ia, q.20, a.3, 4.

20 I Cor. 4: 7.

texts in Gonet, we see that he speaks exactly as Alvarez does, and that he maintains that sufficient grace, which is the subject of dispute, is called sufficient not in reference to the imperfect act of attrition but to the perfect act of contrition. Then every difficulty is dispelled, for grace, said to be sufficient as regards contrition, is infallibly efficacious as regards attrition. And we find this to be the teaching of Lemos, Alvarez, del Prado, also Gonet, even of Massoulié and all the Thomists whom we consulted, verifying from their context the incomplete quotations appealed to from the writings of these authors.

For instance Gonet says: "Both kinds of help, sufficient and efficacious, are included in the expression *auxilii Dei moventis;* because each consists in a certain supernatural motion that applies the faculties of the soul to their supernatural acts; yet with this difference, that the sufficient help merely moves and applies the will to the performance of imperfect acts, thereby disposing and preparing the soul for more perfect acts. But the efficacious help moves and applies the will to the performance of perfect acts of contrition and charity that finally prepare and dispose the soul for sanctifying grace, which is the ultimate and most perfect form of the supernatural order. Hence it is the common teaching of the Thomists in agreement with Alvarez (*De auxiliis,* Bk. III, disp. 80) that every help that is sufficient for one particular act, is also at the same time efficacious for the performance of another to which by an absolute decree of divine providence it is ordained, so that it is unconditionally sufficient and conditionally efficacious." [21]

The last sentence of this quotation shows that this opinion

[21] *De voluntate Dei,* Vol. II, disp. IV, no. 147. In like manner Father del Prado says that for every salutary act, even the one easy to perform, an infallibly efficacious grace is required, which can be called sufficient not in reference to this act, but in reference to the following more perfect act. Cf. del Prado, *De gratia,* III, 423.

does not belong peculiarly to Lemos and Alvarez. All Thomists speak as they do.

Thus everything becomes perfectly clear. Grace said to be sufficient as regards contrition, is infallibly efficacious as regards attrition. It is therefore wrong to say that Gonet and other Thomists declare that imperfect salutary free acts do not demand for their actual performance an infallibly efficacious grace.

But even Massoulié is of the same mind as Gonet, for precisely when explaining and defending the theory of Gonzalez and showing that this same theory does not contradict the one held by Alvarez, he writes: "So grace is said to be efficacious as regards the imperfect effect which it effects, but inefficacious or sufficient as regards the ultimate and more perfect to which it disposes, since, of course, as we explained, it has less efficacy and power than is required for the eliciting of the more perfect act." [22]

If, then, we inspect the contexts from which the quotations of the various Thomists are taken, we do not find in them this doctrine, that infallibly efficacious grace is not necessary for the actual performance of easy salutary acts. They teach the very contrary of this.

The new interpretation cannot be reconciled with the general principles of St. Thomas. It goes against the principle of predilection: "For since God's love is the cause of goodness in things, no one thing would be better than another, if God did not will greater good for one than for another." [23]

If the fact of resisting sufficient grace is an evil that can come only from us, then the fact of not resisting is a good that cannot be attributed solely to us, but which must come from the source of all good. According to the teaching of St. Thomas, if one of two persons rather than the other actually

22 *Divus Thomas sui interpres*, II, p. 206a.
23 *Loc. cit.*, Ia, q.20, a.3.

makes an act of attrition, then the reason for this is that God from all eternity willed it by His infallibly efficacious and consequent will.[24]

From the very fact that these principles are of the metaphysical order, they are without exception. For anyone to say that they do not apply to easy acts, is to say that they no longer are absolutely universal principles. Hence they lose all validity and "are fit to be trodden upon by men." Principles are principles; to deny their universal validity is to compromise everything.

The principle of predilection clarifies all these problems, and the subsequent obscurity pertains not to this life but to the next, in that it is the result of a light too great for our feeble vision. Thus we keep the sense of the mystery without seeking to explain it in too human a way.[25]

[24] *Ibid.*, Ia, q. 19, a.6 ad 1um.
[25] The unity of the doctrine and of the Thomist school on this subject was pointed out by us in the *Revue Thomiste*, March–April, 1926. "Infallibly efficacious grace and salutary acts easy to perform" was the title of the article for the April number. There one will find some important texts of Gonzalez, the Thomist, which are fully in agreement with the principles set forth by St. Thomas.

APPENDIX II

The Opinion of Father Billot, S.J., on the Divine Motion

A THEOLOGIAN who was a disciple of Father Billot, S.J., in reviewing the articles on predestination and premotion written by us,[1] which have been reproduced and recast in this work, wrote as follows:

"Father Garrigou-Lagrange has taken a very objective attitude in the exposition of the systems, quoting texts in support of his statements. Undoubtedly one or other of his conclusions will trouble a theologian who, adopting the theories of Molina or Suarez, claims nevertheless to be a follower of St. Thomas. Is not the repetition of the phrase appropriate here: A friend of Plato, but more a friend of truth? . . .

"When he reminds us of the teaching of the Church in recording the various opinions, evidently he assumes an objective attitude in doing so, but he also shows undisguised sympathy for the Thomism of the Dominican school. We cannot blame him for his preferences. We owe him a deep debt of gratitude for his splendid articles which, notwithstanding a certain long discursiveness of style and repetitions,[2] constitute the finest historical and doctrinal synthesis which we have ever read on this grave problem of predestination. . . .

"The limitations of this article prevent us from vindicating Billot's true point of view, which Father Garrigou-Lagrange

[1] Cf. *Dict. de théol. cath.*

[2] We could have eliminated these in the present work, but we thought it necessary to hark back frequently, as St. Thomas does, to these same principles, so that the deep meaning and universality of the same may be readily perceived by all.

seems to have completely misunderstood in making out that the famous Jesuit believed in an indifferent premotion, as a result of which the free will would determine itself to act and would determine the divine motion to produce this or that particular free act. Such an opinion would have been repudiated (we say that it was expressly repudiated) by the cardinal, and we find no trace of it in his works. In spite of the seemingly contrary statements, Billot's stand, even in the question of physical premotion, differs perhaps less than one might imagine from the thesis defended by Father Garrigou-Lagrange." [3]

At our request, *L'Ami du Clergé,* in one of its later issues (June 20, 1935, pp. 392–94), thus replied to this objection of ours:

Objection. In reviewing the article on physical premotion,[4] the *Ami* of February 21 affirms that Cardinal Billot expressly repudiated the theory of an indifferent premotion attributed to him by the author of the reviewed article.

"I would be thankful to your collaborator if he would justify his assertion, which at first sight seems strange enough."

Reply. In expressing our appreciation in writing of Cardinal Billot, we felt certain of arousing in the minds of some of our readers at least a sense of curiosity. Let us recall first of all what Father Garrigou-Lagrange wrote:

"Would the divine motion by which God would determine us to the performance of an indeliberate act, be an indifferent premotion, so that the free will of itself would determine itself and also the divine motion to this or that particular act? Certain theologians thought so, especially L. Billot.[5]

"This theory and the *scientia media* mutually support each other. There would still be some reality that eludes God's universal causality. There would be a determination that is independent of the sovereign causality. The nobler part in the work of salvation,

---

[3] Cf. *Ami du Clergé,* February 21, 1935, pp. 114–20.
[4] Cf. *Dict. de théol. cath.*
[5] *De Deo uno,* part. II, chap. I, "De scientia Dei."

the determination of our salutary act, would not come from the Author of salvation." [6]

We said and we again say that Billot's view, notwithstanding appearances, does not differ so much as one would think from that held by Father Garrigou-Lagrange.

1) Undoubtedly Billot defends the theory of the *scientia media*. But for anyone who reads without prejudice the thesis he dedicated to this subject, this theory is viewed, in accordance with the very sound Thomism of the author of this thesis, as a means of rejecting what he believes to be the Dominican theory which consists in a predetermination that takes away from the will the possibility of determining itself. Moreover, as Father Garrigou-Lagrange candidly admits, there is a similar sentiment in the opposite direction on the part of the Dominicans to use the term *predetermination* so as to discard the untenable theory of simultaneous concurrence or of an indifferent premotion.

2) The *scientia media* of Billot, in its final analysis, closely approaches the Dominican "knowledge of vision." Billot, indeed, never taught that either a simple or a conditional future is known by God independently of the decree of His will.

Concerning conditional futures he writes as follows: "But, in fact, because we assert that conditional futures are known by God before any actual decree of His will, we do not exclude hypothetical decrees which God would have of moving the created will, and of bestowing all that is required on its part." [7] Let us see now what a Dominican says. Father Hugon writes: "Manifestly . . . God knows nothing as certainly and determinately future, except in the decree of His will. And conditional futures are in some way future, not indeed absolutely, but conditionally. Therefore they are known not in God's absolute decree, for then they would be simple futures; but they are known in His decree that is conditioned by the object. But a decree of this kind extends both to the object and to the free or necessary mode of the same, so that a conditional future would not be posited by man unless he freely determined himself to do so under the influence of the divine motion." [8]

6 Cf. *Dict. de théol. cath.*, XIII, 36.

7 *De Deo uno et trino*, 1910, p. 213.

8 *Tract. dogm.*, I, 212.

We should indeed like to know what difference there is, however slight it may be, between the Jesuit and the Dominican texts, both as to the doctrine and also, very much so, as to the way it is expressed.

3) Let us add that Billot always taught that everything of a positive nature in the determination of our free will depends upon the divine will and the divine motion. This is clearly seen in his argument in proof of the first Mover:

"That which is lacking in some perfection cannot be adequately sufficient to give to itself such perfection, because nothing is adequately sufficient to give to itself what it does not have. But what is mobile lacks the act of perfection to which it is brought. Nor can it be said that although it may be *formally* lacking in that perfection, yet it still has the same equivalently or virtually. For there is only one of two possibilities. Either it has equivalently as precontained in it whatever reality there is in the perfecton formally as such, and then there can be no movement to acquire such perfection, because a positive movement by which nothing positive is acquired is repugnant to reason. Or else it virtually has the perfection, that is, only in the first actuality, and then it is not of itself adequately sufficient for the second actuality, which by far exceeds the first; but it needs to receive this, and the need of receiving excludes the perfect sufficiency of giving, as the terms evidently denote." [9]

Can there be a clearer declaration of principles? Indifferent premotion would be implied in this *"virtually,"* this application of the will only in the first actuality. Now this is what Billot never admitted. Such an indifferent motion is a contradiction in terms. Billot was faithful to the Thomist conception of the divine motion to the second actuality of the will in his other treatises, most especially in those that closely concern the question of physical premotion.

Right away we have evidence of this in his treatise *On Sin*. The question at issue is to explain how, notwithstanding the dependence of whatever positiveness there is in our free acts upon the divine causality, God nevertheless is not the cause of sin. He

[9] *Loc. cit.*, pp. 55 f.

writes: "Immediately a difficulty presents itself; for if the substance of the evil act even as a moral entity is something positive, and if it is bound up with the very notion of sin, then one of two alternatives follows: either sin is from God or else not everything that actually exists depends upon the first Cause." [10] Now Billot was absolutely against admitting the hypothesis of this latter alternative.[11]

We find the same doctrine in his tractate on grace: "In theology the question comes up for examination concerning that motion by which the will passes from the first actuality of the salutary act to the second and deliberate actuality, and it posits the presence of that which for the will to act freely presupposes what has already been proved." [12] The eminent theologian gives us a brief summary of his opinion on this question in the following passage: "We propose to declare with certainty how every being and every mode of being comes from Him whose essence is His existence; likewise how nothing brings anything into existence except in so far as it acts by divine power; likewise how God is the cause of operation in all beings, at the same time for each secondary cause retaining intact its specific and proper activity, and, in fine, we shall declare whatever pertains to the universal dependence of creatures upon God and their community of relativity toward Him." [13] When Billot speaks of secondary causes determining God's general motion, he speaks as St. Thomas did. It is not a question of determining an indifferent motion, but of explaining how in the secondary cause the divine motion, which is capable, because of its universality, of adapting itself to all created activities, is particularized and determined by reason of certain effects that are proper to certain secondary causes. "Existence is the proper effect of the first Agent," says St. Thomas, too, "and all other agents act inasmuch as they act in virtue of the first Agent; but secondary agents, which are, as it were, particular ones and

---

10 *De peccato personali et originali,* p. 20.

11 For his solution of this difficulty consult *L'Ami,* 1928, p. 776, where we translated into French the complete text of the Jesuit theologian.

12 The reference is to the treatise *De Deo Creatore,* which unfortunately the eminent theologian never wrote.

13 *De gratia Christi,* p. 37.

which determine the action of the first Agent, produce as their proper effects other perfections that determine existence." [14]

Father Garrigou-Lagrange could have quoted an author who formally taught an indifferent motion in the secondary act. This was the case with Pignataro, who wrote: "This motion constitutes the will proximately disposed to make the choice." The explanation follows, and is thus formulated: "That the divine motion is determined to one movement in those things which by nature are determined to one thing, I concede; that it is so in contingent things, I deny." [15] There we have the motion that is undetermined as to its effect. But in that he would have been but a far echo of Billot who did not hesitate to declare the opinion of his confrère when it appeared in print as absolutely unintelligible. Undoubtedly Father Billot truly considered himself to be the opponent of the Dominican thesis; in truth, he had a wrong conception of it. But expressing himself in different terms, though retaining the mental attitude which his Jesuit training imposed upon him, he was in truth quite in agreement with the best of Thomists.

So writes the learned reviewer of the *Ami du Clergé*.

I shall reply here as I did in this same periodical. I am happy in coming to a better understanding from the texts just quoted that Cardinal Billot, "though retaining the mental attitude imposed upon him by his Jesuit training," was more like a Dominican Thomist in his doctrine than at first sight he appeared to be. My conversations with him induced me to see considerable differences of meaning in the terms he employed and not sufficiently to perceive certain profound similarities in doctrine, which I am very happy to note. I noticed especially that he defends the theory of the *scientia media*, but it must be admitted that in his explanation of it, he seeks to approach as near as possible the teaching of Dominican theologians.

However, in the leading text quoted in the preceding

---

[14] *Contra Gentes*, III, 66. The reference is to the unwritten tractate *De Deo Creatore*.

[15] *De Deo Creatore*, p. 519.

pages, which is taken from his dogmatic treatise, instead of reading: "We do not exclude hypothetical decrees which God would have of moving the created will, and of bestowing all that is required on its part," [16] a Thomist would say: "which God has," and not "which God would have." Particularly so a Thomist would not add what we read nine lines further on: "Therefore God sees those (conditional futures) dependent upon the condition of His hypothetical motion which, however, cannot at all be predetermining, because thus the proper and specific mode by which free acts participate in the divine essence would be destroyed."

You will say to me: "that is due to the mental attitude imposed by the Jesuit training" upon Cardinal Billot, who was preoccupied in rejecting, as you say, what he believed to be the Dominican theory. On this point he had a wrong conception of their teaching. And, this admitted, as for the rest it can truly be said that we are substantially in agreement.

That is why in this work, when speaking of the indifferent motion, I quoted Father Pignataro, S.J., in preference to Cardinal Billot, as exponent of this opinion.

[16] *De Deo uno et trino*, 1910.

APPENDIX III

A Reply to Some Well-known Objections against Premotion

WE here insert a manuscript bearing no date, which came into our hands some years ago, and which appears to be the work of a sound Thomist. He succeeds well enough in replying to some very well-known objections raised against the teaching of St. Thomas regarding the divine motion.

A BRIEF EXPOSITION OF THE TEACHING OF ST. THOMAS ON DIVINE MOTION

St. Thomas says: "But if we hold that a sacrament is an instrumental cause of grace, we must needs allow that there is in the sacraments a certain instrumental power of bringing about the sacramental effects. . . . But the instrumental power has a being that passes from one thing into another, and is incomplete; just as motion is an imperfect act passing from agent to patient." [1]

Farther on in the same article he says: "A spiritual power cannot be in a corporeal subject after the manner of a permanent and complete power. But there is nothing to hinder an instrumental spiritual power from being in a body, in so far as a body can be moved by a particular spiritual substance so as to produce a particular spiritual effect." [2]

But now it must be pointed out that this spiritual power is something transient in a material subject, for instance, in

[1] *Summa theol.*, IIIa, q.62, a.4.
[2] *Ibid.*, ad 1um.

baptismal water, which remains material. This instrumental power (which is a motion) is of such a nature that it in no way intrinsically modifies the nature of the subject in which it is found: in the present case indeed it is spiritual, and yet the water does not become spiritual, but is elevated for the time being to produce a spiritual effect.

There is something similar to this, as St. Thomas says, in the very voice perceived by the senses "in which there is a certain spiritual power, inasmuch as it proceeds from a mental concept, of arousing the mind of the hearer." [3] The same is the case with the pen of the author in writing something intelligible.

It seems now possible in a general way to understand that it is not the function of motion to modify in any way the nature of the subject in which it is found, but leaving the nature or faculty absolutely unchanged physically, all that the motion does is to actuate the same for its own operation. The motion will be either for a necessary or free operation, according as the agent is either necessary or free. For just as water when moved remains material, so the will when moved remains free; and the action of the will when moved is free and not necessary, because such is the nature of the will.

By this, however, we assert the fact, but we have not as yet the reason for the fact. Moreover, it seems that the reason for this is to be sought in the very nature of this peculiar entity called motion; for it is not properly *being*, but a *becoming*. Why indeed is water not spiritual, although it has a spiritual quality? It is because this quality is fluid, is in the process of becoming spiritual. Why does the will remain free and determinating, although it receives a determinated quality? It is because that quality is not determined to a mode of being, but is essentially fluid, or a becoming, in process of being determined. For it is nothing else but a plenitude of action or power or an activity by which the faculty that previously

[3] *Ibid.*, ad 1um.

was not actually eliciting its act is actually doing so. And just as the power in the pen causes it actually to produce its own action, namely, the writing, so this plenitude of action causes the will actually to produce its own action, which is this particular action rather than a certain other, or it chooses, because its proper action is election. And here we already have a vague idea how motion does not prevent but rather causes the freedom of the act.

It is very difficult to see how under the influence of this motion there is truly freedom of action, while on the one hand the motion is a requisite for action, and on the other that the will is not free to have it or not.

As for this it must absolutely be said that certainly the will has no choice concerning the motion; but this is not contrary to liberty. For this it suffices that the act be under the control of the will, but not the principle of the act. It is indeed absurd and a contradiction in terms for that which constitutes a principle to depend upon this principle. Therefore, just as it is absurd for what constitutes the will as such to depend upon this same will, so it is absurd for what constitutes the will in act as such to depend upon this same will. Now it is motion that constitutes the will in act, or as having power and active indifference in act. Therefore it is absurd for motion to depend upon the will and be under the control of the will.

In other words, so long as the will is considered without the motion, it has not this active indifference actually but merely potentially. Therefore it is absurd to think that previous to the motion it can exercise its active indifference, namely, by accepting or refusing this motion.

Actual liberty is to be sought only where the will is in act. Now the will is in act by means of motion. Therefore the will when moved, and not before it is moved, must be *actually* actively indifferent, and it must have its terminus, namely, its act, in its power.

But you will say: The motion itself is already determined to one thing; therefore the will when moved is already determined to one thing, and therefore is not actively indifferent.

Reply: I distinguish. The motion is determined as an *incomplete being,* or as determining, or as that by which the will determines itself, or as producing the determination, this I concede; that the motion is determined as a complete being, as a form, as *ens quod,* this I deny. I distinguish the consequent: That the will when moved determines itself to one thing, this I concede; that it is determined to one thing by a determination independent of itself, this I deny.

You will insist: How can the will receive from something external to itself a determination that must come essentially from itself?

Reply: I distinguish. It cannot receive from something external to itself a determination, namely, the act that must come essentially from itself; this I concede. It cannot receive from something external to itself that by which it effects its determination, that by which it determines itself; this I again distinguish. If this something external to itself is not the first Cause, then I concede this; if it is, then I deny this. On the contrary, this is of necessity required so that the will may be the principle of its act.

Still you insist: He who has the end within his grasp, has the means also. Now motion is the means required for the act. Therefore this must be within the reach of the will.

Reply. I distinguish the major. He must have within his grasp the means that pertain to the principle of operative power; this I concede. That he must have within his grasp the principle by which the agent is constituted as actually having power; this I deny. For one actually to have the power presupposes that one is already constituted as the principle. I contradistinguish the minor, and deny the consequence. For just as, when we say that the will has dominion over itself, this means that it has dominion over its act and not over its faculty, so when we say that it actually has dominion over itself, this must be understood as meaning that it has dominion over its act, but not over that by which it is actually constituted as having dominion over its act, namely, over motion.

It therefore seems right to conclude that just as, when we speak of matter and form, of essence and existence, we must always correct by means of the intellect that imagination we have of specific being, which is the reason for all the difficulties presenting themselves against a real distinction in each case, so we must always correct the imagination that represents motion to us as being that is complete, determined, and predetermined; and once the imagination is given admittance, immediately inextricable difficulties arise. For what is determined cannot any more be determined; what is chosen cannot any more be the object of choice. But if we take note of the fact that St. Thomas always speaks of motion as a fluid being, as a being that is essentially in the process of becoming (not however as a relation), then all difficulties are easily solved, or rather, of their own accord disappear. These principles established, we may briefly sum up the teaching of St. Thomas as follows:

CATECHISM OF MOTION

1) Can God be the cause of free being?

R. Most certainly: for otherwise He would not be Being.

2) Can God be the cause of the created free action?

R. Most certainly: for otherwise there would not be either action or free action.

3) How can God be the cause of created free action, so that the action of the creature, however, is truly elicited by it?

R. By motion.

4) What is motion?

R. Motion is that activity by which I freely determine myself.

5) Can it be called premotion?

R. Certainly: because that by which I determine myself, that by which I actually exercise my liberty, is by nature prior to the exercise of my liberty; and yet it does not prevent my being free, but even causes me to be free.

6) Is that activity or premotion something that is caused by God?

R. I distinguish: as *ens quo*, I concede; as *ens quod*, I deny. For it is the subjection of the creature to God as regards action.

7) Does God determine the will by causing this activity?

R. I distinguish: He determines the will by taking away passive indifference, this I concede; by taking away active indifference, this I deny. This latter is even actually caused by this motion.

8) Is this activity or premotion something determined?

R. I distinguish: That it is determined as the principle of determination, as that by which I determine myself, this I concede; that it is determined, as the form which is the principle of action, as the impression received in the eye is the principle of vision, this I deny.

9) Can this activity be said to be indifferent?

R. I distinguish: That it is indifferent as the principle of indifference, or inasmuch as it causes this active indifference, this I concede; that it is indifferent as though needing a further determination, or as though the will under its influence is able not to act or to do something else, this again I subdistinguish: if this activity were not precisely that by which the will determinately chooses one particular thing, this I concede; if it is so, then I deny this or subdistinguish: *in sensu diviso*, I concede; *in sensu composito*, I deny.

10) Under the influence of that activity or motion the will can act only in one way. Therefore active indifference is taken away from this motion.

R. That the will when moved acts only in one way, this I concede; that it can act only in one way, I subdistinguish: because it is supposed by this activity already to have chosen freely one particular thing, this I concede; as though it does not always have the power of choosing something else, this I deny.

11) It is a contradiction in terms for God to determine the will to determine itself; for free determination must by its very nature originate from an intrinsic principle.

R. I distinguish: It is a contradiction for God to determine by introducing into the will some determination, namely, a determinate form, this I concede; by introducing that by which the will determines itself, this I deny. Nay rather, it is a contradiction in terms for the will to be able to be determined without a determination.

As for the reason adduced, I distinguish: that the determination, namely, the free act, must originate from an intrinsic principle, I concede; that by which the will determines itself, must so originate, this I deny. For just as that by which the will is constituted as such cannot originate from an intrinsic principle, so neither can that by which the will is constituted *in act:* it is absurd for the will to be able to produce some activity before it is constituted in act.

12) That by which the will determines itself must be within its power.

R. I distinguish: It must be within its power terminatively (the act, namely, to which the will determines itself), this I concede; it must be so formally, this I deny.

13) It follows therefore that the will stands in need of something which is not within its power, so that it may choose freely.

R. Certainly: since for the will freely to act it itself needs to be a free faculty; and for it to be freely the principle of its act, it needs to be the principle of its act; and for it freely to exercise its active indifference, it needs to be actively indifferent. All these things are not within its power, and yet no one says that for this reason the will is not free.

14) What is the cause of the determination cannot be said to be formally the previous determination. Therefore physical predetermination must be rejected.

R. I distinguish: The cause of the determination cannot be said to be determination as a form determining or determined, this I concede; it cannot be said to be determination or motion determining, this I deny. I distinguish the consequent: Physical predetermination must be rejected if the term means that a determinate form is introduced by God into the faculty, this I concede; if the term means a motion determining and predetermining, then I deny it must be rejected. It is not a question of a name but of a thing. If one does not care for the name, give it up. Nevertheless a false meaning must not be attributed to those asserting such a doctrine, even granted that the name may be the occasion of false interpretation.

15) Does the motion determine the will, or does it make the will determine itself?

R. It is in any case both. For God determines the will by giving it that by which it determines itself.

16) Can the will under the influence of this motion determine itself otherwise than God wills?

R. Yes: in just the same way as the will, when it wills, can determine itself otherwise than it wills.

17) It is contrary to the notion of liberty for any external agent to make me will what it may please this agent to will.

R. I distinguish: Unless such be the power of such an agent that it gives the will that by which it wills freely, then I concede the assertion; if the agent gives the will that by which the will chooses freely, namely, the motion, then I deny the assertion. Certainly there can be no conception of liberty without motion. Hence the argument is reversed.

18) That God should decide my choice is unintelligible.

R. That God should decide my choice·without giving me the principle of choosing, namely, motion, this I concede; if He does so, then I deny the assertion. We confess, however, that this is beyond the power of imagination; wherefore he who, as St. Thomas says, wishes to reduce intelligible things to sense perception, never will be able to understand motion.

19) What is meant by saying that God eternally predetermined my act?

R. It does not mean that God predestined or preformed the act that must be mine, so that afterwards somehow He imitates it in me; but it means that God, as the cause of free being, eternally decided to imbue me with that activity by which I am able to actuate or exercise my liberty, as He decided to move a necessary being to perform necessary acts. In such predefining or predetermining He most certainly knew that my act would be elicited freely by me.

20) Can God foresee my free act before He foresees the motion?

R. It is absolutely impossible. To foresee my act before foreseeing the motion would be like foreseeing the act of my will before the will itself is foreseen: which is absurd. The will is in act only by being moved.

21) If God were to foresee my act before He foresees the motion, would my act be free?

R. Not at all. Before God foresees the motion, He can foresee my act only as possible; because, before being moved, the will is not at all determined to one thing rather than another; and if it is determined, it is no longer free but necessary, for evidently the determination in which liberty has no part is necessary by natural necessity.

22) Can free will be retained by not admitting motion?

R. Not at all, philosophically speaking. For if, before the exercise of my liberty or of that which implies such exercise (which is motion) my act is supposed to be determined to one thing rather than another, evidently my act is one of necessity. Therefore, motion not admitted, the logical outcome is fatalism.

In conclusion we must say that the whole explanation of the difficulty in reconciling the divine motion with free will seems to proceed from a false notion of divine motion. For the divine action is conceived as being like created action. God, however, and the free will are conceived as *two co-ordinated causes* operating to produce the one effect. Once this view is taken, there is no possibility of any rational solution of the problem. Either free will is denied or else the divine action. It follows as a consequence of this that both are denied.

But, on the contrary, in the doctrine of St. Thomas, God and the free will are simply *subordinated causes*. The entire action is from God and also from the free will; and it is entirely from the free will because it is entirely from God. To withdraw the free will from the influence of the divine action is the same as to withdraw it from its own activity, and this is therefore the same as to destroy it. The divine motion, however, is precisely that by which the free will is subjected to the divine action that it may be constituted in act.

But no created intellect can by its own power acquire a knowledge of the divine action as it is in itself. Wherefore the obscurity in this doctrine is an argument in favor of its truth. Whereas in the other opinions the difficulty is fundamentally removed—for God would be acting only in a human and created way—yet those of the opposing camp have to contend with inexplicable difficulties and even absurdities in explaining, namely, how the free will and the divine foreknowledge are to be reconciled. And these difficulties or

absurdities strike at faith itself when from the divine the trans-
fer is made in a natural way to supernatural motion, or to
grace.

So ends this manuscript.

All the preceding discussion is tantamount to saying with
Bossuet that "God eternally wills all the future use of free
will as to all the goodness and reality there is in it. Nothing
is more absurd than to say a thing does not exist because God
does not will it. Must we not say, on the contrary, that it exists
because God wills it? And just as it happens that we are free
in virtue of the decree which wills us to be free, so it happens
that we act freely in this or that act, even in virtue of the decree which extends to all this in detail." [4]

Briefly then, what is more absurd than to claim that the
actualization of liberty destroys it?

[4] *Traité du libre arbitre*, chap. 8.

APPENDIX IV

The Thomist Origin of the Doctrine of Predetermining Decrees and Dr. H. Schwamm's Recent Work

WE take the opportunity here to thank our former pupil, Julien Groblicki, for having written the following note, and it gives us pleasure to publish it. It concerns Dr. Schwamm's recent work already mentioned in this book.[1]

In this present work the author sets out to prove what he unhesitatingly asserted in his two previous works,[2] after what Father Pelster, S.J.,[3] had written. It is that the doctrine of the present-day Thomists concerning the divine predetermining decrees, as the medium in which God knows contingent futures, is not to be attributed to St. Thomas but to the Subtle Doctor, and that he is the author of the same.[4] Although, to be sure, Scotus did not explicitly speak of the predetermining decrees, yet by his having presented the state of the question in a new light, and by his inquiry into the root cause of the contingency of things (contingency of the divine will) he necessarily and proximately prepared the way for this explanation.[5] The author endeavors to prove three things concerning this thesis:

I. *John Scotus is the originator of this doctrine.* Scotus presented the problem in a new light [6] (kernel of the prob-

---

[1] See *supra*, p. 278 note 77. *The divine foreknowledge according to Duns Scotus and his first followers*, Innsbruck, 1934.

[2] Magistri Joannis de Ripa, O.F.M., "Doctrina de praescientia divina." *Analecta Gregoriana*, I, Romae, 1930. Robert Cowton, O.F.M., "Uber das gottliche vorherwissen," Innsbruck, 1931.

[3] Thomas von Sutton, O.P., "Ein Oxforder verteidiger der thomistischen lehre," in *Zeitschr. f. Kat. Theol.*, XLVI (1922), pp. 383 f.

[4] Cf. *Ibid.*, pp. 330, 334.

[5] *Ibid.*, p. 2.

[6] *Ibid.*, p. 1, and generally throughout article 1.

lem) inasmuch as he showed the connection between God's will and His knowledge. Just as God in all His operations *ad extra* brings things into being by an act of His will, so also He knows all that actually exists by and in the determination of His will, or, according to modern terminology, in the decrees of His will. The decrees are what make contingent futures determinately true for God. The system of predetermining decrees had as a necessary and logical consequence to be evolved from this explanation of the Scotist solution. The disciples were not always in agreement in interpreting their master's doctrine. Some indeed asserted that Scotus spoke not explicitly but virtually of *concomitant* or *condetermining* decrees,[7] so that Mastrius and many saw that the freedom of the human will is jeopardized by the theory of predetermining decrees, which were admitted by others and attributed to the Subtle Doctor.

II. Schwamm asserts that this doctrine is not to be found in the works of St. Thomas, nor can it be deduced from his assertions, nor can it be reconciled with his view of the eternal presentiality of all things before God.

III. The Scotist doctrine of predetermining decrees was adopted by the Thomists from Bannez. That he will prove this last point in his next work is clearly enough foretold by him at the end of the book.[8]

As for the first question, whatever may be said about it (concerning Scotus and his disciples) and the first disciples of St. Thomas—and this will be taken up by him in the work which he has in preparation—it is certain that the author entirely misunderstood the Angelic Doctor. Now I am not speaking of his method of procedure, in that he selected only one article for discussion,[9] giving but a passing mention to the other passages; nor do I say anything of the way in which

---

[7] See pp. 330, 331, and in various places.
[8] See p. 334.
[9] Cf. I *Sent.*, d. 38, q.1, a.5.

he treats the problem. For when he comes to explain the opinion of St. Thomas which, as he sees it, "is irreconcilably in opposition" to that of Scotus, he says:

"But perhaps the first objection that presents itself, in seeking for the teaching of St. Thomas, is that these passages must be accepted as a starting point, in which he speaks more in favor of later Thomists. Is it necessary so as to justify oneself, as to the meaning of any author, concerning any question we wish to know, that we seek the explanation in those passages in which the author expressly wishes to answer the question?"

I pass this over, therefore, without comment, but I assert and prove that the author, in the single text from St. Thomas which he accepted, has still misunderstood the Angelic Doctor and explained him contrary to what he meant.

For he says that not only it cannot be affirmed that St. Thomas presupposes predetermining decrees, but that he "positively excludes them." St. Thomas rejected, so Schwamm contends, even every explanation of this problem by referring to the divine causality as insufficient and impossible. And he deduces this conclusion from the Doctor's words. He writes: "But there still remains a greater doubt concerning the secondary cause, because the first and necessary cause can co-exist with the defect of the secondary cause, just as the action of the sun can co-exist with the barrenness of the tree. But God's knowledge cannot co-exist with the defect of the secondary cause; for God cannot at the same time know that this particular person will run, and that he fails to run. To have certain knowledge of this, we must find, indeed, some certainty in the thing known." [10]

And this, adds Schwamm, is St. Thomas' "foundation" [11] for his further inquiry by which he seeks for the determination in contingent things that actually exist, but not in God.

[10] *Loc. cit.,* p. 94.
[11] *Ibid.,* p. 95.

Hence there can be no question of explaining the divine knowledge by an appeal to the infallibly efficient causality of the divine will. The statements of St. Thomas are evidently in opposition to any explanation of this kind.

CRITICISM

Dr. Schwamm's interpretation is false. For what St. Thomas posited in his objection, which he explained three times in this article, Dr. Schwamm accepted and proposed as the opinion of St. Thomas. This method of procedure is contrary to sound exegesis.

Moreover, Schwamm overlooks the conclusion in the first article of this same question, which is as follows: "the knowledge of good pleasure is the cause of things." [12]

The whole article is but a solution of two objections which St. Thomas stated at the beginning of the body of the article.[13] The first of these difficulties arises from the consideration of the divine knowledge, which is the cause of things. Therefore, it seems to impose necessity on things foreknown, and consequently it takes away contingency from things. In his reply to this, the Angelic Doctor does not deny that the divine knowledge is the cause of things and even the necessarily required cause. He fully admits the major of the argument. But he adds that God's knowledge is not the sole cause, but that it includes secondary causes, on account of which the effects can be either contingent or necessary, dependent upon the nature of the proximate secondary causes.

For an understanding of the second difficulty, it is important to notice that it is one thing to inquire about knowledge in general as such, about the notion and definition of the same; and it is another thing to inquire about some particular knowledge, for instance, the divine knowledge. Knowl-

---

[12] Cf. *Summa theol.*, Ia, q.14, a.8, which concludes the same way.

[13] Cf. I *Sent.*, d. 38, q.1, a.5. The same solution is given in his reply to the first and second objections and is again given in the middle of the argumentative part of the article.

edge as such, which, as the Angelic Doctor says in this article, is "certain cognition," pertains to the notion of whatsoever knowledge. It does not pertain to the notion of knowledge as such, that it be the cause of the things known. This applies to divine knowledge precisely as such and according as it is joined to the divine will. Hence after having considered in the previous objection knowledge as the cause of things, which applies to it inasmuch as it is divine, in this objection he considers knowledge in general, according as it is "certain cognition," abstracting from the fact of its being the cause of things. That this is the intention of the Angelic Doctor is evident from his explanation of this difficulty which, as I said, he explains three times in this article. To conclude from this that St. Thomas denies the divine knowledge to be the cause of things, or that he thinks the previous explanation insufficient, is the same as asserting that abstraction is the same as negation. But who can say so? In considering universals, such as the nature of a lion or any animal, shall we deny these exist in the concrete with their individualizing principles? [14]

Hence whatever opinion one may have of the solution of the arguments and difficulties, whether they please one or not, whether one consents to them or not, it cannot be concluded from what St. Thomas said, as Dr. Schwamm did, that the Angelic Doctor rejects the explanation of the knowledge of contingent futures as being the cause of the same.

I think this is the meaning of the article, and it will appeal to anyone who "reads it with an upright mind," as actually the immediate disciples of St. Thomas said.

What I say concerns this text alone. There are, of course, very many others that Schwamm interprets in the wrong sense, and which are known to all. [15]

[14] *Loc. cit.,* Ia, q.14, a.8, c. et ad 1um.

[15] For my part, however, if I may be permitted to say anything in addition to this, the following texts are of the greatest importance: (1) *De veritate,* q.2, a.12, sed contra, arg. 4: "God knows things inasmuch as He is their cause.

We have quoted many texts from St. Thomas which show that for him it was evident that, if God from all eternity knew with infallible certainty St. Paul's conversion, it is because He willed it by "the determination of His will and intellect." [16] If He had not positively willed it, there would be no reason for this contingent future rather than its contrary to be eternally present to the divine vision. Nor would He know future sins without a permissive decree.[17] Dr. Schwamm's thesis is a challenge that can make an impression only on those who never read St. Thomas, or those who never seriously considered the dilemma: God determining or determined; there is no other alternative.[18]

But God is not only the cause of necesary but also of contingent things. Therefore He knows both necessary and contingent things." Cf. *ibid.*, sed contra, arg. 6: "To know means to know the cause of a thing. But God knows the causes of all contingent things; for He knows Himself who is the cause of all things. Therefore He knows contingent things." See also *De veritate*, q.3, a.6. (2) Cf. *Contra Gentes*, I, 68: "God knows the thoughts of the mind and movements of the will in their power and cause, since He is the universal principle of being." *Ibid.*, par. 2: "God's causality extends to the operations of our intellect and will." *Ibid.*, par. 3, "So by knowing His intellect and will He knows every thought and wish." (3) Cf. *Peri Hermeneias*, Bk. I, chap. 9, lect. 14. What he says in this text about contingent things He also applies to the determination of the divine will; and this was written in the last days of his life.

[16] *Loc. cit.*, Ia, q.19, a.4.

[17] See pp. 75–84, 97–101, 248–50, 267–92, 300–9. In these pages texts from St. Thomas have been quoted that refer to determining decrees.

[18] See above, pp. 143, 148 f., 248 f. Let us not forget, moreover, that the influence of the divine motion upon the intellect and the will to cause it to will infallibly a determined thing is affirmed not only by St. Thomas, but also by Leo XIII in his encyclical *Providentissimus Deus* (Denz., no. 1,592), which is as follows: "For by supernatural power He (the Holy Spirit) so moved and compelled them (the sacred writers)—He was so present to them—that the things which He ordered, and those only, they first rightly understood, then willed faithfully to write down, and finally expressed in apt words and with infallible truth, otherwise it could not be said that He was the Author of the entire Scripture." Now if once, in this case of the inspiration of the Scripture, the infallible efficacy of the divine motion does not destroy liberty, then it does not destroy it in other cases. Cf. J. M. Vosté, *De divina inspiratione et veritate sacrae Scripturae*, Roma, Angelicum, 1932, pp. 46 ff.

INDEX

FR. REGINALD GARRIGOU-LAGRANGE, O.P.

**Fr. Garrigou-Lagrange, O.P.
1877-1964**

Fr. Reginald Marie Garrigou-Lagrange, O.P. (1877-1964) was probably the greatest Catholic theologian of the 20th century. (He is not to be confused with his uncle, Père Lagrange, the biblical scholar.) Fr. Garrigou-Lagrange initially attracted attention in the early 20th century, when he wrote against Modernism. Recognizing that Modernism—which denied the objective truth of divine revelation and affirmed an heretical conception of the evolution of dogma—struck at the very root of Catholic faith, Fr. Garrigou-Lagrange wrote classic works on apologetics, defending the Catholic Faith by way of both philosophy and theology. Fr. Garrigou-Lagrange taught at the Angelicum in Rome from 1909 to 1960, and he served for many years as a consultor to the Holy Office and other Roman Congregations. He is most famous, however, for his writings, producing over 500 books and articles. In these he showed himself to be a thoroughgoing Thomist in the classic Dominican tradition.

Fr. Garrigou-Lagrange was best known for his spiritual theology, particularly for insisting that all are called to holiness and for zealously propounding the thesis that infused contemplation and the resulting mystical life are in the normal way of holiness or Christian perfection. His classic work in this field—and his overall masterpiece—is *The Three Ages of the Interior Life,* in which the Catholic Faith stands out in all its splendor as a divine work of incomparable integrity, structure and beauty, ordered to raise man to the divine life of grace and bring to flower in him the "supernatural organism" of Sanctifying Grace and the Seven Gifts of the Holy Ghost—the wellsprings of all true mysticism. Among his other famous theological works are *The Three Ways of the Spiritual Life, Christian Perfection and Contemplation* (a forerunner of *The Three Ages of the Interior Life*), *The Love of God and the Cross of Jesus, The Mother of the Saviour and our Interior Life,* and *Christ the Saviour.* His most important philosophical work was *God, His Existence and Nature: A Thomistic Solution of Certain Agnostic Antinomies.*

The works of Fr. Garrigou-Lagrange are unlikely to be equalled for many decades to come.

Spread the Faith with . . .

TAN·BOOKS

A Division of Saint Benedict Press, LLC

TAN books are powerful tools for evangelization. They lift the mind to God and change lives. Millions of readers have found in TAN books and booklets an effective way to teach and defend the Faith, soften hearts, and grow in prayer and holiness of life.

Throughout history the faithful have distributed Catholic literature and sacramentals to save souls. St. Francis de Sales passed out his own pamphlets to win back those who had abandoned the Faith. Countless others have distributed the Miraculous Medal to prompt conversions and inspire deeper devotion to God. Our customers use TAN books in that same spirit.

If you have been helped by this or another TAN title, share it with others. Become a TAN Missionary and share our life changing books and booklets with your family, friends and community. We'll help by providing special discounts for books and booklets purchased in quantity for purposes of evangelization. Write or call us for additional details.

TAN Books
Attn: TAN Missionaries Department
PO Box 410487
Charlotte, NC 28241

Toll-free (800) 437-5876
missionaries@TANBooks.com

 **TAN · BOOKS**

TAN Books was founded in 1967 to preserve the spiritual, intellectual and liturgical traditions of the Catholic Church. At a critical moment in history TAN kept alive the great classics of the Faith and drew many to the Church. In 2008 TAN was acquired by Saint Benedict Press. Today TAN continues its mission to a new generation of readers.

From its earliest days TAN has published a range of booklets that teach and defend the Faith. Through partnerships with organizations, apostolates, and mission-minded individuals, well over 10 million TAN booklets have been distributed.

More recently, TAN has expanded its publishing with the launch of Catholic calendars and daily planners—as well as Bibles, fiction, and multimedia products through its sister imprints Catholic Courses (CatholicCourses.com) and Saint Benedict Press (SaintBenedictPress.com).

Today TAN publishes over 500 titles in the areas of theology, prayer, devotions, doctrine, Church history, and the lives of the saints. TAN books are published in multiple languages and found throughout the world in schools, parishes, bookstores and homes.

For a free catalog, visit us online at
TANBooks.com

Or call us toll-free at
(800) 437-5876

Made in the USA
Lexington, KY
06 November 2017